1986

COLOR MODEL ENVIRONMENTS

COLOR MODEL ENVIRONMENTS: COLOR AND LIGHT IN THREE-DIMENSIONAL DESIGN

Harold Linton

Illustrations: Richard Rochon

 VAN NOSTRAND REINHOLD COMPANY _____ New York

This book is dedicated to my wife, Nadyne, our sons, Joshua and Jonathan, and to our parents, Ruth and Leonard and Barbara and Leon.

Printed in the United States of America
Designed by Joel A. Lutz

Published by Van Nostrand Reinhold Company Inc.
135 West 50th Street
New York, New York 10020

Van Nostrand Reinhold Company Limited
Molly Millars Lane
Wokingham, Berkshire RG11 2PY, England

Van Nostrand Reinhold
480 La Trobe Street
Melbourne, Victoria 3000, Australia

Macmillan of Canada
Division of Canada Publishing Corporation
164 Commander Boulevard
Agincourt, Ontario M1S 3C7, Canada

16 15 14 13 12 11 10 9 8 7 6 5 4 3 2 1

Library of Congress Cataloging in Publication Data

Linton, Harold.
  Color model environments.

  Bibliography: p. 243
  Includes index.
  1. Color in architecture.   2. Light in architecture.
3. Architectural models.   I. Title.
NA2795.L5 1985   720′.2228   84-27112
ISBN 0-442-25893-3 (cl.)
ISBN 0-442-26073-3 (pbk.)

Every attempt has been made to describe the construction procedures in this book in a clear and straightforward manner. Because of the variations in skill and experience of each reader and because of the possible variation in materials and workmanship, neither the author nor the publisher can assume responsibility for the proper application or suitability of these techniques to a particular project. The use of trade names throughout the book for specific products is not intended as an endorsement by either the author or the publisher. Trade names are included to indicate the specific type of product or building material being described and to suggest a possible source for such materials.

Contents

List of Tables

Foreword

During the last two decades there has been a quiet but dramatic revolution both in designers' attitudes toward color and in the use of color in all aspects of design for the man-made environment. From an architectural point of view, this revolution was spearheaded by the spontaneous wall-painting movement occurring in the early sixties—an international phenomenon that was to reintroduce an exuberance of color into our towns and cities not witnessed since the Renaissance. In gaining a generally recognized public acceptance, and in exploiting higher levels of color intensity in urban space, artists and environmental designers were spurred toward a serious engagement in the creation of a more diverse and a variegated architectural setting.

In tandem with this resurgence of interest in color as a vital tool of design, a renewed dialogue between the disciplines of art and design has been taking place. As a result, the traditionally evolved "languages" of design are no longer considered exclusive. Furthermore, the often divisive approaches to the teaching of light and color as separate phenomena have been called into question: those institutions with existing color courses are refining their programs while other programs are being initiated or await initiation.

Most concepts of color treat its phenomenon as a three-dimensional experience. A division has existed between the artist and the architect, however. For example, while the former exploits three-dimensional color qualities on a single plane, the latter tends to use a two-dimensional process in the dynamic light and many dimensions of architectural space. Also, an underlying and singular association of color as the property of surface has led many designers to overemphasize the form-giving qualities of light at the expense of any recognition of its color-rendering properties and its spectral characteristics. Many of these limited design attitudes stem directly from design courses and their attendant literature, which promote the impossible—the concept of color and light as separate disciplines. More dangerously, such attitudes can isolate color from the understanding of basic design principles, a situation that had led to a widespread misconception that views the articulation of form in space as a colorless science.

Color Model Environments is a timely and important landmark because of its major contribution to the interdisciplinary design dialogue. Its central purpose is threefold: to present a structural order underlying the effective use of color and light; to communicate this order based on three-dimensional design principles; and to relate these aspects to the planning stages and concepts for model forms used by students and professionals in several design disciplines.

The reader will find the ideas in this study presented in the spirit of a workshop. Its reward is an insight gained via exposure, discussion, and experience that leads to a deeper awareness of the spectrum of design principles and ultimately to a closer union of color, space, and surface in the design process.

Color Model Environments focuses on the developments in color education for artists and designers who work in three dimensions. The viewpoint maintained throughout this book is that an awareness of the vocabulary of design and the fundamentals of color and light are basic to all personal explorations in three-dimensional design and that incorporation of these elements, including knowledge of the properties of materials, lends direction and support to individual expression.

Many of the student examples herein cover the first decade in my color classes at the Lawrence Institute of Technology. Several student projects, however, have been loaned from design instructors throughout the United States and Europe. I am grateful to all these individuals whose involvement represents a wider experience than my own.

To begin thinking about color, light, and form we must first of all recognize that although these subjects are the fundamentals of the designer's education and background, together they represent an interdisciplinary involvement. The disciplines of physics, chemistry, psychology, and art all have a special interest in the subject of color and light. The physicist has an interest in the theories and sources of the sensation of color and the related principles of optics. The chemist is involved with formulations relating to the physical composition of pigments and their applications. Psychologists acquire information about how color is perceived and how it influences one's emotional responses; and physiologists are interested in how one senses color. The artist and the designer are also concerned with these factors but must seek an understanding that leads to the development of a personal and distinctive visual vocabulary that will lift the human spirit. Together, at the point where science and art meet, their common cause has resulted in a greater assimilation of information touching many of the disciplines concerned with the subject of color.

Many artists and designers have a background of early experiences that have provided lessons aimed at self-discovery, the development of the power of perception, the ability to analyze spatial relationships, and an understanding of the principles of design that contribute to the unified organization of form. A basic question asked by students concerns the relative value of the "languages" the designer works with: words, drawings, and models. The use of many methods is an essential requirement, and all are prerequisites for the thinking process needed to deal with the complexity of three-dimensional objects.

To aid those who are beginning three-dimensional design, an opening presentation of many of the fundamental resources and materials of the design studio is provided. In addition, discussion has been extended to include direction for the construction of basic forms, description of the principles of three-dimensional design, and introductory projects that explore perception and planning. Each of these projects focuses on specific forms in individual and group studies and are illustrated by drawings that express the subtlety of values that define form.

All the projects have been ordered into groups that relate to the elements and principles of design; the structural sense of color; the interaction of light and form; the application of color and light to linear, planar, and volumetric form; and the plan of color and light in an environment. In addition, examples from practitioners of the design disciplines—art, architecture, and interior design—from the United States and Europe have been assembled. Some of these designers are already familiar, while others are just beginning to gain significant exposure for their work. The works of student and professional artists and designers have been organized within the subject areas of the book to reflect a relationship between the visual and physical properties of dimensional form and to support the following criteria for the role of color in design education:

• To experience the qualities of color and light and their combined effect on form in planning and practice.

• To acquaint one with the special possibilities of color

materials and their methods of application in three-dimensional design.

• To understand the structure and planning of color as a fundamentally rational and visual process interwoven in the act of design.

• To utilize drawing as a means of furthering an analysis of the qualities of form and composition in the design process.

• To realize a complex form in its entirety as a harmonic whole.

• To increase awareness of the methods used for color and light planning by professional artists, architects, and designers.

Attempts should be made to adapt suitable methods of design representation to these background goals—of fully appreciating any idea that satisfies the initial criteria of a design problem. Although the materials used in model making will differ from those used in actual construction, they will provide the designer with the tactile experience of shaping physical space and thereby influence the quality of form it replicates. Within the framework of a creative and developing design dialogue, design tools can be harnessed to serve each individual in his or her pursuit of unique concepts of form.

Harold Linton

Acknowledgments

I would like to extend my acknowledgment and appreciation to the following people:

Richard Rochon, to whom I am profoundly indebted for his unyielding friendship and magnificent illustrations—and for invaluable assistance from those in his office, Joel Rochon, Jerome Rochon, and Carol Kaffenberger.

Bob, Toni, Michael, and Matthew for their love, support, and kindness;

Galit Zolkower and Bruce Kutz, not only for their translations from French and Spanish to English but also for their love and support;

Stan and Kris Tracy for a deeply valued and colossal effort in photographing student projects, preparing the many group photographs, and lending photographs of their work;

Joel and Lela Lutz, Graphic Services, not only for the beautiful layout and design of the book but especially for care and guidance throughout the project;

Edwina Delbridge, Communication Services, for her virtually faultless typing and her patience and kindness;

Morris Jackson and Cesar Pelli for their interest and valued support at the outset of the project;

Tom Porter for his insight, encouragement, and invaluable contributions;

Charles N. Smith, who passed his delight in color on to me and for contributing to and reviewing my early manuscript;

Faber Birren for taking time to review and lend advice on my early manuscript;

Larry Hager, Susan Munger, Wendy Lochner, and Stephanie Salomon, editors, Van Nostrand Reinhold Company;

Karl Greimel, dean, School of Architecture, Lawrence Institute of Technology, for providing the opportunity to evolve my teaching methodology and for continuous support and constructive advice;

Dr. Richard E. Marburger, president and chief executive officer, Lawrence Institute of Technology, for providing consistent encouragement and support;

Rosemary Hodges, assistant to the president, Lawrence Institute of Technology, for interest and support during the project;

Dennis Selke and Tong Cheung for creating demonstration plates and assisting with all the visual preparations of the project;

The undergraduate architecture students in my color classes at the School of Architecture, Lawrence Institute of Technology, whose names are listed on page xii;

Gary R. Cocozzoli, director, Lawrence Institute of Technology Library;

Gail Nastwold, director, College Bookstore, Lawrence Institute of Technology, for help in preparation and facilitation of the manuscript;

Karen Clark, Kathleen Gilman, Monica Tombers, and Judy Wegener, for assisting with preparation of the manuscript;

Walter G. Bizon, director of photography, Lawrence Institute of Technology, for his kind assistance;

Gary Steffy, lighting designer, Ann Arbor, Michigan, for valued advice and support during the project;

Will Allen, landscape architect, for assistance and advice on early portions of the manuscript;

Ken Paul Associates, Detroit, Michigan, for generously lending services and professional work;

Paul Stevenson Oles, AIA, for generously providing guidance and advice;

Tony Horne, President, and David Miller, Manager of DMI Industries, Madison Heights, Michigan for their generous information and advice;

Dennis R. Kapp, President, and Dick Cooper, national sales manager, Martin F. Weber, Martin Instrument Company, Livonia, Michigan for their generous information and advice;

Marc Winkelman of the I-Browse Bookstore, West Bloomfield, Michigan;

Ray Socha and Color Detroit Inc., Photographic Laboratory, Ferndale, Michigan, for their generous support, commitment to the project and professional service;

Hazel and Bill Tucker, Grossman Knowling Co., Color Photographic Laboratory, Southfield, and Detroit, Michigan, for kind support and generous advice;

Mal White, White Reproduction Inc., Birmingham, Michigan, for kind and valued support;

Mel Etenson, President, Ain Plastics, Detroit, Michigan, for generous support and advice;

Al and Barbara Serman for graphic services;

and my colleagues from the School of Architecture, Lawrence Institute of Technology, for advice, encouragement, and noted project contributions: Robert A. Benson, Richard Bolton ("Collage and Space"), Robert D. Champlin, Patrick H. Corcoran, Leonard Else, Paul Chu Lin ("Basic Studies of Mass"), Henry A. Matthews ("Mass Studies in Color and Light"), Gretchen Maricak, Thomas J. Nashlen ("Spatial Activity Module"), George E. Quinn ("Mass and Void"), Thomas Regenbogen, Betty-Lee Seydler Sweatt, Roy J. Strickfaden, and Richard Hall.

Special thanks to my students for their involvement:

Michel Allen	E. Jane Halliday	John Savitski
Olympia Apostolakou	Ryad Hammou	Michael S. Schiepke
Carlos Arnini	George Hopkins	John Stanley
Christopher G. Barnas	Martin K. Hoye	Jeff H. Sherman
Frederick P. Bartlett Jr.	George A. Kachadoorian	Steven A. Sproul
Kevin Bennett	Kelly Kerlin	John B. Stock
Jeff Birgbauer	Keith Kilroy	Barbara Tanney
Lee Boman	Donald C. Kuntz	Rosalind Tieleman
Darryl S. Brill	Jun R. Leobrera	Molley J. Tooze
Carmen Brunone	Paul R. Lewis	Susanne Trewhitt
John J. Carrick III	Michael Lueder	Elaine Vedrody
Jamie J. Chiatalas	Paul J. Marcus	Steven T. Volz
Kimberly Combs	John McCann	John Waldrop
C. Brian Cook	Chris Merceier	David Wawrzyniak
Daniel Cragel	Frank Muehlenbein	Teah Ann Weyers
Richard Droste	Eric A. Murrell	
Steve Dumont	Chris Onwuzurike	
Aydin Erhan	Glenn Phillips	
Beth E. Freudenburg	Jack Putti	
Duane Fueslein	Mohsen Rahimi (in fond	
Lynne Garms	remembrance)	
Brian J. Gorzynski	Peter F. Reed	
Deborah K. Gregory	Raymond J. Romeo	
Lisa Grenn	Richard G. Rounds	
Todd Gute	Elie Samaha	

COLOR MODEL ENVIRONMENTS

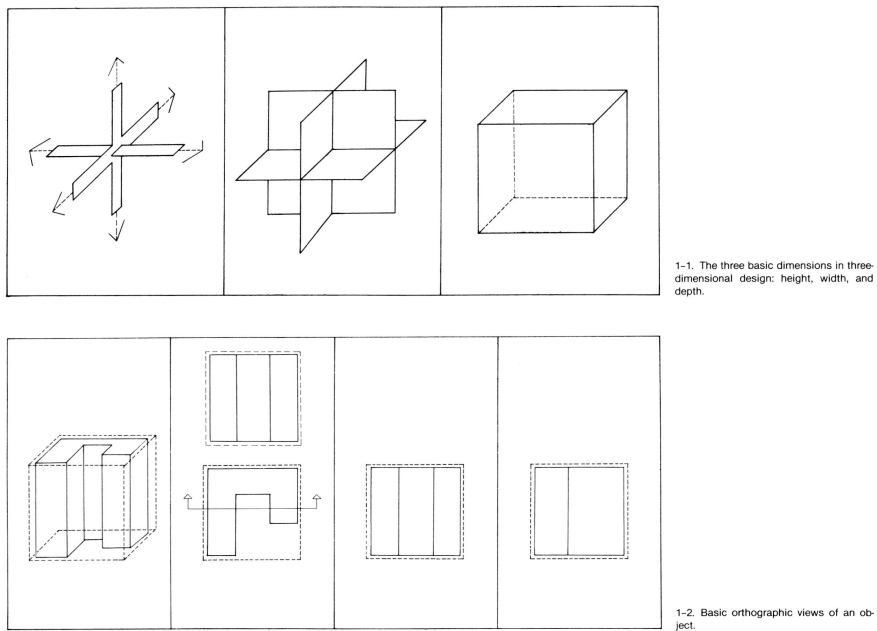

1-1. The three basic dimensions in three-dimensional design: height, width, and depth.

1-2. Basic orthographic views of an object.

1 The Elements of Design

A two-dimensional vocabulary of design concerns a single plane and its relationship to the observer. The organization of elements occurs on the length and breadth of the plane of reference, the main purpose of which is to convey order and harmony and to express visual interest and meaning. This process of human creation exemplified by the forms of drawing, painting, printing, and photography all communicate images that contain flat marks with little visible depth except for an illusory kind.

This concept is not altogether valid when one transfers ideas and patterns into actual space. If one examines any object that is small, lightweight, and close at hand, each turn of the object reveals a different face or plane. A three-dimensional object cannot be completely understood at first glance, as it involves time and movement in space. What appears to be a cube viewed at a distance may on closer investigation turn out to be a pyramid, a rectangular solid, or any shape with a square base. A three-dimensional object often requires views from different distances and angles to understand the reality of the complete form.

To organize compositions, one must consider many viewpoints. Most important, one is not dealing with a single set of relationships but with a plan for several sets of relationships. The problem is no longer a flat picture that contains length and breadth only, but an expanse with physical depth—the third dimension. One composition has many different aspects that must be composed in themselves, and each view must lead to an exploration of the next view and its changing relationships. One's previous understanding and sensitivity must be extended to include the challenge and the expanding set of relationships of a new problem.

For the same reason, sculpture stands are mounted on swivels that continually turn and enable a form to be studied from all angles. All the elements of form change in relation to the sculptor and as the sculptor moves in relation to the form. Similarly, architects use orthographic projection and perspective drawing to distinguish important views of a subject and to study

relationships among them. They also develop scale models in order to visualize these relationships more accurately. Industrial designers create small plastic models and larger mock-ups in plaster and other easily formed materials for the same purpose. All these approaches to the study of three-dimensional form are both important and very helpful in visualizing complex relationships.

Initially, three basic directions in three-dimensional design can be acknowledged: height, width, and depth. In each direction, one has the opportunity to measure the expanse of a form horizontally, vertically, and throughout its depth. If one initiates planes that cross at the center of these directions, horizontal, vertical, and oblique planes will occur. By adding another set of planes and moving each to opposite sides, the solid form of a cube can be created (fig. 1–1).

Although this is not the place to explore the technical aspects of orthographic drawing, an understanding of its principles will help to visualize three-dimensional relationships. The basic idea is to break down the form into the important views that can be drawn in two dimensions. The manner by which the views are interpreted on paper shows how they arrange themselves in space. By placing a three-dimensional object inside an imaginary cube, three basic views can be established. The simplest view is the plan, which appears as a pattern the form makes on a base. With a plan diagram as a beginning, elevations can be constructed from remaining or given directions. These views of the object can be further amplified with cross-section drawings of the form to express relationships that are not easily visible or understood. In many types of structural design, the ability to analyze form in this manner is both an essential and invaluable technique for visualizing a concept (fig. 1–2).

In three-dimensional design, there are three groups of elements: theoretical, visual, and organizational. Included in the theoretical elements are the concepts of point, line, plane, and volume. These elements are often perceived in the designer's mind before they are given physical form. The visual elements—shape, size, color, and texture—are affected by the conditions under which we see them and establish the final appearance of a design. The organizational elements—position, orientation, space, and gravity—influence the overall structure and internal aspects of the visual elements.

THEORETICAL ELEMENTS

A three-dimensional form can be visualized and mentally rotated in the mind. In all directions, the entire form can be conceived of before it is given physical shape. Each designer's concept for a form begins with theoretical elements (fig. 1–3).

POINT

A point indicates a position in space. Because it has no length, breadth, or depth, it is a single place. It may indicate the place where the ends of two lines meet and intersect, as in the corner of a plane or the angle of a solid form (fig. 1–3A).

LINE

The extension of a point in a given direction is a line. It has length without breadth or depth. Having direction and position, it may define the edge of a plane or solid or a place where they might intersect (fig. 1–3B).

PLANE

The extension of a line from its origin of direction changes the line to a plane. Conceptually, a plane has length and width without depth. The shape of a plane is determined by the contour of the line that forms its edges. Planes may also define the limitations of volumes (fig. 1–3C).

VOLUME

The extension of a plane from its origin of direction changes the plane to a volume. Conceptually, a volume has dimensions of length, breadth, and depth. As a three-dimensional element in the vocabulary of design, a volume can be a solid, which has length, breadth, depth, and bulk. It may contain or enclose space by planes and may also be space itself displaced by mass or void (fig. 1–3D).

VISUAL ELEMENTS

It should be assumed that three-dimensional forms appear different from various angles, distances, and types of lighting. The following discussion of the visual elements is offered independently of a later discussion in this chapter of the variable conditions of lighting (fig. 1–4).

SHAPE

An area that is perceived as having defined boundaries because of differences in value, color, or texture is considered a shape. Drawings of three-dimensional forms can be made on paper by repeating flat shapes. Our awareness of their distinct and related views as forms is important in understanding three-dimensional objects (fig. 1–4A).

SIZE

Size is a measurement or series of measurements from the length, breadth, depth, or thickness of a form, which may also allow for the calculation of a volume measurement. Although three dimensions may determine the proportions of a form, the scale of a form is determined by its size in relation to other forms in its context (fig. 1–4B).

COLOR

Hue, intensity, and value (light to dark) serve to distinguish a form from its environment. Color may be applied artificially to a form through the use of paint and material lamination or may be a natural result of the color of a selected material. In either circumstance, color affects the visual weight of a form (fig. 1–4C).

TEXTURE

The surface characteristics of forms in design may be natural or specially treated to create smooth, rough, mat, glossy, and other tactile qualities. Whether actual, invented, or simulated, the tactile and light-reflective qualities of a surface are transformed by the manipulation of design materials and elements (fig. 1–4D).

ORGANIZATIONAL ELEMENTS

In three-dimensional design, the elements of organization become more complex than in two-dimensional design on a flat surface. The cube again serves as an example of the basic elements of organization, position, orientation, space, and gravity (fig. 1–5).

POSITION

In order to establish the location of a point, we must know the relationship between the point and all our planes of reference. In the case of a point within a cube, the relationship of distance between sides, front and back, and top and bottom are necessary to understand the position (fig. 1–5A).

ORIENTATION

Orientation is also best understood by selecting different angles of view of the volume. A line that is parallel to the front and back planes may not be parallel to either the top and bottom or side planes (fig. 1–5B).

SPACE

Space defined by an actual cube as opposed to a drawing is real and not illusory. One can orient both a drawing and an actual cube to suggest space continuing or being contained, as in a hollow cube, space contained within a volume, or a volume concealing or occupying space (fig. 1–5C).

GRAVITY

In three-dimensional design, we deal with the constant effect of gravity on the fabrication and stability of forms. The materials selected determine the ability of a form to support loads from above. Often structural diagrams are helpful in the plan and choice of materials for many arrangements, while others are simply not possible. Beyond the scope of the physical stability of form, the visual stability or Inertia of a form is controlled by its geometry and orientation to the ground plane, as well as by the viewer's line of sight (fig. 1–5D).

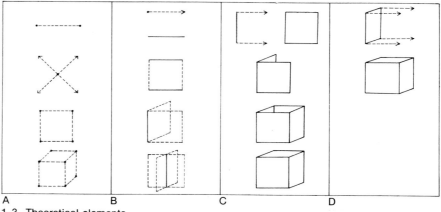

A   B   C   D
1–3. Theoretical elements.

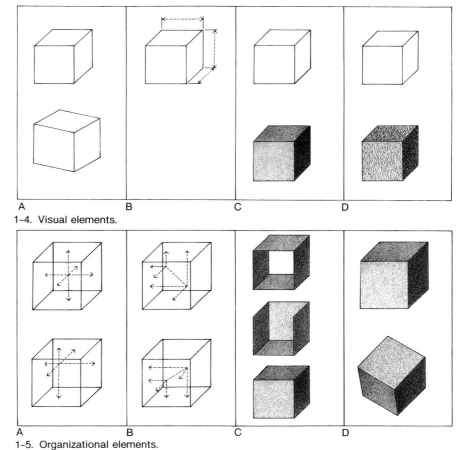

A   B   C   D
1–4. Visual elements.

A   B   C   D
1–5. Organizational elements.

STRUCTURAL ELEMENTS

Structural elements are important to our understanding of the construction of three-dimensional volumes. Along with the plastic elements, they are also useful as a reference to the conditions of lighting under which they are seen (fig. 1–6).

VERTEX

Three planes that come together and meet at one point are considered a vertex. Within the wide variety of possible solids, vertices can have varying degrees of inward and outward projection (fig. 1–6A).

EDGE

Edges are formed by nonparallel planes that meet at one line and may also be projected inward or outward (fig. 1–6B).

FACE

A plane of physical substance or material is considered a surface. External surfaces that enclose volumes are considered the faces of a volume (fig. 1–6C).

The formal structure of a geometric solid relies on the fact that the elements have sharp, straight edges where planes join and smooth, flat surfaces as the faces of a volume. The proper selection of materials and techniques contributes to the attainment of these attributes, which results in precisely defined volumetric forms.

PLASTIC ELEMENTS

Materials that can be formed or molded with one's hands—paper, clay, wax, and plaster—are all considered pliable or plastic. In addition, our perception of three-dimensional form under general conditions of lighting is the result of a pattern of light and shade. The term *plastic elements* refers to those visible aspects of a three-dimensional pattern, a configuration of value contrasts and gradations. The plastic elements therefore include any three-dimensional material that can be shaped by hand or tool and the visible relationships in arrangements of value gradations, contrasts, depth, and space (fig. 1–7).

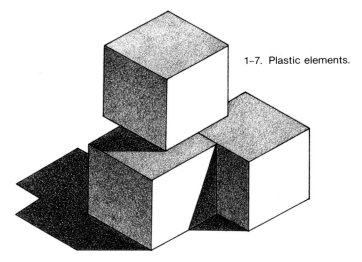

1–7. Plastic elements.

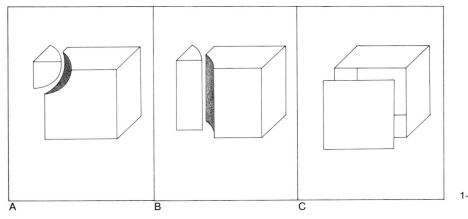

A   B   C

1–6. Structural elements.

PERCEPTION OF FORM

Our perception of form is governed by variation in the field of vision. (By drawing a form on paper, one makes part of the paper different from the rest through contrast.) If the field is constant, our perception will be uniform throughout, a sensation of light in space. Conversely, if we perceive form, there are differences in the field of vision. These differences account for large and small levels of contrast and are the basis for our perception of form. We therefore create relationships and forms through the use of contrast. By lighting an object from opposite sides, we can reduce levels of contrast and make the object almost disappear (fig. 1-8). Our perception of form is weakened as contrast in the visual field is lessened. If we aim one light at the side of an object and another at the paper behind, one side of the object will be light against a darker ground and the other side dark against a lighter ground (fig. 1-9). The result is a strong perception of form.

BASIC STUDIES

The following are introductory exercises that demonstrate the effects of light upon basic geometric forms. Our perception of the qualities of edge, plane, mass, and volume are measurably influenced by the direction, distance, and intensity of a light source to its subject.

A flat surface reflects light without a great range of light-to-dark variation. Any object with combined concave and convex or wrinkled surfaces, however, may reflect light with varied intensity, depending upon its substance and the way its surfaces are turned toward the light source.

When we first create a physical form, we think of it as the complete "object." The challenge remains, however, to use the light sources (or move the object if the light source is fixed) in such a way that the light defining the object communicates the dimensional potential of the form. Each addition or variation of shape, as well as other types of material—shiny, opaque, or transparent—affect the qualities of form and are the product of the individual's own ingenuity, dexterity, and interest.

1-8. Lighting an object from opposite sides.

1-9. Lighting the object and background from opposite sides.

BAS-RELIEF PAPER STRUCTURES

For this exercise with a graduated relief, sheets of three-ply white bristol board are used. By subdividing each composition into basic geometric shapes, designs are organized and glued into place with dots or by a thread of glue along the edges. Various layers of board in playful arrangements provide an important dimension of interest for the exercise (fig. 1–10). Because the shapes have thickness and their edges are exposed to light and shade, the study in relief is not two- but three-dimensional. The plastic appearance of the study may be enhanced by the size and thickness of the base to which it is adhered. A relation between these elements should be investigated as an important and final consideration. Although cutting thick bristol board may require patience and care, the degree of mechanical and technical skill required is not great (figs. 1–11A to 1–11H). As the project is turned in front of a fixed source of light, highlights and shadows change according to the pattern of higher and lower planes of paper facing the light.

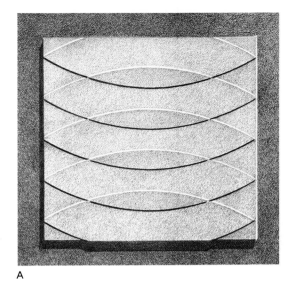

A

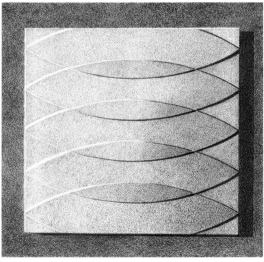

B

1–10. Cross section view of bas-relief paper structure (see fig. 1–11A).

1–11A–H. Bas-relief paper structures reflect different patterns of highlights and shadows turned in various ways in front of a single light source.

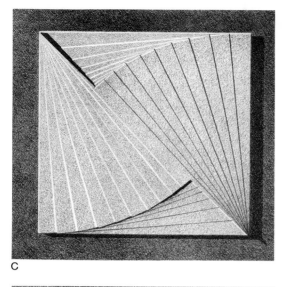

C

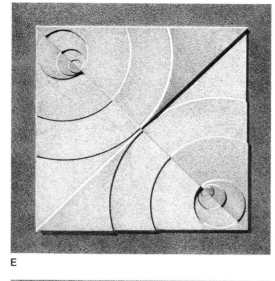

E

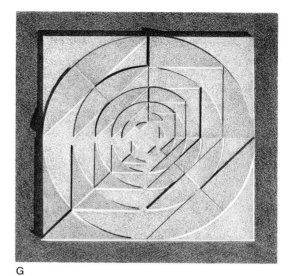

G

D

F

H

1-11A-H *continued.*

EFFECTS OF INCREASING AND DECREASING SPACE

These studies are first organized as a flat composition, using vertical and horizontal rows of five squares each. Both the top chamber and constructed base are made from four-ply white bristol board (fig. 1–12). From the top, portions of each shape are cut out and scored or creased to bend inward and outward at gradual angles. An effect of increased space is achieved by slightly raising or lowering the tabs on the surface to varying positions.

As the project is turned in front of a fixed source of light, the pattern of highlights and shadows increases (value contrast is greater) and decreases (value contrast is lessened), depending on the direction of light to the angle and position of the tabs on the surface of the chamber (figs. 1–13A to 1–13H). Additional grid patterns, unit shapes, and shape groupings—twisting, overlapping, and stacking—provide further awareness of the many possibilities and how they may be realized. The following variations in the surface design of the top chamber include:

- Organizing elements by grouping toward the center, edges, opposite sides, and corners.
- Cutting and bending a portion of the square from the top at any angle.
- Bending and slanting more than one portion of a raised tab at increasing or decreasing angles.

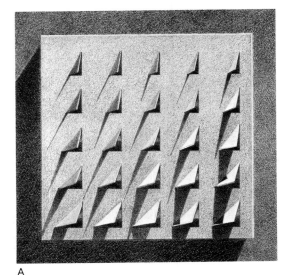

A

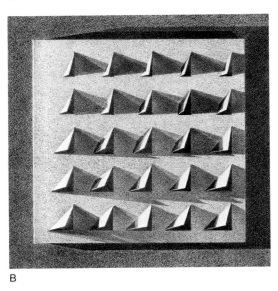

B

1–12. Cross section view of paper structure with tabs (see fig. 1–13A).

1–13A–H. Paper structures with sequences of raised and lowered tabs increase and decrease the effects of space depending on the direction of light to the angle and position of the tabs on the surface.

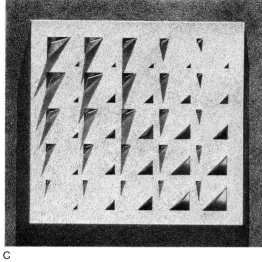

C

E

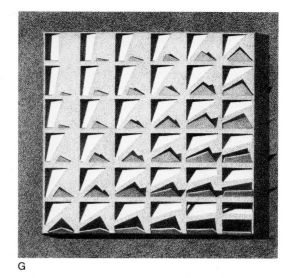

G

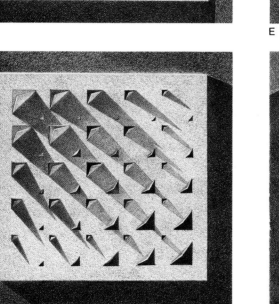

D

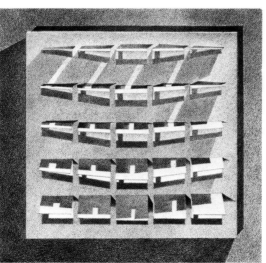

F

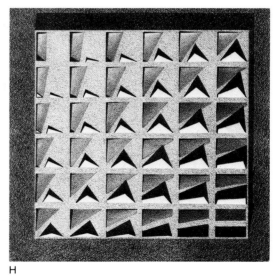

H

1–13A–H *continued.*

FREESTANDING PAPER FORMS

For these experiments, lightweight bristol and softly textured papers can be used. An assortment of processes—scoring, bending, and rolling—together with a plan for basic solids, transforms a sheet of paper into a three-dimensional form (fig. 1–14). Some of the forms are designed with tabs and glued into basic volumetric shapes, while others are left freestanding for flexible arrangement and experimentation (fig. 1–15).

Creasing a sheet of paper in the middle provides enough stability to enable the paper to stand upright. Note the vertical centerline, the angles, their proportions, and the refraction of light defined by shadows on and around the forms (figs. 1–16A to 1–16H). In this introductory exercise, notice how a form rests on its base, and how, by moving the light source closer and farther above it, the light on the form brightens and shadows shorten and lengthen. By grouping a few related solids in front of the light, we can better understand how their appearance, texture, and sense of volume are altered. Dark shadows in contrast with strong highlights measurably affect our perception of form and space.

The marvel of communication lies in its perpetual innovation and variation. The creative designer strives to increase the scope of vision, create new relationships between familiar elements, and employ the expressive dimensions of surprise growing out of the potential of materials and means. The study of bas-relief and freestanding paper forms is therefore integral to the training of the designer within a chosen discipline. Photography, sculpture, painting, and architecture take on new meaning if they are understood as light modulators.

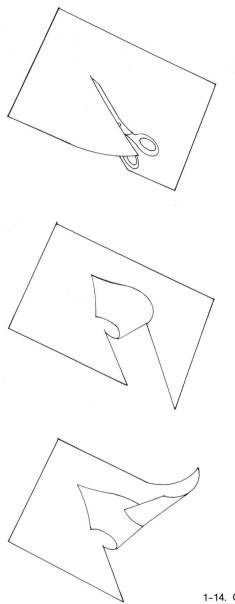

1–14. Creating a three-dimensional paper form for experimentation with light.

1–15 (See p. 11). Light modulators made from sheets of creased, rolled, and folded paper for experimentation with patterns of highlights, shades, and shadows.

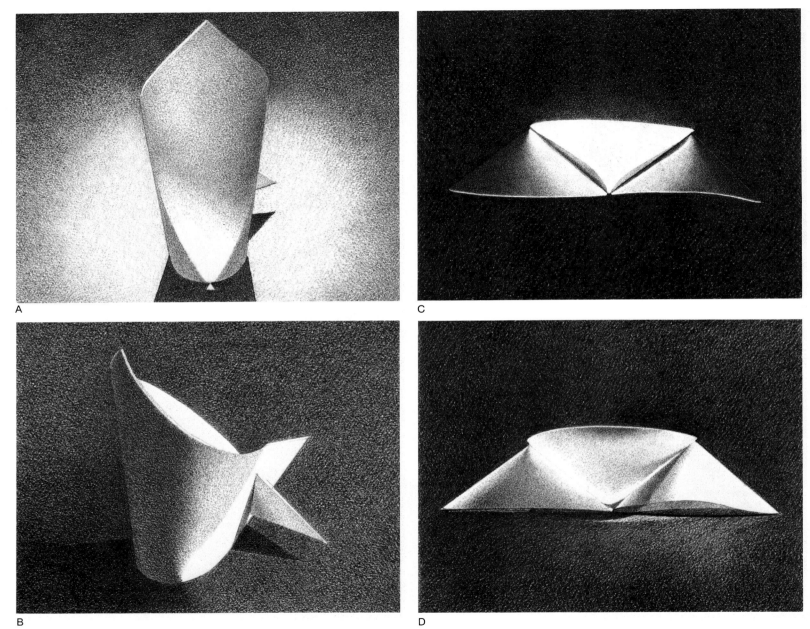

A

B

C

D

1-16A-H. A group of basic forms made from sheets of paper is useful to a study of how light affects a form's appearance as a volume.

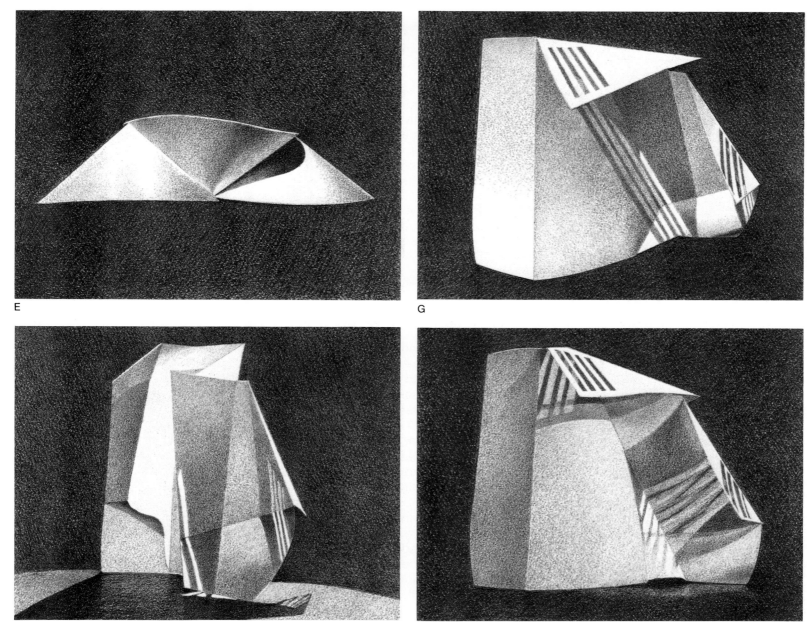

E

G

F

H

1-16A-H *continued.*

2 Materials, Methods, and Techniques

Designers often select materials for study that are easy to handle. Of the variety of design media, paper and cardboard are among the least expensive and most versatile of all materials to work with. A careful selection of materials based on color, texture, light reflection, scale, and the inherent use for which they are intended will influence the quality of form they represent. Many manufacturers have produced papers and boards in a wide assortment of primary, secondary, and tertiary hues, as well as in a range of surface finishes, such as dull, textured, and glossy. Design media can therefore be selected and applied with an awareness of methods and techniques appropriate to a particular type of form. Several groups of design media enhance these purposes.

DESIGN MEDIA

The most important of the materials groups comprises papers and cardboards. These are useful for lightweight structures and accept the applied media from many other groups of materials. A brief description of the physical properties, construction techniques, and uses of the materials in this group is included in the first section of this chapter, along with a reference table. Table 1 illustrates their common sizes, thicknesses, surface textures, and colors.

The materials of the second group, color papers and films, are best suited for opaque and transparent color overlays and the refinement of surface treatments. Many of these materials will also accept applications of liquid and dry media with proper handling. These materials are produced and purchased for their special characteristics of color range, surface finish, size, and application; therefore, they are grouped and discussed according to their physical properties, application techniques, uses in design, and their manufacturers. The third group, plastics and woods, contains materials often used as structural elements in three-dimensional design. However, several of these materials have application only as laminates, while others can be used as laminates and construction materials for dimensional form. These are also organized according to their manufacturers and described in relation to their special characteristics of color range, surface finish, size, and application.

The last group, liquid and dry media, extends the range of color, texture, and possible effects for surface treatment and refinement. Included is information about the physical properties of each medium and suggestions for mixing and application.

PAPERS AND CARDBOARDS

Bristol Board. This is a versatile, white, paperboard that has many applications in two- and three-dimensional design. It is made by many manufacturers, is available in both a hot- and a cold-press surface, and is commonly stocked in a range of thicknesses from one- to four-ply. Cold-press is a mat finish surface, and hot-press has a hard, smooth surface similar in character to poster board. Black and gray bristol boards come in two-ply thicknesses in only a cold-press surface. Hot- and cold-press surfaces will accept liquid media, drawing tools, and overlays of paper and film. They are easy to cut and score and have many possible applications in model construction. Heavier weight bristol, three-ply and thicker, will accept most liquid media without buckling and is rigid enough to use in constructing freestanding solid forms.

Canvas Board. Canvas board is used in the fine arts for painting. It is designed as a single-surface, white board, with a woven canvas texture for the acceptance of acrylic and oil-base media and may be adapted as a color and textural element for surface refinement in model construction. It is available in a double-thick weight in a wide range of sizes. Cutting this material is more difficult than cutting many of the other boards. Its density and fabric lamination require slow and patient cutting with a sharp blade, razor, or saw with a fine-tooth blade.

Chipboard. Chipboard is a dense, gray cardboard used for study rather than presentation purposes. It is available in a variety of thicknesses and sheet sizes and is an excellent material for experimentation and testing of elementary concepts of form. The material properties of the surface are not particularly suited for drawing or liquid media, but chipboard may be used as a core to which paper and other boards can be adhered. It is relatively easy to cut with a utility knife.

Corrugated Board. Corrugated board is found in box construction and packing materials. Although it is only useful for rough studies in mass and volume, the brown-paper face can be stripped away to reveal a ribbed paper texture that extends the range of textural effects in the most basic model forms. It is relatively easy to cut with an art knife or razor, but it is not suited for liquid or drawing media.

Display Blanks. Display blanks, or railroad boards, are available in a basic range of colors. Their purpose in design and model construction, however, is limited. They may be used for beginning studies but lack the material characteristics necessary for surface treatment and further refinement. They are relatively easy to cut and useful only for beginning study concepts.

Foam Board. Foam board is a sandwich of two paper faces laminated to a white polystyrene foam inner core. It is available in either a kraft paper face similar to brown butcher's paper, or as a white, plate-finish bristol face. Foam board is available in three thicknesses and several sizes. The boards are easily cut with an art knife, razor, bevel mat cutter, or band saw using a fine-tooth blade. Foam boards are often used in study models as a material for the skeleton construction of a model form and base. They may be covered with many other types of papers and boards for finishing treatments.

Foil Board. Foil board is a single-thick material, with a thin metallic gold or silver foil applied to one side, and is available in both smooth and textured surfaces. The smooth metallic surface has high reflective properties but lacks the crisp reflective definition possible with mirrored glass or metalicized acetate. Gold and silver foil boards are available in one thickness and sheet size. They are easily cut with art and utility knives and function well as decorative surfaces and reflective details.

Illustration Board. Illustration board has one working surface (single-surface) and carries the manufacturer's name printed on the reverse side. It is made in white and many colors, including a wide variety of neutral and earth colors. In white and off-white, it is available in single- and double-thicknesses and in either hot- or cold-press surfaces. Double-thick illustration board will accept all of the liquid and drawing media without buckling and is useful as a base and support in model construction.

Mat Board. Mat boards offer a rich variety of color, texture, and surface finishes for design. These are all single-surface design boards that carry a white or neutral color on the reverse side along with the manufacturer's name. They are used as supports for mounting flat work and as a base for the application of liquid and drawing media. They may be cut with art knives and used as structural supports and decorative surfaces in model construction.

Mounting Board. White mounting boards or mechanical boards are used for paste-up and key-line and pencil drawing. They are similar in character and handling to many mat and illustration boards, but offer an additional advantage of resisting staining from rubber cement adhesives. Many are available in single- and double-thicknesses with a gray reverse side, which is also usable. Museum mounting boards are a 100 percent rag board, useful only for matting, mounting, and preservation of original drawings and prints.

Watercolor. Watercolor paper and boards extend the range of color and textural effects in design. They provide several grades of rough to smooth finish in a range of light- to heavyweight stock. These are ideally suited for the liquid media and provide a foundation surface for opaque and transparent color effects.

EXPLANATION OF TABLE 1

Type. The generic names have been used for paper and board products listed in the table. These materials are generally available through more than one manufacturer. Refer to the source code for the names of distributors for each material. On page 241, the List of Manufacturers includes complete sources for all the materials mentioned in this book. (Many additional manufacturers of quality materials are also available.)

Surfaces. The paper industry uses many terms to describe the same surface quality. For example, smooth bristol board is

Table 2-1. Commonly Used Papers and Boards for Design and Construction

	Bristol Board	Bristol Board	Colored Bristol Board	Canvas Board	Chipboard	Corrugated Board	Display Blanks (Railroad Board)	Foam Board	Foil Board	Illustration Board	Illustration Board
Size	22" × 30"	22" × 30"	22" × 30"	4" × 5" up to 30" × 40"	30" × 40" 32" × 40"	30" × 40"	22" × 28" 28" × 44"	30" × 40" 32" × 40" 40" × 60" 48" × 96"	28" × 44"	30" × 40"	30" × 40"
Thickness	1 ply up to 4 ply	1 ply up to 4 ply	2 ply	Double-Thick	1/32" 1/16" 1/8"	1/4" up to 1"	6 ply 12 ply 14 ply	1/8" 3/16" 3/8"	Single-Thick	Single- and Double-Thick	Single- and Double-Thick
Color	White Off-White	White Off-White	T.V. Grays	White Gray	Gray	Neutral Tan and Colors	White and Colors	Kraft White	Metallics	White Off-White	White Off-White
Reverse	Prime	Prime	Prime	Printed Chip	Gray	Variegated	Prime	Prime	White	White Chip Printed Chip	White Chip Printed Chip
Texture	Smooth	Medium	Smooth	Canvas	Smooth	Medium	Smooth	Kraft Smooth	Smooth	Smooth	Medium
Source	B,BA,BI, C,M,N,S	B,BA,BI, C,M,N,S	B,BA,C, M,N	F,M,N	BA,BI,F,N	F,M,N	B,BA,BI, C,F,M	BA,BI,C, F,MO,P	BA,C,N	B,BA,BI,C, M,N,S	B,BA,BI,C M,N,S
Adhesive	A,B,C, D,E,F,	A,B,C, D,E,F	A,B,C, D,E,F	A,B,C	A,B,C, D,E,F	A,B,C D,E,F	A,B,C D,E,F	A,C,D,E,F	A,C,D,E,F	A,B,C, D,E,F	A,B,C, D,E,F
Acceptance of Media	A,C,I,O, P,W	A,C,D,I,O, P,T,X,W	A,C,D,I, O,P,W	A,C,D,I, P,W	A,C,I, O,P,W	A,C,O, P,W	A,C,O, P,W,X	A,I,P	A,I,P	A,C,I,O, P,W	A,C,D,I, P,T,X,W

Key for Sources. Letter abbreviations correspond to the following list of companies.

B = Bee Paper Co.
BA = Bainbridge Co.
BI = Bienfang Paper Co.
C = Crescent Cardboard Co.
F = Fredrix Co.
M = Morilla Co.
MO = Monsanto Co.
N = National Card and Mat Co.
P = Primex Plastics Corp.
S = Strathmore/Hammermill Co.

Key for Adhesives. Letter abbreviations correspond to the following list of common types of adhesives.

A = Spray adhesives
B = Cellulose cement
C = White glue
D = Rubber cement
E = Paste-up sheets (double-sided adhesive sheets)
F = Double-coated tapes

	Colored Illustration Board	Mat Board (Pebbled)	Mat Board (Colored)	Mat Board (Linen)	Mounting Board	Museum Mounting Board	Poster Boards	Tag Boards	Watercolor	Watercolor	Watercolor
Size	30″ × 40″	30″ × 40″ 32″ × 40″ 40″ × 60″	32″ × 40″	32″ × 40″	30″ × 40″	30″ × 40″ 32″ × 40″ 40″ × 60″	22″ × 28″ 28″ × 44″ 40″ × 60″	22″ × 30″	22″ × 30″	22″ × 30″	22″ × 30″
Thickness	Single-Thick	Single- and Double Thick	Single- and Double-Thick	Single-Thick	Single- and Double-Thick	1 ply 2 ply 4 ply	8 ply 14 ply 22 ply	4 ply	Extra Heavy	Extra Heavy	Extra Heavy
Color	Colors	White Cream Gray Black	Colors	Earth Tones	White	White Colors	White Colors	Tan Brown	White	White	White
Reverse	White Chip Printed Chip	White Cream Gray	White Chip Printed Chip	White Chip Printed Chip	Chip	Prime	Gray Brown or Prime	Prime	Prime	Prime	Prime
Texture	Medium	Rough	Medium	Linen	Smooth	Medium	Smooth	Medium	Smooth	Medium	Rough
Source	B,BA,BI,C, M,N,S	B,BA,BI, C,M,N	B,BA,BI,C, M,N,S	BA,C,F,N	B,BA,BI,C F,M,N,S	BA,C,S,N	B,BA,BI C,F,M,N	B,BI,M	B,BA,BI,C F,M,N,S	B,BA,BI,C, F,M,N,S	B,BA,BI,C,F, M,N,S
Adhesive	A,B,C, D,E,F	A,B,C, D,E,F	A,B,C, D,E,F	A,B,C, D,E,F	A,B,C, D,E,F	A,B,C, D,E,F	A,B,C, D,E,F	A,B,C, D,E,F	A,C,D,E,F	A,C,D,E,F	A,C,D,E,F
Acceptance of Media	A,C,D,I,O, P,T,X,W	C,D,I,P,W	C,D,I,P,W	C,D,P,W	A,C,I,O, P,W	A,C,D,I,O, P,T,X,W	A,C,I,O,P, X	A,C,D, O,P	A,C,D,I, O,T,W	A,C,D,I,O, T,W	A,C,D,I,O, T,W

Key for Acceptance of Media. Letters correspond to the following list of design media.

A = Acrylic colors
C = Crayon and Contè
D = Pastel and chalk
I = Pen and ink
O = Opaque or designer's Gouache

P = Permanent markers
T = Transparent watercolor
X = Tempera or poster paint
W = Water-based markers

Media and material combinations are traditionally thought of as permanent when their properties are compatible and do not deteriorate in time. The column Acceptance of Media is not descriptive of the means by which the media are handled in combination with paper and board materials, but simply suggests a number of possibilities that provide a broad range of effects.

described by manufacturers as hot press or high or plate finish. Rough bristol board is described as cold press, medium, regular, or vellum.

Size. The sizes of papers and boards are indicated in inches and represent common dimensions of materials available through art and drafting supply stores.

Thickness. Materials are purchased in various standards of thicknesses. Different industries use different standards; for example, the printing industry specifies thickness in point sizes; the art material industry specifies thickness in plies (single- or double-thick are also common terms); and metric measurements are often used.

Color. These terms indicate the color or range of colors available from the manufacturer.

Reverse. The term *prime* indicates that the same color and texture as the front is also used on the underside.

Texture. The terms smooth, medium, and rough identify the relative coarseness or smoothness of paper and board surfaces. When applicable, a specific term, such as canvas, is used to identify the texture of a material.

COLOR PAPERS AND FILMS

Bourges is the original producer of transparent color film for the artist and designer. Based on the early color matching system of Albert Bourges, designed and produced in 1918, printing ink colors on transparent film have become the accepted art medium for graphics. Bourges sheets, first manufactured in 1944, now feature a clear heat-resistant adhesive backing so that they are easily applied to any smooth surface, cut out to shape, and the unwanted color film quickly removed.

Bourges color sheets are keyed to many ink-matching systems for graphic reproduction. Transparent color sheets called Cutocolor are available in twenty basic hues in five tint values of each color: 100 percent, 70 percent, 50 percent, 30 percent, and 10 percent; as well as a range of designer colors, whites, and nine values of transparent grays. These sheets are sold in sizes of 20″ × 25″ and smaller sizes, through dealers or direct from Bourges if a local supplier is not available.

Bourges also produces Kleerkote, a glossy plastic sheet with a special transparent coating that accepts gouache, ink, and watercolor without crawling or chipping. This film is available in single sheets or 12-sheet pads of up to 20″ × 25″. A pressure-sensitive mat film without a color coating, called Bourges Dultop, is available in a sheet size of 20″ × 25″. Dultop is produced with an adhesive backing in relatively thin guages for overlay purposes and will accept ink and pencil.

Canson & Montgolfier of France manufacture several lines of papers for fine and commercial artists. Widely available in North America are:

• Canson Mi-Teintes, 160 GSM. A finely woven rag paper suitable for work in pastel, acrylic, tempera, gouache, pencil, and felt-tip markers, available in 35 colors, in sheets 19½″ × 25½″ and 21½″ × 29½″, in rolls 59″ × 11 yards, in 24-sheet pads, 9½″ × 12½″ and 11½″ × 16½″, and mounted on boards 19″ × 25″ and 29″ × 43″.

• Canson Ingres. A fine-textured rag paper suitable for use with charcoal, pastel, pencil, and markers, available in 21 colors, in sheets 19½″ × 25½″, and in 24-sheet pads, 9½″ × 12½″ and 11½″ × 16½″. Both Canson Ingres and Canson Mi-Teintes require an adhesive for mounting purposes.

• Canson Vidalon Tracing Vellum. Available in four basic weights, each in a wide assortment of sheets, sketching pads, and rolls.

Cello-Tak produces both a line of color film and a matching line of color paper. The color film line contains 241 colors in either a low-tack adhesive backing or a wax adhesive backing. Because the colorant on the wax adhesive sheet is on the "bottom side" of the sheet, most art media, including ink, pencil, and gouache, can be used on this material. Color film is available in three sizes: 10″ × 13″, 13″ × 20″, and 20″ × 26″. The color paper line has a selection of 220 colors and is available without adhesive backing and with a wax adhesive backing. Related art media are acceptable to the color paper line. Papers are available in one size, 20″ × 26″. A 3″ × 4″ film swatch book is also available from Cello-Tak.

Chartpak manufactures a variety of color papers and color films useful to the designer. Chartpak color papers are available in a range of 194 mat surface colors and require an adhesive. In addition to this line, an adhesive-back coated (ABC) color paper is made in a range of 82 vivid colors, including metallic gold and silver. A matching line of translucent color films is also available and has been coordinated to match Chartpak color paper. This line offers 194 mat finish colors, 12 transparent colors, and all of these sheets have a repositionable adhesive. The sheet size of these products measure 14″ × 17″, and 2″ × 3¼″ swatch books are also available. Because the color paper is made with water-resistant inks, it repels any water-based medium, but will accept solvent-based permanent inks.

Color-Aid Corporation, manufacturers of Color-Aid Products, offer 202 color papers in a smooth mat surface finish. A complete color wheel consists of 24 hues with four tint and three shade values for each hue, 16 gray values, and black and white. The sheets are produced in individual sizes of 18″ × 24″, 24″ × 36″, Color-Aid Packets of 202 coordinated colors in 6″ × 9″ sheets, and swatch books in 3″ × 5″ sheets containing the complete line. Gray sets containing 16 values are also available in 9″ × 12″ sheets. These sheets will accept other media such as ink, pastel, and gouache and have been in use for over 25 years. An adhesive, such as spray cement, rubber cement, or double-sided adhesive films, is required.

Color-Vu produces a line of 212 coordinated color papers that contains 24 full-strength hues, followed in order by four tint and three shade values for each hue. These are number coded from 1 to 192. Also available are 16 neutral grays coded G–1 to G–16, a white, a vivid red, and two blacks, one of which is printed on black paper to eliminate the need for retouching after it has been cut. Individual sheets are sold in a size of 18″ × 24″. A complete Color-Vu Packet contains 212 sheets at a size of 6″ × 9″. These papers are mat finish and will accept other media such as ink, pastel, and gouache. Color-Vu features its own double-sided adhesive sheet, Twin-Tak, which has been found to be an excellent substitute for rubber cement and spray adhesives. This adhesive material is produced in two sizes: 18″ × 24″ and 24″ × 36″.

The Crescent Cardboard Company manufactures both color papers and a matching line of color mat and drawing boards. Fifty-six colors are available in papers at one size, 22″ × 32″. These offer a rich selection of mainly intermediate and tertiary hues. They are useful with most art media such as pastel, pen and ink, felt-tip markers, and designer's gouache and have been coordinated to match 56 colored mat boards in the Crescent line. The Crescent mat board line is quite large and offers a superb range of subtle to bright hues, soft textures, and reflective and fabric surface boards in sizes 32″ × 40″ and 40″ × 48″. Applicable adhesives for work with paper include spray adhesives, rubber cement, and double-sided adhesive sheets. Adhesives for work with mat boards include spray adhesives and white glue.

Mecanorma produces a line of self-adhesive transparent mat surface color films, a line of self-adhesive transparent gloss surface color films, and a line of mat finish color papers. There are 161 colors available in either of the Normacolor transparent film lines and 159 colors available in the Normacolor paper line. The color paper line requires an adhesive and will accept ink, pencil, dry transfer lettering, and designer's gouache. Paper sheets are sold singly and measure 500 mm × 600 mm. (about 19½″ × 23½″). The adhesive films are also sold singly and measure 350 mm × 490 mm. (about 14″ × 19″). Swatch books are available for all product lines, including the recent addition of a line of 20 graduated paper colors that have the appearance of a diminishing tonal change, similar to an airbrush effect.

Pantone (Pantone, Inc.'s check-standard trademark for color reproduction and color reproduction materials) Color Products by Letraset offer a wide variety of color papers and transparent sheets. The Pantone color paper line is the widest range of color sheets available in 505 colors in an uncoated stock. Pantone coated color papers are available in 135 self-adhesive colors. Pantone color overlays are available in 275 Pantone Colors, 58 of which are Pantone screen tints. These are translucent, self-adhesive films that can be easily repositioned.

Presstype produces the ChromaRama Color System, which consists of 220 coordinated silk-screen printed color papers. These papers are available in a standard sheet size of 18″ × 24″. A complete packet of all 220 color sheets is available in a 6″ × 9″ size. Double-size sheets, 24″ × 36″, may also be specially ordered. A 2″ × 6″ swatch book is also available, which contains the entire range of the 220 colors. The system is organized around a 24-hue color wheel with 4 tint and 3 shade values accompanying each hue. Additional elements of the ChromaRama line consist of a 16-value gray scale, black, white, and a range of 10 bright colors. All ChromaRama sheets are sold on an individual basis. These papers will accept almost any art and design medium including pastel, ink, gouache, and most important, will not crack after scoring or folding. ChromaRama also offers a high resistance to fingerprinting. In addition to the standard paper line of Chroma-Rama sheets that require an adhesive such as double-sided film, spray cement, or rubber cement, a new limited line of pressure-sensitive adhesive-backed ChromaRama sheets has just been introduced. As with all ChromaRama sheets, colors are consistent from sheet to sheet and batch to batch.

Zipatone produces a range of 142 transparent color sheets in both a mat or glossy finish. A complete color wheel consists of 21 hues, 2 tints, and 3 shade values for each hue, 14 gray values, and black and white. Zipatone offers a choice of two sheet sizes, 10″ × 14″ and 20″ × 28″. The mat color surface will accept other art media such as ink, pencil, gouache, or dry transfer lettering. Both the mat and glossy lines have a low-tack adhesive coating and are repositionable on most any surface.

LIQUID AND DRY MEDIA

In addition to dry color papers, boards, and transparent color sheets, liquid color media extend the range of possible effects and experience for three-dimensional design. Included in these are the traditional water-based media—gouache, water-color, tempera, acrylic paint, and ink (fig. 2–1) and the color drawing media—pencil, pastel, and markers (fig. 2–2). These descriptions are simply an overview of their characteristics, handling, and associated tools.

Gouache. Gouache is an opaque, water-based paint that completely covers the underlying surface. One of several manufacturers, Winsor & Newton produce a professional line called Designer's Gouache, which contains 78 colors and is widely used for art and design purposes. Other manufacturers produce reliable lightfast gouache, also referred to as designer's colors or opaque watercolor. Although many similarities in handling and

2–1. Liquid media.

2–2. Dry media.

technique exist between Winsor & Newton and other brands, the special characteristics, as well as the price and color range of the brand chosen, should be investigated.

A broad range of paper and board supports (see Table 1) can be used with gouache. Opaque applications and surface building through overpainting are possible along with a dimension of transparent effects. In the Winsor & Newton line, there are two whites, permanent white and zinc white. Permanent white is for maximum opacity and is not recommended for diluting colors, while zinc white makes the "cleanest" and clearest tints. There are also three blacks in the line, jet, lamp, and ivory black. Jet black is a very opaque, cool black that gives blue-grays when mixed with white. Lamp black produces cool grays when mixed with white. Ivory black, a brownish-black, gives warm grays and sepia tones when mixed with white. The range of colors are classified into four grades of permanence. The codes AA (extremely permanent), A (durable), B (moderately durable), and C (fugitive) indicate which colors are most suitable for extended periods of lightfastness. Some of the colors are more opaque than others, depending upon the opacity of the basic pigment. They are classified in four degrees of opacity. Additionally, some colors have better bleed resistance than others and have been classified into four degrees of staining. (Staining is the ability of individual hues to leave pigment stains after rinsing with water.) A second coat should be applied thinly to avoid cracking or flaking—a little gum arabic added to the top color will give greater protection. For gouache to adhere to acetate and suitable film surfaces, simply mix in small quantities of a noncrawl additive. If not added, such surfaces may cause "crawling," the forming of globules, instead of spreading evenly.

Ideally, gouache colors are thinned with water and best applied with a good-quality sable brush, although less expensive watercolor brushes will also work. These colors can be used with a lettering pen, ruling pen, or airbrush. There are many possible techniques and advantages to gouache that are worthwhile experimenting with. Among liquid media, gouache is one of the fast-drying color paints.

Watercolor. Well known for its freshness, watercolor is a transparent water-based medium that provides a vibrant color range and value control and allows large surface areas to be covered quickly. One of the important features of this medium is that color values are reduced only by the addition of water and not by the use of white paint. A vital characteristic of watercolor is also the use of the wash. By thinning the paint with water, washes are applied to achieve flat tones, variation within a single tone, and changing effect from one tone to another. The watercolor artist must work dark on light and not light on dark as is possible with gouache. Strictly speaking, the number of transparent wash overlays should not exceed three, as the overall result will begin to appear muddy. Through experimentation with related drawing and painting materials, a number of effects are possible. A few of the many possible approaches include pen-line and watercolor wash, masking fluids and candle wax as resist techniques with wash overlays, and using the fine to broad spray of an airbrush.

A wide range of watercolor is available. It is common to find several lines of watercolor produced by a single manufacturer, one of which will be more expensive and of better quality than the others. The less expensive paints usually will have different characteristics in terms of tinting strength, permanence, and the quality of pigments. Watercolors are available in pan forms as well as in sets and tubes. A few of the major brands are Winsor & Newton, Speedball Professional Watercolors by Hunt Manufacturing Co., and Grumbacher. Fully liquid watercolor can also be purchased in bottles with an eyedropper provided to transfer paint to palette. Luma and Dr. Martin's are two brands that offer wide color ranges of liquid watercolor.

Tempera. Many artists and designers choose this medium over others because the paints dry much truer to the original pigment color, allowing the artist to work more accurately and control the final color of his work. There are two approaches to the practice of using tempera. The first is to mix one's own by combining egg yolk, a nondrying oil, and lecithin. When these ingredients are mixed with dry pigments and distilled water, the egg tempera medium is formed. One may further explore this method and its many variations by investigating the process in an artist's materials and techniques book.

Ready-mixed tempera paints, also called poster paints, can be purchased in bottles through art supply stores and differ in character and handling from the homemade tempera. This form of tempera, normally used for signs, posters, and commercial illustrations is thinned with water and applied by brush for opaque and transparent effects. Overpainting is usually done only after the first coat has dried. Tempera is ill-suited for use in an impasto or heavy surface application, which can result in the paint cracking. A rigid surface, such as a heavy bristol board or illustration board, makes an excellent painting and design support for this medium. Rich Art Color Company and Iddings Paint Division of Rosco Labs are both major manufacturers of this form of tempera paint.

Acrylic. Acrylic paint is normally sold in tubes or in bottles. Similar to gouache, watercolor, and tempera, when diluted with water and used on paper acrylic paint dries to an even mat (semigloss) finish. A number of related products—gel medium, mat medium, and gloss medium—may be added to affect the thickness, handling opacity, and surface finish of the paint. Acrylics afford the artist an opportunity to work in either opaque or transparent effects or a combination of both. When dry, they will not change in color or texture, and overpainting is possible without altering the preceding coat. The drying time for this medium may be slowed by adding a retarder or small amounts of propolene glycol to the paint on a palette. These paints are recognized for their versatility and may be applied to a wide variety of paper, board, and canvas products. It is necessary in most cases to prepare the surface with an acrylic primer. Liquitex, Winsor & Newton, Grumbacher's Hyplar, Permalba, Atalier, and Chromacryl are among the well-known brands.

Inks. A broad variety of drawing inks is available to the artist. Inks are generally classified as one of two types: water-resistant and nonwaterproof. The water-resistant inks dry to a glossy film and can be overlaid. Many manufacturers use shellac as a waterproofing agent and various dyes (not pigments) which are not lightfast. Inks based on dyes should not be used for work that is intended for display in lighted areas for any period of time. Where a high degree of lightfastness is required, the artist should use watercolor or gouache. Grumbacher makes a range of 17 colors; Pelikan makes 18 colors, and Winsor & Newton have 24. There are also several nonwaterproof inks available in a range of colors. They give the effect of diluted watercolors, dry to a mat finish, and are also more readily absorbed by paper than the others. Some nonwaterproof carbon inks are useful because they dilute easily with water, giving tones that can be further diluted when water is washed over them with a brush. When ink is left for a period of time, pigmented inks will settle, requiring the bottle to be shaken before use. If the ink has evaporated and the color has become deeper and thicker, a small amount of distilled water will thin it again for easier flow. All of these drawing inks are used with both brush and dip pen. A wide assortment of colored inks are sold through art and drafting supply stores, including Higgins by Faber-Castell, Winsor & Newton, Grumbacher, Koh-I-Noor, and Pelikan by Koh-I-Noor Rapidograph.

Pencils. Until the development of the graphite pencil, preliminary sketches and designs by artists were created with charcoal or brush. It was not until the seventeenth century that the potential of graphite was fully realized. Today, manufacturers provide a wide range of graphite, charcoal, carbon, and colored pencils. The graphite or "lead" pencil is manufactured in common grades according to a range of softness or hardness. This range normally extends from 6B (the softest) through HB (middle range) to 9H (the hardest). Charcoal and carbon pencils both produce very black lines and are also available in soft and hard ranges. Unlike graphite, however, even the hardest of these will produce a high degree of blackness. The traditional ingredients of colored pencils—filler, binder, lubricant, and pigment—result in reasonably soft marks that can be completely removed only by the use of a blade, although kneaded rubber followed by a standard rubber eraser will usually remove enough for recoloring. In addition to their line of color pencils, Berol Corporation now produces Prismacolor Art Stix. Because the ingredients of these uncovered color sticks are identical to those in Berol Prismacolor pencils, they may be used in combination with the pencils or individually for broad-stroke blending and shading effects. Berol, Eagle, Faber-Castell, Pentalic Corporation, and Staedtler all market a wide variety of pencils.

Pastel. From the moment pastels are applied, their effect is easily noticed. Their soft, bright, and fresh hues make them one of the most attractive color media. Color can be blended directly on the paper. Unlike water-based media, pastels cannot be mixed on the palette to form other colors and tones. They are made from a paste composed of powdered pigments bound together by weak gum or resin and should not be confused with harder chalk crayons, which are made with wax or oil.

Pastels are produced in three forms: pastel pencils, and round and square pastel sticks. Up to 600 tints are available from some manufacturers. Manufacturers normally label their colors by name and number utilizing a scale from 0 to 8 to indicate the relative lightness to darkness of a tone. To a considerable extent, pastel work relies on the color and texture of the paper for its effect. A good-quality watercolor or drawing paper with sufficient "tooth" is normally recommended. Ingres papers are a most reliable support for work in pastel and are available in 15 colors. Pastels may also be applied over paper that has been tinted with watercolor or over drawings in ink and gouache. The well-known Conté pastels are manufactured in France and are imported only by Hunt Manufacturing Company. Grumbacher, Talens-Rembrandt, and NuPastel are also major brands that produce an extensive range of pastel colors.

Markers. Today, felt- and fiber-tip pens are increasingly used by professionals for drawing and design projects. Because they are produced in a wide assortment of sizes and colors, they can be used in every stage of work, from rough layout to a finished presentation. Several companies produce pens in water- and spirit-based inks. The coloring ingredients are usually a combination of aniline dye and xylol solvent, which is transparent on paper and dries quickly. Because the color dyes in markers fade after being exposed to light, drawings that are to be displayed should be protected by a clear plastic sheet or glass that contains ultraviolet-light-screening agents.

Additional specialized pens are made for overhead projection drawing; ball-tip pens for carbon copying; and clear-solution pens with various tip sizes and shapes, including chisel, wedge-shaped, and razor-point. Several of the manufacturers offer a selection of over 150 colors. Major brands for markers include Pentel of America, Ltd., Magic Marker Industries, Design Markers, and Mecanorma Art Marker.

PLASTICS AND WOODS

Georgia-Pacific Corporation produces tinted transparent acetate called XCEL Cast Cellulose Acetate tinted sheets. These are available through art and drafting stores in a variety of standard colors—amber, blue, green, red, yellow, pink, and orange. They are also produced with a one-side or two-side tint in gauges from .003″ to .010″. Georgia-Pacific also manufactures XCEL Extruded Cellulose Acetate sheets, known for their toughness and optical clarity and used extensively in the manufacture of protective shields for the eyes and face, splash shields, grinding shields, and welding shields. Standard colors in this line include clear transparent, light-green, medium-green, or dark-green transparent, yellow transparent, brown transparent, and gray smoke transparent. Thicknesses in this line extend from .020″ to .100″. Various surface finishes are also available in both product lines.

Transilwrap Plastics is a single source for a broad selection of plastic sheets, rolls and assorted transparent materials. Clear acetate is available in several thicknesses from .003″ to .015″ and in many sheet sizes from 8½″ × 11″ to 40″ × 50″. Transparent colored acetate sheets in red, blue, green, and yellow are available in thicknesses of .003″, .005″, .0075″, .010″ inches, and in sheet sizes of 25″ × 40″ and 20″ × 50″. Also available is Transil G.A., a precoated acetate, which is coated to accept ink, watercolor, and almost any liquid medium without beading or crawling. These sheets are produced in one thickness of .005″ and in sheet sizes of 20″ × 25″ through 40″ × 50″. Thinner gauge acetate, colored cellophane, rigid vinyl sheets in colors, acrylic sheets in assorted colors and finishes, acetate grid sheets, and metallic polyester films are among other products available through Transilwrap Plastics.

E. I. Dupont Co. is the manufacturer of Mylar polyester film. This material is a flexible, exceptionally strong and durable transparent film with an unusual balance of properties that make it suitable for many applications. It has high tensile, tear, and impact strength, resists moisture vapor, and does not become brittle with age. Its ability to lie flat without wrinkling or buckling is an additional reason why this material is useful to artists, architects, and engineers. In the graphic arts, its many uses include as a layout base for preparing color separations and lithographic plates, as a surface for technical drawing capable of reproduction, and as a support sheet in silk screening. Ultraclear, mat, and pigmented films are available in either roll or sheet form and in a variety of gauges and widths. Mylar polyester film, type ERM, is suitable for drawing with technical pen and with colored and lead pencils. Other varieties are available that can be laminated, embossed, metallized, punched, dyed, or coated, as well as vacuum-formed.

The Rohm and Haas Company manufactures a wide variety of products, including a brand of acrylic sheet that carries the trade name Plexiglas.

Translucent color sheets are available in 25 hues. They transmit light that is diffused so that an object behind the sheet cannot be clearly distinguished. Their color will vary according to the amount of light transmitted through the sheet or reflected from its surface. Transparent color sheets provide "see-through" visibility and are available in 10 hues. The solar control tinted sheets offer a range of five color densities or tints in either bronze or gray colors. In addition, 15 opaque color sheets are available, 6 mirror color tinted sheets and an assortment of clear and colored patterned surfaces. Information on the handling of these materials is offered under Construction Methods in this chapter as a general background. It is important to note that product, health, and safety information are available from the manufacturer and should be reviewed prior to using these materials.

Colorants. The following discussion is an overview of the material properties of acrylic and plastic colorants. In the plastics field, colorants are classified into three categories: dyes, organic pigments (although chemists often refer to these as dyes as well), and inorganic pigments. A major distinction between dyes and pigments is that dyes transfer their colors to the host, and pigments carry or impart their own colors. A further difference is that dyes absorb certain wavelengths of light while transmitting others, and pigments absorb some wavelengths while reflecting others. Both dyes and pigments can be synthetic or natural; dyes, however, are characterized by excellent clarity, transparency, and high saturation, while inorganic pigments are insoluble in resins and are usually opaque with few exceptions. Dyes are also less stable under extreme conditions of light and heat than inorganic pigments, which have excellent heat- and lightfastness. Organic pigments fall between those two categories, with some having very good heat- and lightfastness as well as transparency, while others are opaque and dull. Transparent organic pigments (vat dyes) can be obtained for polyesters to yield stained-glass-quality colors. Acrylic monomer-based color dyes are available for tinting acrylic sheets and forms through a dipping process, which can provide very uniform and high saturation through repeated immersions.

Woods and Accessories. A variety of woods and metals are commonly found in art and hobby supply stores, and are very useful in three-dimensional work. Balsa wood is the most frequently used wood because of its light weight and flexibility. It is available in sheets, sticks, dowels, blocks, planks, moldings, and triangles. Harder woods, such as bass, cherry, maple, walnut, and mahogany are also available and provide the designer with greater durability, more attractive color and grain, plus a smaller amount of splintering. Hard woods are available in an equally wide range of sizes and shapes. Because of the porous nature of wood, the most effective adhesives are the cellulose cements and wood glues. Metal tubing, sheets, and rods in copper, brass, and aluminum are often combined with wood when constructing a model to lend variety in appearance and support to other forms. When bonding metals together, special epoxy and super-strength glues or a soldering tool may be required.

MEDIA TOOLS

The use of design media requires an understanding of the tools and traditional approaches directly related to their application. The appropriate selection of an adhesive for paper products, plastic, and wood contribute to the desired appearance and durability of a design. The texture and finish of a surface with which liquid media will be used depend upon the selection of an appropriate tool and its handling. Many papers and cardboards require the selection of an adhesive that provides durability, flexibility of use, and ease in application. It is often advantageous to select a repositionable adhesive for thin papers, such as spray mount or double-sided paste-up sheets, to provide strength and convenience in handling their unprotected surfaces. White glue and aliphatic resin glues are useful for heavy paper and cardboard materials, while special adhesives for bonding plastic, wood, and metal are also available.

The liquid media are applied for a smooth flat finish with a soft-hair brush such as sable or, for textural effects, with a coarse bristle brush. The airbrush is also capable of creating flat surface finishes without brush strokes as well as rich textural effects when used with masking devices.

ADHESIVES

Many adhesives are suitable for design work. Those generally used for light paper applications, of one- and two-ply thickness, are rubber cement, double-sided tapes, double-sided adhesive sheets, spray mount adhesives, and solid glue in stick form. Appropriate adhesives for heavier materials—four-ply paperboards, single- and double-thick boards, include white glue, aliphatic resin glue, contact cement, and spray cements (fig. 2–3). In addition, there are adhesives especially suited for work with acetate, acrylic sheets, wood, and metal. The following descriptions include several common adhesives and a reference table for their applications to various materials (table 2).

Double-sided Adhesive Films (Paste-up Sheets). A paste-up sheet consists of a sheet of paper coated on both sides with a thin membrane adhesive and protected by two sheets of easy-to-remove release paper. They are used for permanent mounting of flat materials and adhere to paper, plastic, wood, and metal. Surfaces can be joined by simply pressing materials onto the exposed adhesive surface by hand. Sheets are available in several sizes from 9″ × 12″ up to 27″ × 36″ through Kent Adhesive Products.

Rubber Cement. Rubber cement is available in tubes, bottles, and cans and is used on a wide assortment of materials. It is a low-strength adhesive most often used with lightweight materials such as paper and cardboard. For a temporary bond, coat

2–3. Adhesives.

one surface and join materials while cement is wet. For stronger bonds, both surfaces should be coated, allowed to dry, and then joined together. Bonds made with rubber cement are temporary. The solvent for this product is volatile. When mounting flat art materials, rubber cement is often thinned first with a solvent and two coats are applied to each surface. When thoroughly dry, the art work and mounting board are joined. Best-Test and Sanford's Rubber Cement are both major brands.

Table 2.2 Common Adhesives and Their Applications

Adhesive	Paper	Cardboard	Light Wood	Heavy Wood	Metal	Plastics	Fabric
Paste-up Sheets	X	X					
Rubber Cement	X	X	X				
White Glue	X	X	X	X			X
Aliphatic Resin Glue	X	X	X	X			X
Cellulose Cement	X	X	X		X	X[1]	X
Contact Cement		X	X		X	X	X
Epoxy Cement			X	X	X	X	

[1] Use when cementing celluloid and acetate to other materials

White Glue. White glue is water soluble, clear, and fast-drying. It is sold in liquid form in plastic containers and bottles. It is compatible with paper, cardboard, fabric, and wood, but not with plastic or metal. Use clamps to hold materials together for about thirty minutes until glue has set. Excess glue should be cleaned off immediately with a damp rag. This glue may also be slightly diluted with water for transparent joints. Elmer's Glue-All adhesive, by Borden Inc. and Uhu are two major brands.

Aliphatic Resin Glue. Aliphatic resin glues are water-resistant when dry and are available in liquid form. They are a permanent form of white glue and are used for joining heavy paper, cardboard, and wood. Light work requires five-minute clamping and heavier jobs in wood require up to 45 minutes of clamping and drying.

Cellulose Cement. Cellulose cement is a clear, quick-drying, waterproof cement commonly packaged in tubes. Model-airplane glue and household varieties are available. They can be used to bond porous and nonporous materials. The solvent for this type of cement is acetone. Applications should permit air circulation around the joint to allow the solvent to evaporate and the cement to thoroughly dry. Nonporous materials may be coated on one side and adhered, while porous materials require coating on both surfaces before materials are pressed together. Uhu is one of several major brands.

Contact Cement. Contact cement is a quick-drying, water-resistant liquid. It is normally packaged in cans and aerosol sprays. This cement is designed to make materials adhere on contact without clamping. Apply a coat to both surfaces, allow it to dry, apply a second coat, and allow this to dry for thirty minutes. The bond should be made within a three-hour period. If not allowed to thoroughly dry, this adhesive will separate when exposed to normal sunlight. Contact cement is made with neoprene and naphtha or toluol. It is also available in a nonflammable water-based form. The 3M Company and Weldwood both manufacture this adhesive.

Epoxy Cement. Epoxy cement is made up of two parts, a resin and a hardener, which, when combined, form a high-strength bond. This cement will bond most materials, including plastics and metals. Epoxy is applied to both surfaces that are to be joined. Parts are then pressed together without the aid of clamps. The excess should be removed immediately with

denatured alcohol prior to the adhesive setting. Hands should be cleaned immediately with nail-polish remover or denatured alcohol. Also available is an instant epoxy that hardens in approximately one minute. Duro E-POX-E Adhesive and Duro Super Glue are both made by the Loctite Corporation.

BRUSHES

Artist's brushes are made in many sizes and shapes and of several different materials, each for a variety of purposes (fig. 2-4). A versatile group of brush shapes for water-based media are brights, flats, rounds, and filberts. A range of coarse- and soft-hair brushes are also useful for a variety of textural effects. The following descriptions of the shapes and composition of brushes are included to offer a basis for comparison and a means of selection.

Brights. Brights are square-cornered with short bristles that are only slightly longer than the width of the ferrules. The shortness of their bristles makes them relatively stiff, providing control of thick acrylic paint. The stiffness tends to impress the bristle ends into the paint, leaving marks that provide texture.

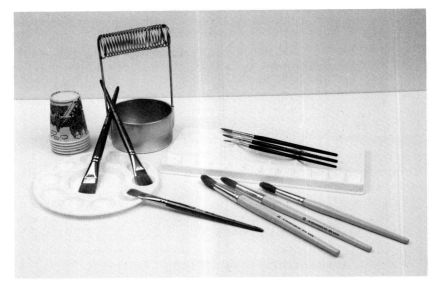

2-4. Brushes.

Flats. Flats are square-cornered with hairs approximately one and one-half times longer than the width of the ferrules. The added length makes the hairs more flexible, allowing for a softer impression left in the pigment, and therefore fewer brush strokes in the application of a flat color.

Rounds. Rounds have hairs tapered from a round ferrule to a point. These are generally useful for line work, preliminary sketching, and for outlining shapes over broad areas. They are also used for making variable-width strokes, which widen as pressure is applied to the stroke.

Filberts. Filberts are similar to brights and flats in length, but have rounded corners. This shape accommodates a variable stroke but in a broader range than the round. It is useful for blending edges and can achieve a controlled line definition.

There are a variety of types of hairs that influence the smooth or textural appearance of liquid media. The following descriptions survey both the soft and coarse varieties and their applications.

Red Sable. Red sable comes from weasel and Kolinsky tails, both grouped under the name red tarter marten. A top-quality red sable brush must have the finest-quality hair and be uniform in strength, thickness, and elasticity or spring. It is expensive but makes the very best brush for flat application of water-based media without brush strokes.

Ox Hair. Ox hair used in brushes is taken from the ears of oxen and comes in many qualities. It has great tensile strength and does not break off under strenuous use with any medium. These are light blond hairs that have relatively long-tapered points and are springy in character. They are useful for textural effects. Darker ox hairs are also available but vary more in quality.

Sabeline. Sabeline, a light ox hair that has been dyed reddish has handling characteristics similar to that of red sable. It is a sturdy and durable soft hair that is often combined with a blend of red sable during manufacturing.

Camel Hair. The term *camel hair,* when applied to brushes, is somewhat misleading as a trade term. The finer grades actually are made of squirrel hair with other varieties made of pony and goat hair. They may be used for flat applications with a wide range of liquid media including watercolor, tempera, and ink.

Bristle. Bristle is taken from hogs and boars. The terms *hair* and *bristle* are not interchangeable words and have distinct differences. The important difference is that a hair has a single, individual, natural point, while a bristle has multiple natural tips called flags. (A magnification of the end of a hair appears as one strand from the root to the tip, while the tip of a bristle has multiple tails or flags.) The bristle also has a unique taper from the root to the tip, and the hair is less consistent, thickest in the midsection. Bristles make relatively stiff brushes, which are advantageous for creating textural effects with water-based media.

Synthetic. The synthetic varieties are available when the budget does not permit the purchase of high-quality hair or bristle brushes. Synthetic hair brushes provide an excellent substitute and simulate both the fine hair of watercolor brushes as well as the coarser varieties that are useful for acrylic and oil. They are made in several shapes such as rounds, flats, and brights and come in a variety of sizes.

AIRBRUSH

Today, the airbrush has become an important addition to the designer's equipment and has application to both graphic and three-dimensional design (fig. 2–5). It is a highly sophisticated tool and requires considerable practice for proper use. Principally, the airbrush functions on compressed air that is pressurized in a container at 30 pounds per square inch. The air passes through a narrow chamber into a wider one, where it expands to create a partial vacuum. Paint in the brush reservoir is pulled into the chamber to mix with the air and is atomized.

There are several choices for air containers that may be

2–5. Airbrush.

used with an airbrush. The common ones are an electric compressor, an aerosol can, and a refillable canister such as those used by skin divers. Of these sources, the compressor is preferred because the air supply can be maintained at a constant pressure (fig. 2-6). Other sources may be used if properly regulated.

Basic Models. Essentially, there are two types of airbrush operating mechanisms. In the single-action model, the artist cannot alter the pattern of spray. He may increase or decrease the flow of color or change the distance between the brush and the surface being painted. This type of airbrush is relatively simple to maintain and is used largely for simple background work where precise detail is unnecessary. For more sophisticated work, an airbrush with a double-action lever is required. This type of lever allows the artist to control and vary both the air and color flow. By pressing the lever down, air is released and by simultaneously pressing down and pulling the lever back, a greater proportion of paint is mixed with air.

Preparing and Mixing Color. It is important that paints and inks to be used for airbrush work are correctly and carefully prepared. A desired medium should be thinned to resemble the consistency of milk. If a mixed solution is too thick, a coarse, stippled effect will result, which may clog the nozzle, distort the

needle action, and possibly damage the brush. Each time a pigment is changed, the paint reservoir should be cleaned out with an appropriate solvent.

A wide range of media varying in color and consistency may be used with an airbrush. Among the suitable media are gouache or designer's colors, concentrated liquid watercolor, waterproof drawing inks, and acrylic paint. Liquid and friskets are commonly used with the airbrush to create a variety of textural, reflective, or atmospheric effects or to block out larger areas. A frisket can be made by tracing an image exactly onto film before cutting. Liquid masks are applied with a paintbrush and rubbed off when paint is dry. A torn paper mask can be used to create patterns, textures, and varying line qualities. Paasche is one of the major manufacturers of professional airbrush equipment and compressors.

CONSTRUCTION METHODS

Materials that relate to three-dimensional design have properties of rigidity, flexibility, and durability. They cannot sustain stress, tension, and load beyond their ultimate strength without buckling or breaking. Because gravity exerts a force upon all materials, constructed relationships in increasing sizes have limitations beyond which they will collapse. Wood is a flexible and fairly elastic material that can be used as a linear, planar, and volumetric element. Wood, cardboard, and heavier papers can all be laminated together to increase their thickness and stability. They may be used as structural elements and as spans across spaces, which transmit their loads through vertical supports to a construction's base.

The basic principles of construction for three-dimensional objects from any material include methods of cutting, scoring, folding, bending, laminating, and joining. Although the type of tool and the manner in which it is used may vary from one material to another, the basic methods are essentially the same. Drafting tools and art knives are necessary for three-dimensional work in most materials, especially paper and cardboard. The additional tools—saws, drills, sandpaper, and polishing equipment—are often used for work in wood and plastic.

2-6. Compressor.

PAPER MODELING

The beginning principles and processes of paper modeling are to form a three-dimensional object from a flat piece of paper by curving, cutting, folding, and bending. A completed model may be fashioned with simple tools such as a utility knife, T-square, and glue. Intricate geometric volumes, pleated forms for interior or exterior treatments, laminations for contour forms, and structural elements can all be made. It is also possible to wet-form curvilinear surfaces from some types of cardboards. Neither extensive practice nor a high level of skill is necessary to construct study models from these materials. By following simple guidelines and procedures, one can easily manipulate a piece of paper.

Whether freestanding or relief, a concept can be adapted from sketches and photographs, although ideas should be simplified in the beginning with a minimum of detail. Generally, the size of the model determines the thickness of paper to consider; large models may collapse if the materials are too thin. Bristol papers in various sizes are suitable for many model applications; however, models for architectural and theater design are usually made from thicker cardboard. Many freestanding forms are made from a basic vocabulary of two-dimensional shapes, such as squares, triangles, and rectangles and, for additional strength, are often constructed around an armature such as a thicker cardboard or a wooden support.

WORK AREA AND EQUIPMENT FOR BASIC FORMS

A well-arranged work area will facilitate your results. It is important that your table be completely flat, preferably a large drawing table covered with gray chipboard or illustration board, about 30″ × 40″ and 1/16″ thick. The board should be secured to the table with double-sided tape.

Tools for working with paper and cardboard are less specialized than those for many other types of design. Tools should include a utility knife, X-Acto knife and new blades, scissors, 2-H hard lead pencils, a compass with arms measuring four to five inches, a metal ruler, a clear plastic ruler, a 45-degree and a 30 to 60-degree clear plastic triangle, a clear plastic protractor, a kneaded eraser, a plastic eraser, masking tape, white glue, and a

T-square. Additional tools worthwhile to consider are a can of spray cement and a flexible drawing curve (fig. 2–7). Your work area should be kept clean with all tools, containers, and scraps of paper off to the side of your space. When performing jobs such as cutting and scoring, it is best to stand at the desk in order to have a clear overview. Good lighting is also necessary for your work area, and daylight is most preferable. For working at night, artificial lamps with flexible arms, in addition to ceiling lights, are advantageous.

ADDITIONAL EQUIPMENT

In order to facilitate more sophisticated model design and construction, the basic set of tools used for study models can be expanded to include a comprehensive range of equipment (fig. 2–8). Many of the following items are well known to the designer, while others are the relatively recent results of technological developments.

Drawing Instruments and Equipment. A set of drawing instruments is an important tool for the designer. A small kit in-

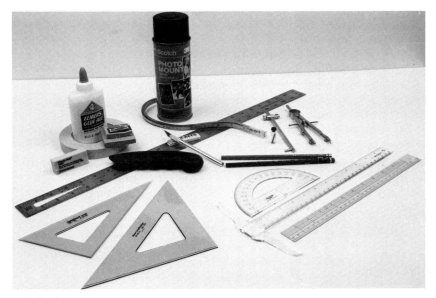

2-7. Basic equipment.

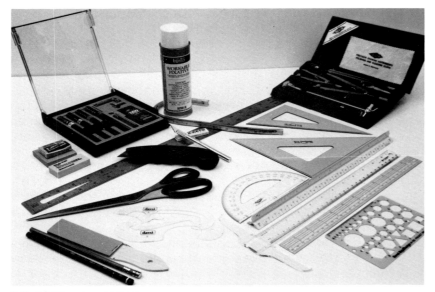

2-8. Additional equipment.

cludes two sets of spring bow compasses, a small radius compass, and an extension bar for drawing large arcs and circles. Among the various useful attachments for the compass are a lead holder, a cutting blade, a ruling pen, and an attachment for a stylus or technical pen. Alvin and Company, Inc., Martin Instrument Company, and the C-Thru Ruler Company are all major manufacturers of drawing instruments and kits.

Ruling Pens. Ruling pens are useful for doing line work of a constant thickness. The standard pen is designed so that the ink is held between two prongs, and an adjustable screw setting varies the line thickness. A variety of other liquid media may also be used, provided the medium is thinned down to a consistency of ink. For continuous ink flow, a technical pen is recommended.

Technical Pens. Technical pens are useful for very detailed drawings and designs. These are tubular nib pens that enable the designer to draw consistent ink lines. They may be used with rulers, stencils—and by means of a special attachment—with a compass. Many nib units are interchangeable and provide different line widths. Special inks in black and several

colors are available and will give precise, dense lines that can be reproduced. Major brands include Reform by Alvin and Company, Inc., Faber-Castell, Koh-I-Noor, and Mars-Staedtler.

Rulers and Guides. Of the many templates, rulers, and guides common to the designer's equipment, a scale, a metal straightedge ruler, and a T-square are the most basic. A plastic scale is useful to enlarge or reduce the size of technical drawings. Used in conjunction with a T-square, the 45-degree, 30/60-degree, and adjustable triangles are useful for lines of varying degrees of angles. Also common for this purpose is a protractor with calibrated degrees of angles, 0 to 180 degrees. French curves, flexible drawing curves, and a wide assortment of templates are also available for creating complex curvilinear shapes.

Cutting Tools. A selection of cutting tools are most important for the designer. For fine cutting, artist knives with interchangeable blades, scissors, a utility knife, and a parallel cutter are all necessary. A utility knife and guillotine are useful for heavier cutting work. X-Acto precision knives and tools is a subsidiary of Hunt Manufacturing Company and is a major source for cutting tools.

Sharpening. One of the most reliable and controllable methods of sharpening pencils is with a utility or artist knife. A pencil that has been properly sharpened with a blade will reveal more lead and retain its point longer than if sharpened with a pencil sharpener. A sandpaper block is often used for final shaping. Pencil sharpeners are also useful but cannot be as effectively controlled as a blade and have the unfortunate habit of breaking off the lead just as it reaches a suitable point.

Erasers. Most erasers will have an adverse affect, however limited, on the surface of the paper. Plastic and art gum erasers are helpful in avoiding smudging but may crumble and damage a drawing. Kneaded or putty erasers are most useful because of their pliability and are helpful in revealing areas of white paper to pick up highlights. For erasing India ink from mat films, prepared acetate, and hard surface papers, the Koh-I-Noor number 9600 Imbibed Eraser is recommended. J. S. Staedtler Co. and Eberhard-Faber, Inc., are also major manufacturers of erasers.

Fixatives. Fixatives can be purchased ready-made, either in aerosol spray cans, or in bottles to be used with an atomizer. For graphite, chalk, charcoal, pastel, and watercolor, fixatives play the role of a binder similar to that of oil and glue in paint.

Palettes. There are a number of palettes available in art supply stores, including ceramic, plastic, metal, and white porcelain enamel trays (see fig. 2–4). Those with pockets for mixing individual hues and with larger areas provided for blending colors are preferred. Mixing is enhanced on a white surface where color can be judged easily. I often require my students to use paper cups when mixing large quantities of paint and plastic wrap to prevent the paint from drying too soon. Plastic pails, bowls, and cups are useful for mixing color and as water containers for rinsing brushes. Brushes should always be cleaned thoroughly to avoid paint drying in between the hairs or at the root end near the ferrule. Water has less tendency to seep into the ferrule and damage the brush if it is left to dry in a spring cup, with the hairs pointing down and the handle up.

METHODS OF CONSTRUCTION FOR BASIC FORMS

When working with paper and cardboard, an awareness of the basic methods of forming three-dimensional constructions is helpful to produce well-crafted results.

Cutting. When cutting cardboard and paper of substantial thickness, it is important to make several light strokes rather than attempt to cut through with a single stroke. Good cutting is also the result of using sharp tools. A metal ruler and guides should be used whenever possible. Often, less pressure against a surface and several passes of the knife along the same path will produce the cleanest possible form.

Scoring. When a crisp bend in the paper is required, the material is partially cut with a knife to allow the material to fold without separating. Very little pressure on the surface is required as the objective in scoring is to cut through approximately one-half of the thickness of the material. Pleated forms are created by alternately scoring on separate lines, first on one side and then the other to allow the paper to fold in opposite directions.

Bending and Folding. Cylinders, cones, and many tubular forms can be created by bending the material. If a piece of paper is pulled from under a ruler in a downward motion, the pressure will create spiral and wavy shapes. Folding the paper, first by scoring or creasing, allows for a sharper division between different planes and is used to form pleats, cubes, and angular shapes.

PAPER, CARDBOARD, AND WOOD CONSTRUCTION

Laminations. When two materials are joined to form a single unit, the process is generally called a lamination. Laminations are often considered a means of providing support and a variety of surface finishes. They require an adhesive that is suitable to both materials and a plan or procedure for the joining operation. The nature of the adhesive used is often determined by the handling characteristics of the materials and the sequence of application in construction. Prior to cutting the final shape and form, two or more materials are bonded by means of an adhesive application. Occasionally, materials are precut together to ensure a matched fit, and then applied to the structure or surface in sequence, one at a time. Laminations requiring the joining of three or more surfaces of materials may require two or more types of adhesives (fig. 2–9).

Edges and Seams. The formation of a line or edge by two planes coming together from different angles is also an important consideration in the plan for construction. A perfectly matched fit (flush) along edges and corners depend on measurements taken

2–9. Laminations.

that allow for overlap and cover fit. Thinner materials such as paper may be cut with a utility knife to form crisp, sharp edges. Cardboard may require the use of a bevel mat cutter, which is capable of cutting along a line with the blade set at an angle of between 0 and 90 degrees (fig. 2-10). To seam materials together, cardboards and woods are sometimes bevel cut and interfaced to continue a finishing surface along to its conclusion. However subtle, the final appearance of a line or break where the material was joined will still be evident.

Joints. There are several ways in which joints can be made in paper, cardboard, and wood. A lap joint or the overlapping of two surfaces that are then fastened by glue or a double-sided adhesive sheet is a basic technique. In lightweight paper models, this joint is commonly used to join angles (with tabs) where two planes meet (fig. 2-11, left). A variation of this procedure, common to carpentry, is the butt joint.

In paper models, this joint requires additional folding to develop a common surface for gluing and results in a more uniform surface than the lap joint (fig. 2-11, right). Tabs and slots are a preliminary way of joining paper that allows one to view the overall form and relationship of its members before gluing. These are friction joints, which resist a minimum amount of force and are temporary. They may be designed to be more permanent by gluing and/or by using "locking devices" (fig. 2-11, center).

Wood Joints. The following are the basic wood-joining techniques from which many variations have been devised. They are useful for structural support and finish in the design of heavier constructions and model bases. Similar to paper joints, the lap or butt joint offers minimum resistance to failure and may be fastened with glue or hardware (fig. 2-12, left). A combination of lap and butt joints provides a more complex joint of greater resistance to failure and may also be fastened with either glue or hardware (fig. 2-12, center). Similar in principle to slots and tabs in paper, the mortice and tenon (with a pegged variation) provides greater resistance to failure and may also be joined with glue and additional hardware (fig. 2-12, right).

ACRYLIC SHEET FABRICATION

Plexiglas and Fire. Plexiglas acrylic must be used with an awareness that it is combustible. In general, the same fire precautions that are observed in connection with the handling and use of

2-10. Edges and seams.

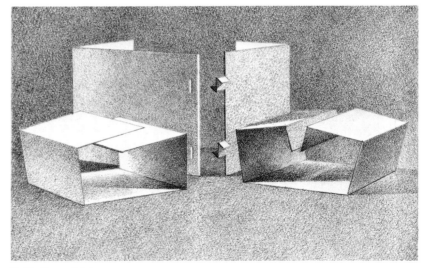

2-11. Paper joints.

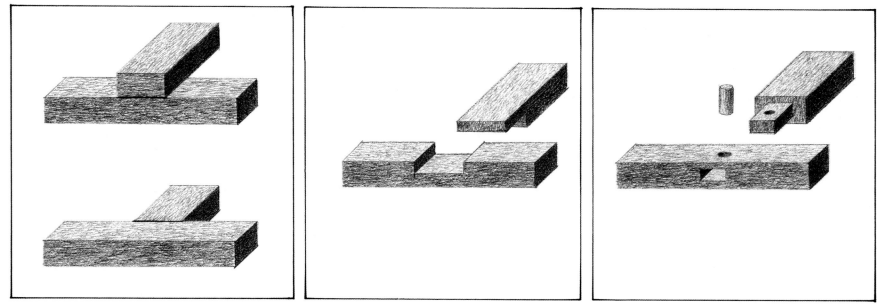

2-12. Wood joints.

any ordinary combustible material should be observed when handling, storing, or using Plexiglas acrylic.

Building codes define good practice in the use of Plexiglas acrylic for light transmission and control on a design and engineering basis, which takes into account the combustibility and fire characteristics of the material. Fire hazards in using Plexiglas can be kept at an acceptable level by complying with building codes and observing established principles of fire safety.

Forming. Acrylic sheets are rigid thermoplastics that become soft and pliable when heated to forming temperatures, much like a pure sheet of gum rubber. The acrylic can then be formed into almost any shape, and when cooled the material retains the shape to which it was formed, except for a small contraction caused by cooling. Before heating, remove all masking paper and masking paper adhesive, and wash with water and dry thoroughly with soft tissue paper. Heating should be done in a forced-circulation air oven or with infrared radiant heaters. One minute of heating time should be allowed for each one-hundredth inch of thickness of acrylic sheet. Soft cotton gloves should be worn to protect not only hands but also the surface of the plastic. Formed parts are generally trimmed to the finished size after forming. For simple shapes, the hot sheet is placed on the form and held by the edges until cool. Cooling should be slow and uniform over the entire surface to minimize internal strain.

Cutting. Acrylic sheets may be cut easily by the use of ordinary band saws, circular saws, or jigsaws. Circular saws should be 8″ to 10″ or larger in diameter, operating at 8,000 to 12,000 RPM. Blades should be $\frac{3}{32}$″ to $\frac{1}{8}$″ thick with 6 to 8 teeth per inch, alternately set and filed radially. For cutting thin sheets, it is preferable to use a hollow-ground blade. Special carbide-tipped blades can be used to cut sheets from .060″ to 1″ in thickness. Carbide-tipped blades are more expensive but will give a better cut and last much longer than steel blades. The height of the circular saw blade should be about $\frac{1}{2}$″ greater than the thickness of the sheet to prevent chipping.

Drilling. Twist drills commonly used for metals can be used for acrylic sheets, but the best results are achieved by re-pointing as follows: The drill point should have the cutting edge ground to a zero rake angle so that it will produce a scraping action. The point-included angle (in which the tip of the drill bit is ground to an angle of 60 degrees) should be 55 to 60 degrees where the sheet thickness is one hole diameter or less. The point angle should be increased for holes where the diameter is less than the sheet thickness. Use moderate speeds and light pressure to avoid "grabbing" when the drill penetrates the sheet.

Cementing. As with other manufacturers of acrylic sheets, special solvent cementing chemicals are recommended for all bonding processes. Rohm and Haas Company produces various cements applicable for bonding for their own product lines of acrylic sheets. Specific instructions for the use of these cements are available from the manufacturer as well as through local distributors.

Installation. Acrylic sheets expand and contract approximately ten times as much as do wood or metal for a given temperature change. Allowance should be made for this difference if the installation is to be exposed to a wide range of temperatures.

Cleaning and Polishing. To clean acrylic sheets, wash with plenty of soap and water, using the bare hand to feel and dislodge any caked dirt or mud. A soft cloth, sponge, or chamois may be used to squeeze water onto the plastic but use the hands to do the actual cleaning. Dry with a clean, damp chamois. To remove oil and grease, use cleanser recommended by the manufacturer. If, after washing, the surface shows a number of minor scratches, it is possible to remove or reduce most of them by hand polishing. Recommended cleansers can be best applied with a small soft flannel pad or soft, grit-free cloth. Excessive rubbing at one spot should be avoided. Several applications may be necessary, but most minor scratches can be reduced and clarity improved within a relatively short time.

Scratches too deep to be removed by the hand application of cleaners are often readily removed by buffing. The best buffing results are obtained with cotton buffing wheels. There are a number of standard commercial buffing compounds satisfactory for use with acrylic sheets. These usually consist of very fine alumina or a similar "abrasive" in combination with wax or grease binders and polishing tallow. Both are available in the form of

bars or tubes for convenience in applying them to the buffing wheel. Such compounds are sometimes referred to as coloring compounds. If scratches are too deep to be removed by buffing alone, it may be advisable to use sandpaper. Sanding should not be used unless some type of mechanical buffing equipment is available, since hand polishing is not sufficiently effective to restore luster to a sanded surface. Since sanding or excessive buffing may introduce objectionable optical distortion, it may be better to leave in deep scratches.

Where sanding must be done, the finest-grade sandpaper that will remove the scratch or other defects (no coarser than number 320) should be used first. Wrap the paper around a hard felt or rubber block and rub the area lightly using water or soap and water as a lubricant. Abrasive paper should be waterproof. Sand with a free circular motion, using light pressure over the area of the scratch. An area having a diameter of two or three times the length of the defect should be sanded in order to minimize local distortion. Initial sanding should be followed by a similar treatment, using progressively finer grades of sandpaper (number 360A to 600A). Wash the sheet after each sanding operation. During each step the scratches left by the preceding grade of abrasives should be removed. Where a large amount of polishing is undertaken, ashing compounds may be used with power-buffing equipment in place of hand sanding.

BASIC FORMS IN PAPER

The demonstrations on pages 35 to 39 include a number of basic exercises that explore eye-hand coordination and an understanding of fundamental three-dimensional forms (fig. 2–13).

MEDIA AND SELECTION

Once one progresses from preliminary design and model concepts to a refined model in finished materials, the question of selecting appropriate materials and methods arises. Two aspects of this question should be considered: What are the materials to be used to support a form or act as a structural surface, and what are the materials to be used as a finished surface? Before making a choice from a wide array of material combinations, one should establish some priorities that will aid in the selection of ap-

2-13. Paper form plastic study.

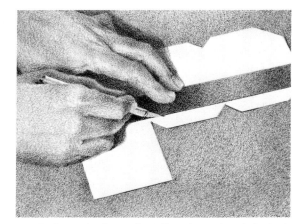

2-14A. On three-ply bristol board, draw six sides, add tabs for glue seams, and cut from a sheet of paper.

2-14. Cube: construction in paper.

2-14B. Score the lines where the tabs and each face of the cube are drawn.

2-14C. Fold the paper along the scored lines, preshape the form, and apply glue to the joining tabs.

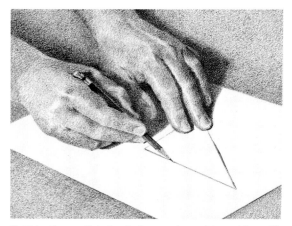

2-15A. From a flat sheet of paper, lay out four sides with connecting base and tabs. A template or compass may be used to draw each of the triangles.

2-15. Pyramid: construction in paper.

2-15B. Score along the seams and tabs.

2-15C. Prefold paper into its shape and apply glue to the tabs.

2-14D. Fold the paper into the cube, and press tabs to the inside of each corner. As you continue to join all six faces, use masking tape to hold seams together until dry.

2-14E. Complete all seams to make the final form.

2-15D. Connect the remaining faces and apply tape to hold seams together until dry.

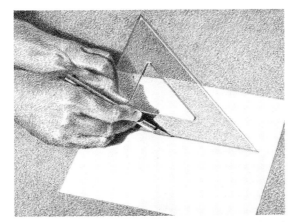

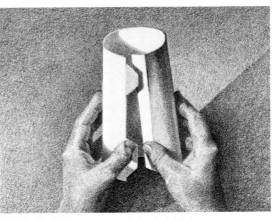

2-16A. Cut a paper rectangle with tabs at one end and fitted slots at the other.

2-16. Cylinder: construction in paper.

2-16B. Roll the paper carefully to initiate a curve.

2-16C. Complete the curve, place tabs inside their slots, glue them, and secure the tabs with tape until they are dry.

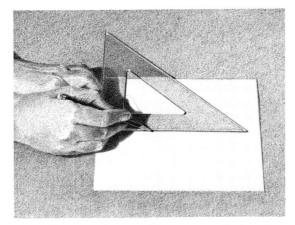

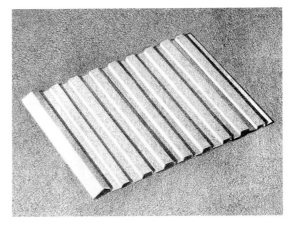

2-17A. Draw equally spaced lines on two aligning sides of a rectangle, and alternately score each line, first on the front and then on the back.

2-17. Pleated folding.

2-17B. Fold along the scored lines, alternating back and forth to create a pleated form.

2-17C. A pleated form can be applied to cylinders, pyramids, and cones or used as surface detail.

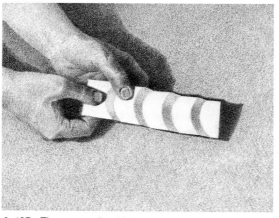

2-18A. A compass is used to draw arcs at a fixed radius. The arcs are scored with a compass and cutting blade attachment, alternating first on the front and then on the back.

2-18. Pleated curves.

2-18B. The paper should be curved gently, one section at a time, folding away from the scored edge.

2-19. Wet forming: cardboard construction. By completely immersing single-thick mat board in a bath of warm water for 10 to 15 minutes, the outside paper surfaces will loosen and float away from the core. Shortly afterward, the remaining beige core will become soft and pliable. It may then be wrapped and formed around a variety of objects to obtain curvilinear shapes. For this procedure the best results have been derived by using pebble-grain mat board. The core should be allowed to dry thoroughly overnight. A formed piece retains spring and flexibility and may be lightly sanded, primed, painted, and glued. After 5 to 10 minutes, the outside paper may be removed.

propriate materials. Although there are no absolutes, the following are standard considerations.

1. *Color Control.* The combination of materials should enable one to create a predictable, specific, and continuous range of colors (and values) for large or small areas.
2. *Texture Control.* The combination of materials should provide a wide assortment of textural effects (from delicate to coarse) in a variety of patterns and grains.
3. *Material Stability.* A finished model should not change in color, texture, or overall quality during its construction, use, or display and, if stored properly, should not deteriorate.
4. *Assemblage and Reassemblage.* The choice of processes and materials for bonding should allow for a clear procedure and ample time to permit parts to be registered correctly, shifted, or removed.
5. *Resources.* The media combination should be as inexpensive as possible and materials should be easily obtainable. Unused materials should not deteriorate when stored.
6. *Portability.* The media combination should be as light as possible and easy to store and retrieve.
7. *Efficiency.* The media combination should provide the sequence of procedures that will most directly produce visual feedback.
8. *Creation and Recreation.* The combination of materials and, if applicable, the base design should accommodate the later use of photography from as many viewing angles as possible.

DESIGN NOTEBOOK

A basic introduction to the differences among materials and their handling can provide a valuable lesson in the methodology of material selection for design. An explanation of the differences between hot- and cold-pressed surfaces; bristol, illustration, and mat boards; and textured and coated finishes leads to a general distinction of the tools and media appropriate to each surface.

Throughout your exploration and experimentation with

2-20. Design notebook.

design processes and materials, you may wish to start a sample collection. You will not only get to know more about materials technically but will be better acquainted with their qualities and the media that favorably interact with them. A hardbound blank page sketchbook, 11″ × 14″, is sufficient for mounting, note-taking, and media experimentation (fig. 2-20). The book itself may be arranged in sections to allow for entries on a variety of subjects including materials, media experimentation, sketching, clippings, and, if applicable, names, addresses, and notes. Samples of materials can be arranged and pasted onto a page to accommodate individual interests in layout and organization. A design notebook can be a valuable tool to refer to in the future for source information, materials, processes, and ideas.

2-21. Package designs by students made with the basic processes of paper and cardboard construction. (Courtesy of Franz Zeier)

3 Composition, Light, and Movement

PRINCIPLES OF COMPOSITION

An understanding of the effects of light on form and color is an essential part of the designer's experience. Whether a designer uses light indirectly or directly, only when its effect is used expressively, as in painting, architecture, or the theater, is it considered. The raking light evident in Claude Monet's *Cathedral of Rouen* is a beautiful example of the perceptive and imaginative handling of light-form composition.

It could be said that light and movement are in themselves vehicles for design and that each affords a wealth of material for exploration. The means of creating unity in material forms in actual space involves movement circuits—rhythm, proportion, and symmetry and the patterns of light. The multiple values and angles of view of these elements make the patterns of relationship an involving experience for the designer and the viewer. This and the following chapters will continue to lay a foundation for the organization of form and the related experience of color and light in three-dimensional design.

The following elements suggest a framework for additional means of ordering three-dimensional composition. These are traditional principles of organization that further express the spatial qualities and arrangements of three-dimensional form.

PRINCIPLES OF ORGANIZATION

Open and Closed Form. Open form contains a central core with an arrangement of elements that work away from the core. In this sense, the central core may or may not be visible and is characteristic of the growth of forms in nature. These forms appear to extend into space and may contain interlocking volumes, separation and continuation of volumes, and volumes that flow into, through, and out of one another.

Some compositions are controlled by a basic geometric volume, where nothing projects beyond exterior faces and all ac-

tivity is contained within. We refer to this as a form envelope, or closed form. Although visual and organizational elements may appear on the external faces of the volume, the exterior form is close-knit, compact, and isolated in relation to the surrounding space (fig. 3–1).

Spatial Closure. A line that fully encloses an area of paper distinguishes the area from the remaining surface as a shape and suggests separation from remaining areas. The degree of enclosure of a two- or three-dimensional space, as determined by the configuration of its defining elements and the pattern of its openings, influences our perception of the orientation and overall form of the space. Equally significant and perhaps less obvious, a solid composed of plane surfaces is an efficient enclosure of space. By itself, a solid does little to define the space surrounding it, but when grouped together, solids have greater ability to limit volume and define space.

A single flat plane has neither an interior nor an exterior and is neutral in space. A flat plane in a horizontal position cannot enclose space, but offers greater potential for exploration of en-

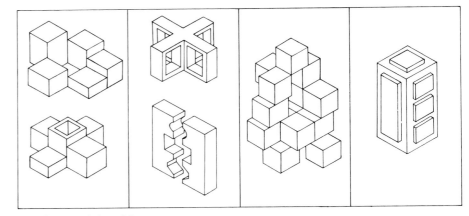

3–1. Open and closed form.

closure than do solids. A curved plane has both interior and exterior expression and begins to define a space volume as it relates to all three spatial directions. Certainly the convex and concave sides of a curved plane extend the qualities of closure as do groups of planes in vertical, horizontal, and diagonal orientations (fig. 3-2).

Implied Planes. Having position and direction, a line defines the edge of a plane and solid, or place where they might intersect. In three-dimensional design, the potential of linear elements and planes to define space is increased when the organization of groups in open space is possible. Perceptually, a fence or a colonnade with intervals of space and linear elements gains significance as an implied plane and form. These elements can also be organized to suggest planes of any shape, position, or size and may be flat, curved, or twisted. Their relatively open organization has the added quality of visual transparency and can be used to separate and join spatial volumes at the same time (fig. 3-3).

Spatial Grouping of Elements. In two-dimensional design, designers bring shapes together by recognizing likenesses in their qualities of form, color, and texture. The problems and resulting values are increased in three-dimensional design by the aspects of various views and angles. In addition, a stronger feeling for the stress and weight of materials exists with three-dimensional form than with comparable two-dimensional forms. Together, within our visual field, parts must appear unified and

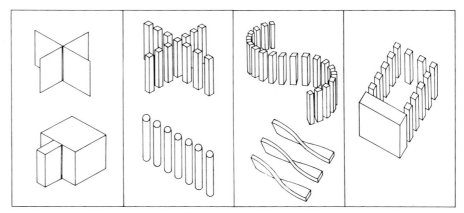

3-3. Implied planes.

have the physical capacity to be unified. Various possibilities for spatial grouping of three-dimensional elements are similar to those of two-dimensional design, with the important exception that elements are now capable of direct physical contact and resulting shadow contrast. The basic possibilities of organizing groups of solids include: spatial tension, faces in contact, edges in contact, points in contact, overlapping, interlocking, and interpenetration (fig. 3-4).

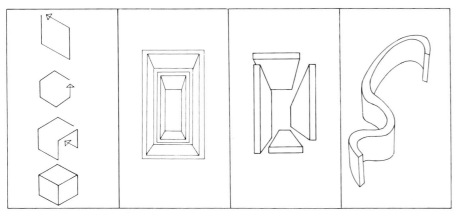

3-2. Spatial closure.

3-4. Spatial grouping of elements.

PRINCIPLES OF ORDERING

Spatial organization and order are created when formal principles and concepts are realized as important and interdependent parts that contribute to the nature of the whole. There are, however, additional concepts of order that also apply to form and space and allow for the development of a natural diversity, complexity, and hierarchy within an organized and unified whole. They include an awareness of axis, symmetry, anomaly, rhythm and repetition, and proportion.

Axis. One of the most basic means of organization, an axis is a line in space by which forms and spaces are arranged in either a regular or irregular manner. Two dimensions allow for a vertical and a horizontal axis. Three dimensions allow for an axis that corresponds to all three spatial directions. We may also have an axial condition of additional orientation within the primary system. Whether an axis is visible or implied, it is a visual force that demands balance through subtle or dominant arrangements of form and space. Because it is a basic linear condition, the axis has attributes of length and direction and suggests movement and views along its path. By definition, an axis must have a place of termination at both its ends. Along a path or direction, the defining edges of lines or planes and the arrangement of form and space serve to establish and reinforce the concept of an axis (fig. 3–5).

Symmetry. In three dimensions, the vertical axis of the front and back of the human body is a general example of symmetrical organization. The axial condition from the front and back consists of bilateral symmetry, a balanced arrangement of equivalent patterns of form and space along a common axis or point. Radial symmetry is composed of a balanced arrangement of elements around two or more axes that intersect at a center point. A three-dimensional construction can be made entirely symmetrical by organizing elements along an axis or point. It may also be organized as a symmetrical part of a composition and allow for the organization of an irregular pattern of form and space around itself (fig. 3–6).

Rhythm and Repetition. Rhythm is a regular and harmonious recurrence of the visual elements. It includes the basic idea of repetition as a means to organize form and space in design. Repetition dictates that there must be a recurrence of visual and organizational characteristic elements. Rhythm establishes the frequency of recurrence of these characteristics. There are many patterns of repetition that help to organize a series of recurring elements and the resultant visual rhythms they create. The most basic form of repetition is a linear pattern of similar elements. Elements may not be perfectly identical, but they may share a physical characteristic of size, shape, color, or texture (fig. 3–7).

Anomaly. Anomaly in two-dimensional design describes a form or space that is visually important to an organization and

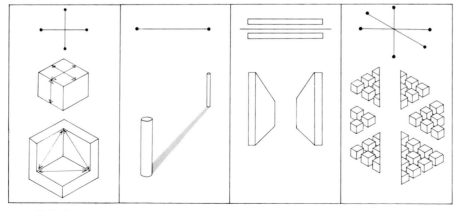

3–5. Axes.

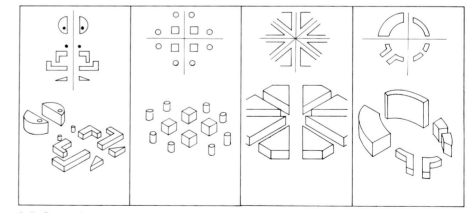

3–6. Symmetry.

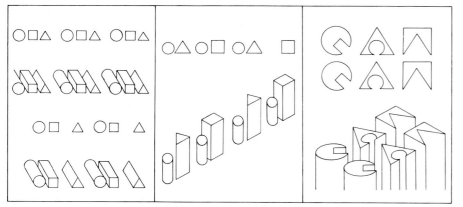

3-7. Rhythm and repetition.

marks a certain degree of departure from the general conformity. An anomaly has necessity and purpose when the designer seeks to attract attention, relieve monotony, or transform or break down regularity. In three-dimensional patterns, a form and space can also follow similar purposes by contrast of size, a unique shape, and the significant placement or location of a form or space. In every situation, the relevant meaning of an anomalous condition is created by an exception to the established pattern (fig. 3–8).

Proportion. Many concepts and theories of proportion share a similar purpose in design. They all speak to an ideal sense of order among the elements in a visual construction. The basis of a system of proportion is a fixed ratio. A ratio suggests a quantitative comparison between two things, such as the number of times the first contains the second or the ratio of three to one. A proportioning system establishes a consistent set of relationships among parts of a design and incorporates a fixed quality of ratio that is transmitted from part to part and from part to whole.

Proportioning systems unify many elements in a three-dimensional design by having all parts belong to the same family of proportions. They provide a sense of order and continuity to a sequence of spaces and relationships between the exterior and interior elements of a construction. Among the well-known systems of proportion are the Fibonacci Series, the Golden Section, and Le Corbusier's The Modular, based on the aesthetic dimensions of the Golden Section and the Fibonacci Series (fig. 3–9).

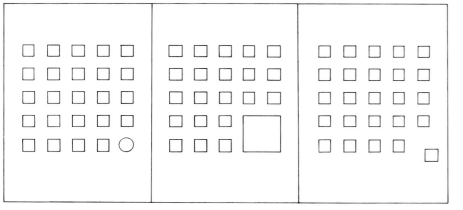

3-8. Anomalies.

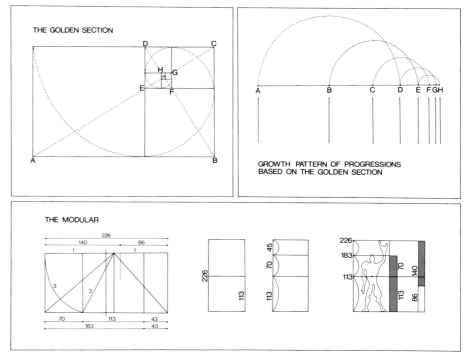

3-9. Proportion.

BASIC STUDIES IN LIGHT AND MOVEMENT

PLASTIC QUALITIES OF MASS AND VOID

Illustrated in figures 3–10 to 3–12 are the basic solids—cube, rectangular solid, pyramid, and cylinder—constructed from three-ply white bristol board. These form a vocabulary of building units for individual and group studies and studies dealing with light. You may wish to increase the degree of complexity and make more than one size of each type of solid. It is also possible to use one or more proportional systems for the unit size and one or more proportional systems for the relationship of space between the unit solids. In this exercise, solids that combine a multiple of 1″ × 1″ × 1″ increments to determine their dimensions, and multiple increments of ¼″ × ¼″ × ¼″ to determine the relationship of space between units have been used. By resting the flat side of a cube on a table, notice that it occupies and claims space by its orientation to the base plane, by the shape of its geometric form, and through light and shadow from a directed light source. Not only do these forms have characteristics of gravity, they have alternative ways of standing on a plane, for example, tipped at any angle on any axis. It is important to discover other, less obvious orientations to the base plane.

Compare the common and dissimilar attributes of the various shapes in order to discover harmonic and discordant relationships among the units. Compositions that tend to demonstrate harmony have similar characteristics. Compositions that tend to be discordant have dissimilar characteristics. The proportional systems used to establish the size of unit forms and the relationship of space between forms can differ. A one-inch module for both systems (form size and space between) will result in unit groupings that have face-to-face, corner-to-corner, and point-to-point relationships and that repeat the proportional system to a point of redundance.

There are several compositional schemes for investigation. As natural building blocks, solids may be stacked in any number of combinations. When solids are grouped together, they may form a negative or enclosed space. An enclosed void has shape and is either a harmonic or discordant element within the total organization of the composition. Partially enclosed spaces

A

3–10A–F. Plastic qualities of mass and void: A light source from one direction provides maximum contrast between light and dark values, while two light sources from different distances and directions provide more even tones and gradation of values.

D

B

3-10A–F *continued.*

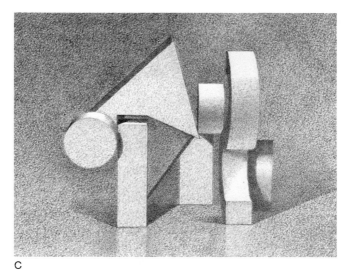

C

E

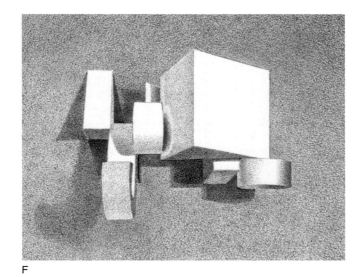

F

A

B

3-11A-D. The qualities of form are expressed through the relationships of highlight, shade, and shadow.

C

D

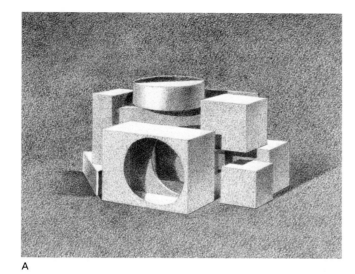

A

B

3–12A–D. Views from above a design and from a variety of angles are helpful to an understanding of the directions and amount of light that serve to enhance the harmony of shape and space in a composition.

C

D

may be linked with others to form more complex conditions of enclosure and negative shapes.

By moving a light source (100-watt reflector flood bulb) to various positions around and above the composition, levels of contrast change on the solids, base plane, and within enclosed spaces.

Several angles of a single light source provide maximum contrast between light and dark values, while two light sources can provide more even tones and gradation of values throughout and around the mass model. Try to find an angle of light that enhances the harmony of shape and space for each composition of solids.

THE PLATONIC POLYHEDRA

To aid the beginning student and as a review for those more advanced, figure 3-13 includes illustrations and construction patterns for the Platonic solids: the tetrahedron (4 faces), the cube (6 faces), the octahedron (8 faces), the dodecahedron (12 faces), and the icosahedron (20 faces). These are fundamental geometric solids that can be adopted as basic structures for three-dimensional design (figs. 3-14, 3-15).

3-13. Group of polyhedra.

3-14. Platonic polyhedra.

3-14A. Tetrahedron.

3-14B. Cube.

3-14C. Octahedron.

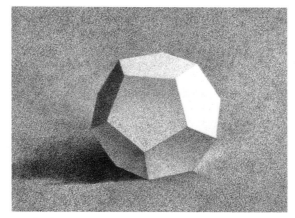

3-14D. Dodecahedron.

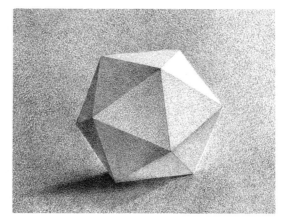

3-14E. Icosahedron.

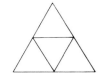

TETRAHEDRON

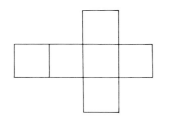

HEXAHEDRON

3-15. Plan diagrams for each polyhedron.

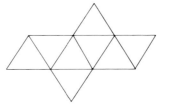

OCTAHEDRON

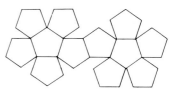

DODECAHEDRON

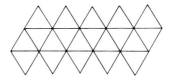

ICOSAHEDRON

A

B

3-16A-C. Grouping study with tetrahedron (two views and plan diagram).

A

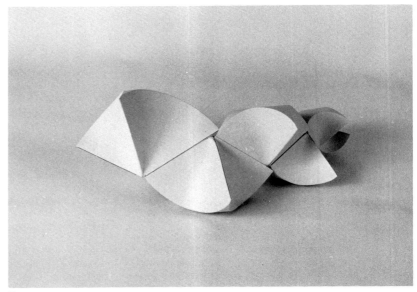

B

3-17A-C. Grouping study with concave polyhedron (two views and plan diagram).

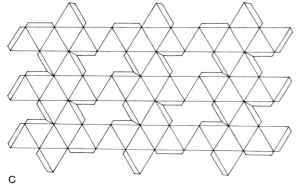

C

3-16A-C *continued.*

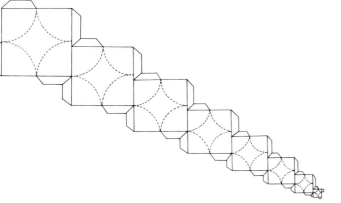

C

3-17A-C *continued.*

GROUPING OF PLATONIC POLYHEDRA

Once the plan drawing for the Platonic polyhedra is understood, many variations in form and three-dimensional groupings are possible. These projects are constructed from a single sheet of paper in a repeating pattern of geometric solids (figs. 3-16, 3-17). It is important to have a careful drawing of the form and a plan for the layout of closing tabs. Voids can also be arranged between solids in the overall composition to reduce the impression of a totally closed form and to allow for the opportunity to further explore the plastic qualities of mass and form.

ISOAXIS

The inventive work of Wallace Walker, author, designer, and originator of the IsoAxis, provides a fascinating example of the principles of polyhedra construction applied to a model form that can be rotated about its center to five unique states, each one creating a different star-shaped polyhedron (fig. 3-18).

IsoAxis is a three-dimensional construction that begins as a two-dimensional rectangle, triangulated into 60 isosceles right triangles. After the rectangle is folded in a prescribed man-

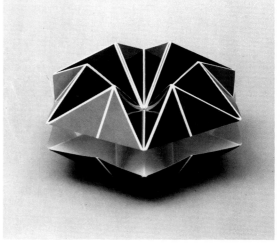

3-18. IsoAxis, designed by Wallace Walker.

ner along the edges of the triangles, two ends of the triangle are joined. The cylinder thus formed is then forced by the creases into a three-dimensional star shape, with the triangles becoming the faces of the model. The construction acts somewhat like a torus (plate 1).

The unique pattern of folds that creates the edges and vertices of the construction permits the model to turn about itself. The IsoAxis combines the surprise of a kaleidoscope with the beauty of an unfolding flower. In its closed position it can serve as a container. As the IsoAxis is opened, the contents appear.

PROJECT TEACH

Robert Seeburger, an art teacher at Waterford-Kettering High School in Drayton Plains, Michigan, working in collaboration with Wallace Walker, has carried Walker's concept into the realm of design education through Project Teach, a program begun by the Michigan Art Education Association with the aim of fostering new and better ways of teaching. Project IsoAxis was presented to Seeburger's design and color classes. Emphasis was placed on the selection of ideas that could be depicted in se-

quence. Color progressions and spatial relationships played an important part in the many successful solutions that underscore the need to think in both two and three dimensions.

Of the many directions pursued by the students, one solution depicted the life cycle of a human being from embryo to old age, while others planned sequences around historical themes, geometric tesselations, photographs, and magazine clippings (figs. 3-19A to 3-19D). At the conclusion of the project, the results were presented to the Project Teach Committee in Michigan and received the highest award for high-school projects.

PLASTIC QUALITIES OF GROUPING WITH COLOR AND PATTERN

The further possibilities of voids within individual solids and the exploration of plastic qualities by varying color and pattern are shown in the student projects on pages 55 and C1 from Franz Zeier's design course at the Zurich School of Art and Design in Switzerland.

In the first project, figure 3-20, a group of three-

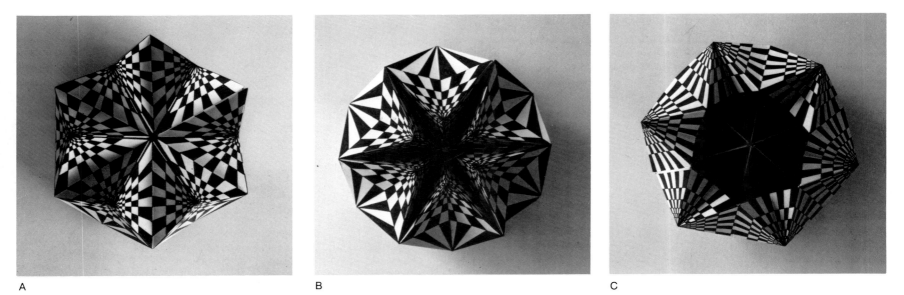

A   B   C

3-19A-D. Four views of an IsoAxis, from Project Teach, by Robert Seeburger and Wallace Walker.

dimensional solids have been related to the interior space of a cubic volume. This study suggests variety within a form and the further potential for the grouping of different solid forms. The containment of these forms within a transparent volume of space allows for the perception of contrast across their planes.

Another method of defining contrast between forms includes the use of surface color. In plate 2, surface color is used to create the effect of anomaly within the overall pattern of three-dimensional organization. Note how the use of black on one solid decreases perception of its form and how red not only arrests our attention but allows for the reflection and contrast of shadow across its surface. Our perception of it as a solid remains visible.

Black reduces our perception of the contrast of light and dark values across a solid form. A set of flat triangles in plate 3 have been colored black and grouped together in the composition. Because the edges of the black triangles reflects less contrast than either of the red and white triangles above, the group of three black triangles appear as a unit or as the new shape of a trapezoid. The reverse of this relationship can be seen in the next example, plate 4. A geometric color pattern is applied to the surface of a single three-dimensional cube. Compare the white cube

behind with the patterned cube. Note how the patterned cube is transformed in appearance and partially loses definition as a solid. The pattern evokes a strong visual influence on the structural edges and vertices while introducing a diminishing scale of gray value across the form. The white cube behind and the red cube below both reflect value contrast across their surfaces and at the edges of their planes.

Inherent in these projects are strong elements of contrast and color against which our perception of form has been measurably altered. As experiments and student exercises, they clearly introduce the basic potential of color as a form giver to design. An appreciation of the application of color to three-dimensional form is relevant to graphic, interior, and architectural design and the fine arts. As Tom Porter has pointed out in *Architectural Color,* "Colour experiments place emphasis on training the eye to see how colour behaves relatively and to demonstrate that an understanding of colour interval is very important to colour prescription; they are also designed to stretch the imagination." In the following chapter, we will explore the nature of color, the roles of light and pigment, and the creative problems of color and design.

D

3-19A-D *continued.*

3-20. Several solids within the interior space of a cubic volume suggest variety within a form and the potential of grouping different solids. (Courtesy of Franz Zeier)

4 Color Structure and Design

Before the creative problems of color and design can be solved, a few basic concepts about the nature of color require understanding. An awareness of what color is and the particular roles of light and pigment will be of value. It is also important to understand how the eye functions in response to color stimulus and to become familiar with the language and graphic means for the classification of the qualities of color.

THE DIMENSIONS OF COLOR

Our perception of color occurs as a vibration of energy in the form of light radiations within the visible spectrum. The human eye receives a small segment of the total range of vibrant energy and conveys it to the brain as the sensation of color. A change in the quality or strength of a light source will result in either a loss or alteration of color. We therefore receive the sensation of white light when the visible range of light vibrations are active and in balanced proportion.

In Isaac Newton's famous experiment, a beam of sunlight passed through a glass prism was broken into an array of colored bands, later known as the spectrum. When the bands were reunited by the use of a reversed prism, the beam of white light was reconstituted. This experiment clearly demonstrated that white light is composed of the many colors included in the spectrum and that each of the particular vibrations of any color are present in the form of white light (fig. 4–1).

The individual color bands in the spectrum are called hues. The colors of the spectrum progress from red, with the longest wavelength, through orange, yellow, green, blue, and finally to purple, with the shortest wavelength. Achromatic light, or light that is perceived as colorless, is the result of equal stimulation of our hue sensitivities. By mixing red, green, and blue lights in various amounts, we create the entire spectrum of hues and white or achromatic light. Chromatic stimulation results in the sensation of hue when some of our hue sensitivities are stimulated more than others.

Newton's celebrated use of a prism to split a beam of sunlight into the visible spectrum led to a second finding that white light could also be obtained from mixing only red, green, and blue light. This discovery was later enlarged by the work of Thomas Young (1801) and others, and expanded in 1867 by Hermann von Helmholtz into the Young-Helmholtz theory.

The Young-Helmholtz Theory proposed that color receptors in the eye respond to red, green, and blue wavelengths of light, which today is still a widely accepted theory by physicists

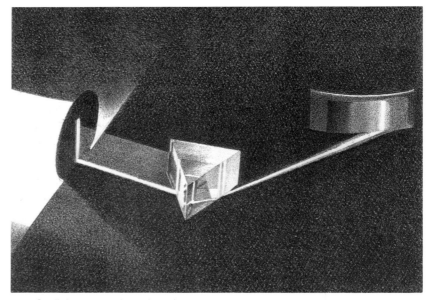

4–1. Sunlight passes through a glass prism and is separated into an array of colors called the spectrum.

and scientists for their measurements of color. The three primary colors used for color photography and color television can be traced back to early experiments with this theory. A rival theory by Ewald Hering in 1874 proposed three pairs of color receptors (red-green, blue-yellow, and black-white). His theory has many supporters throughout the United States and Europe and has been the basis for several European color atlases, beginning with one by Wilhelm Ostwald.

A color sensation may be received directly from a light source such as when we look at billboard lights or through a stained glass window, but more often we experience color sensations as a reflection of light from a pigmented surface. The medium of pigment in both situations has an integral role in the transformation of white light into the colors that we see.

PIGMENT AND LIGHT

Pigments have the special capacity to reflect or conduct vibrations from the spectrum. White pigment will reflect the whole spectral range, while a red-colored pigment can only reflect the particular vibration that is inherent in its substance. A red surface that receives white light will reflect only the red portion of the spectrum. If the red surface were to receive either a green or blue light, it would appear neutral or grayish since there would be no red vibrations to reflect. When a white light shines through a red-pigmented gelatin, only the red vibrations pass through. The other hue vibrations carried by the white light are in a manner absorbed by the red pigment substance.

The effects of pigment and light combinations are common in nature. They are readily observed during a sunset as the colors in the sky or as reflections on the water. Our sensation of color from pigments is the result of light vibrations reflected from their surface.

COLOR VISION AND THE HUMAN EYE

The human eye receives light vibrations and conveys them to the brain as the sensation of color. Anatomically, the eye is a dark chamber that admits and collects light and also reacts to its presence. The eye does not register sensations of color in the absolute fashion we might expect from a laboratory device or the film in the back of a camera, but is an extremely adaptable organ that adjusts to the relative qualities of color and light. Color sensation conveyed to the brain as an apparent color that we experience is affected by the surrounding conditions of light and also by adjacent areas of other colors.

Figure 4–2 and plate 5 demonstrate the adaptability of the human eye to different levels of color contrast. In figure 4–2 the same value of gray is juxtaposed against two different background values. The gray against the darker background has been altered and appears lighter while the same gray against a lighter ground has darkened in appearance. In plate 5, a similar gray is placed against a green-yellow background and appears subtly purple, while the same gray placed against a red background appears to have a faint blue-green cast. These slight changes in our perception of color occur when colors are placed in similar viewing areas. A true orange, for example, will shift in appearance to a slightly yellow-orange cast when placed next to a red, while the same orange in association with yellow will appear to have a slight orange-red cast. This phenomenon of color vision is called simultaneous contrast; color differences in areas of adjoining

4–2. Simultaneous contrast.

hues are exaggerated, thus having a functional relation to our perception of all the qualities of color. These examples adequately demonstrate that color sensation is relational and always depends on the color perceived in context with its environment.

COMPLEMENTS OF COLOR VISION

By contrasting a strong color area with a neutral gray, plate 5 provides an additional example of how the eye selects hue. If our gaze rests on the red color area for a minute or more, the neutral will begin to intensify as a blue-green hue. By shifting our gaze to a neutral area, the image of the red area will persist as an afterimage but will appear as blue-green. The appearance of the blue-green hue, which the eye has created, is an opposite or complementary hue to the red. Similarly, the eye responds to all strong hues by providing afterimages of their complements for all the hues in the spectrum. This suggests that the eye has a dynamic structure that demands an equilibrium of hue sensation in order to avert fatigue and the impairment of color vision. It also implies a necessary relationship of complementary hues in opposition to the spectrum hues, based on an awareness of the behavior and structure of the eye.

Another related color experience, "successive contrast," is caused by the alternating perception of differing colors found opposite one another on the hue circle. A resulting negative afterimage is induced by the perception of the first hue and visually heightens the color impression of the next.

MAPPING THE DIMENSIONS OF COLOR

The hues discerned by the eye can be arranged according to their sequence in the spectrum in a hue circle, with each of the colors in a complementary pair directly across from one another. Five hues can be arranged equidistantly around the circle with intermediate hues in between (fig. 4–3). This alignment of hues on the circle, based on the perceptual experience, is useful not only as a graphic depiction of the perceptual relationship of hues but also for recording mixtures of colored light. In addition to variations of hues, colors may vary in measure according to their attributes of lightness and darkness and also in measure of their dullness and brightness. A green hue may appear light or dark and

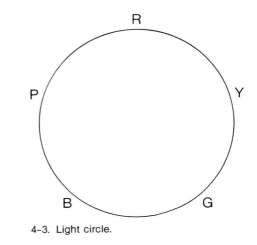

4–3. Light circle.

may also appear dull green or bright green. In order to be able to describe this color, we require a means to indicate and name all of these factors, including its hue, its degree of lightness or darkness, and its strength or saturation as a pigment.

We often speak of color combinations in broad generalities—for example, yellow-orange and red-violet—which serve to identify mixtures. Other colors have been given names characteristic of objects, such as candy-apple red or baby blue. Numerous variations, however, have no accepted or common names. If a color is in question and has no particular name, it can be identified in relation to its direction on the color wheel and by a combination of numbers or letters.

Color systems with a selection of samples are not only the best way to find out what products, materials, or paints are available but enable the designer to discover what colors exist and how they relate to one another. Without a system of classification, it is difficult to plan in terms of color or to match existing materials and colors with any precision. Classifications have been devised with great care to include as many shades and variations of color as possible. Sometimes color systems have samples or chips to illustrate its colors. They are coded with numbers or letters according to the principles on which the system is based.

There are several principles by which color systems have been organized. Some systems have been structured to reflect the controlled properties of pigment mixing, while others have been ordered more closely to the perception of color under stable conditions of light. Systems that organize color according to the attributes of perception (hue, value, and chroma) are the following: The Munsell Color System, published by the Munsell Color Company of Baltimore, Maryland; the Swedish Natural Color System (NCS), developed over the past few years largely through the efforts of Anders Hard and the Swedish Standards Institution of Stockholm (about to be distributed in the United States); and the Acoat Color Codification (ACC) System as applied in the Sikkens Color Collection 2021, published by Akzo Coatings of Amstelveen, Holland.

Of the many systems that chart and describe the qualities of color and are widely available, the Munsell system offers an ample range of hues and a simple means of description and classification. The Munsell system is also appropriate to discuss because it organizes color visually. It is based on measured qualities of colored light, which is significant because color relationships must also be arranged in terms of how they are seen together. Systems based on the principles and behavior of pigment mixing are not entirely appropriate for charting visual relationships.

The Munsell system was founded on several principles of organization and perception. By focusing on an area of strong-chroma red for a few minutes, then shifting focus to a neutral gray area, you will notice an afterimage of blue-green. The blue-green hue is perceived by the mind's eye as the visual complement of the red. In a similar manner, the opposites (or perceived complements) can be found for the four remaining principal hues in the Munsell system: yellow, green, blue, and purple. There are a total of ten hues in the system (five principal and five visually opposite and intermediate hues). They are arranged in a hue circle with the five complements facing the five principal hues. Adjacent hues on the color wheel are chosen in such a way that they appear equally spaced visually. Color wheels are available from Munsell that further divide each of the principal and intermediate hues into 10 subhues, producing a 100-hue color wheel.

The Munsell system uses the terms *hue, value,* and *chroma* to specify the three qualities that describe a color.

Hue. Hue is the attribute by which colors are distinguished from one another, the property that makes red different

from blue. Hue is therefore a specific reference to the quality of color variation noted in the spectrum. The basic hues that our eyes discern are red, yellow, green, blue, and purple, with the perceived complements included in the scale as follows: red, yellow-red, yellow, green-yellow, green, blue-green, blue, purple-blue, purple, and red-purple. White, gray, and black are distinguished by our perception of them as colorless or as having no characteristic hue. Because they are without hue and chroma, they are often referred to as achromatic or neutral colors.

In the Munsell system, the hue (H) notation of a color indicates its relation to a visually equally spaced scale of 100 hues. The hue notation is based on the preceding names (red [R], yellow-red [YR], yellow [Y], green-yellow [GY], green [G], blue-green [BG], blue [B], purple-blue [PB], purple [P], and red-purple [RP]) and given consecutive numbers: red = 5, yellow-red = 15, yellow = 25, and so on and continues around the color wheel to red-purple = 100 (fig. 4-4).

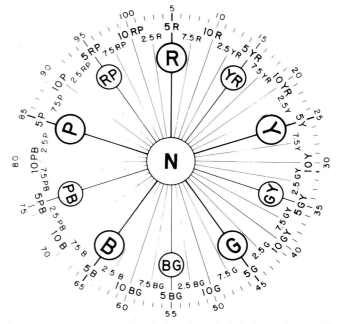

HUE SYMBOLS AND THEIR RELATION TO ONE ANOTHER

4-4. Munsell 100-Step Color Wheel. (Courtesy of Munsell Color)

Value. The second attribute by which color is distinguished is value, a range from light to dark. The value of a color may be determined by comparing a color to a varying scale of grays with white at the top and black at the bottom, called a value scale. By holding a swatch of any color next to a value scale and squinting your eyes, you can reduce the impression of hue, making the value of the color sample more obvious.

In the Munsell system, the value (V) notation indicates the degree of lightness or darkness of a color in relation to a neutral gray scale, which extends from absolute black to absolute white. The value symbol 0/ is used for absolute black; the symbol 10/ is used for absolute white; and the symbol 5/ is used for middle gray and all chromatic colors that appear halfway in value between the absolutes of black and white.

Chroma. In addition to the attributes of hue and value, a third dimension, chroma, is needed to complete the description. The meaning of this term indicates the brightness or dullness of a color. The term *chroma* also borrows its meaning from chemistry, where it is used to describe the strength or saturation of a solution. When discussing color, chroma describes the amount of pigment in a medium: the stronger the amount of pigment, the more saturated a color becomes. A strong-chroma red is very bright and pure, while a weak-chroma red is dull and grayish. The range of chroma extends from neutral or gray to the brightest and most intense color that a pigment can give.

In the Munsell system, the chroma (C) notation indicates the degree of strength or saturation of a given hue from a neutral gray of the same value. The scale of chroma extends from /0 for a neutral gray to /10, /12, /14, or higher, depending on the strength of the sample to be evaluated. For example, a color commonly called "vermilion" might have a chroma as strong as /12 or as vivid as /16, while another color of the same hue and value referred to as "rose red" might have a chroma as weak (dull or grayish) as /4. The complete Munsell notation for a chromatic color is written symbolically: H V/C. The notation for a sample of vermilion might be 5R 5/14, while the notation for rose red might be 5R 5/4. A finer division may also be indicated by decimals; for example: 2.5R 4/12.

The Color Solid. To illustrate the interrelated qualities of the three dimensions of color, it is necessary to show the field of color on a three-dimensional chart. For this purpose, Munsell has suggested a color tree (fig. 4–5). The scales of hue, value, and chroma can be visualized in terms of this tree or color solid (fig. 4–6). The neutral value scale, arranged in visually equal steps from black at the bottom to white at the top, forms a central vertical axis. The hue scale is arranged in visually equal steps around the neutral vertical axis. Chroma scales radiate in visually equal steps from the neutral axis outward to the periphery of the solid. The outward shape of the Munsell color solid is quite irregular because the shape is based on the absolute limits of reflecting color pigments, each of which has an ultimate chromatic strength of varying limitation when compared with other hues. As new and stronger pigment sources become available, one can expect the chroma range to increase to accommodate them. For the purpose of this study, it is important to know at which value level each hue may achieve its maximum intensity. This will be discussed in conjunction with a scale of spectrum values in the following sections of this chapter, which are devoted to the sources and behavior of pigments.

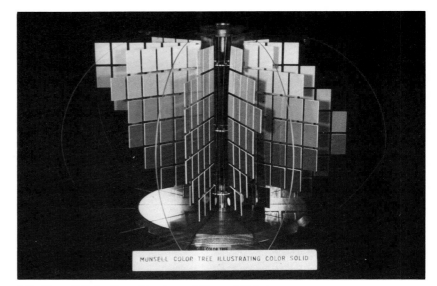

4–5. Munsell Color Tree. (Courtesy of Munsell Color)

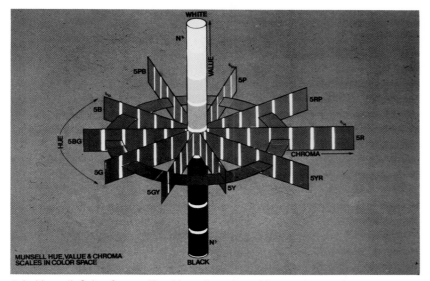

4-6. Munsell Color Space: The Munsell scales of hue, value, and chroma can be visualized in terms of a color space. The neutral value scale, graded in equal steps from black to white, forms the central, vertical axis. Chroma scales radiate from the neutral axis outward to the periphery of the color space in visually equal steps. (Reproduced by permission of Munsell Color)

THE RESPONSE TO PIGMENT

A pigment has the capacity to reflect a limited band of the light spectrum in a selective manner and cancels those vibrations that are not inherent in its substance. Although pigments are used to produce the colors to which we respond as colored light, they are a physical substance different from light, and their behavior in mixture is also quite different from that of light. The physical principles of pigment mixture and light mixture differ greatly and are best understood by examining their individual characteristics of behavior. Scientifically, light mixes according to the additive principle, while pigment mixes according to the subtractive principle.

The process of mixing colored light is called additive mixture, first discovered in Newton's experiment using a prism to split a beam of sunlight into the spectral bands of light. White or colorless light is the addition of the individual wavelengths—red, blue, and green—in balanced proportions. Subtractive mixture results when pigments, dyes, and paints are mixed. It is called subtractive because the spectral energy of one pigment will usually neutralize parts of the energy (wavelength) of another pigment. If red, yellow, and blue, the subtractive primaries, are mixed, they neutralize one another to produce a dull or gray result. Because the mixture of light is a specialized problem and related to designs in which colored light is directly involved, it is explored in depth in chapter 5. A discussion of pigment mixture, however, is of central importance at this point.

The effect of the subtractive mixture of pigments that neutralize the strength of hue is important. A dramatic example occurs when complementary hues are mixed together. The strength of each is cancelled, resulting in a mixture of neutral gray. This mixing concept is often used as a principle for testing colors to determine pigment complements.

In subtractive mixing, a special hue circle is required to map the behavior of pigments (fig. 4–7A). An increased distance is present between red and yellow, allowing for intermediates on either side of orange, and also a new alignment for the complements is presented. If the intermediate steps, OR, YO, GY, BG, PB, RP, are included, the result is a total of 12 hues for the pigment circle as compared to the 10 hues of the light circle (fig. 4–7b).

The pigment circle is a reliable device that allows for any two points to be connected by a straight line, showing the path of the mixture between these pigments. A line drawn between R and Y will move through the orange section of the hue circle. In order to understand why these pigments produce an orange hue, it is necessary to understand more about the nature of pigments.

The portion of the spectrum reflected by a pigment is a limited band of vibrations rather than a precise point. A pigment, therefore, can reflect the related tones of those colors that are directly next to it on the hue circle. When neighboring hues are mixed together, their combined strength dominates and the original pigments become subordinate to the new color. The yellow pigment has a capability of reflecting a certain amount of the neighboring hue, OR, and similarly the Y can reflect an amount of

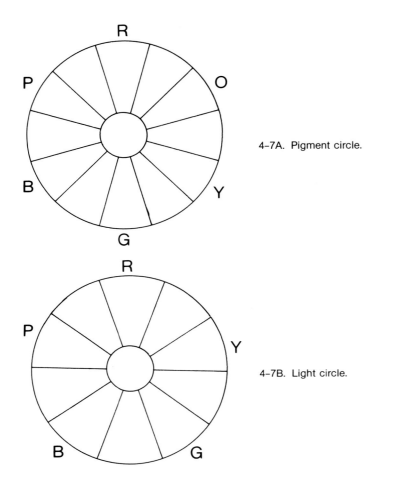

4-7A. Pigment circle.

4-7B. Light circle.

pigment, the following experiment is included. A beam of white light is passed through a red-pigmented gelatin. The red pigment will cancel all other hue vibrations present in the white light except red, which passes through as red light. If one attempts to send the red light through a green gelatin, no light will pass through. The green-pigmented gelatin will have cancelled or subtracted the red light. However, if there are separate light sources, one green and the other red, and they are focused on the same area of a white surface, the result will be a mixture of light and not pigment. The color formed on the screen by the addition of green and red light vibrations will be yellow as illustrated on the light circle (fig. 4-7b).

For the purposes of this study, it should be understood that pigment mixing will produce mixtures that generally correspond to the arrangement of hues on the pigment circle. For the purpose of the use of color in composition, however, colors that are viewed together in a scheme, we must rely on the light circle that takes account of the balance and perceptual experience of hues. Pigments are mixed in relation to a pigment color wheel. Designs are composed with an awareness of how colors behave together, a phenomenon called interaction, which also accords with the light circle.

By following some general guidelines, pigments can be mixed to produce any color of desired quality.

Hue. Hue alteration with a minimum loss of chroma can be controlled by the mixture of analogous or neighboring pigments on the pigment circle.

Value. Values are lightened or darkened with mixtures of white and black. This results in little change of hue but an appreciable reduction in chroma. Values may also be increased or decreased by mixtures with lighter or darker pigments, in which case all three attributes—hue, value, and chroma—are altered.

Chroma. Chroma may be reduced when mixed with the pigment complement or with a neutral without alteration of its hue. Chroma can be increased or intensified only by the addition of a higher-chroma pigment. The mixture of two pigments will gradually or significantly reduce the chroma. Therefore, the random mixing of multiple pigments will surely impede the control and potential for chroma. It is always best to mix purposefully, using as few pigments as necessary to create a desired color.

YO. Therefore, both pigments have a common capability of reflecting orange light. Their combined capability makes orange the strongest force in the mixture and reduces the original strength of the pigments R and Y to approach the neutral center of the pigment circle. This neutral factor is actually a slight reduction in the chroma strength of the mixture to less than that of the original pigments.

To further differentiate between the behavior of light and

SPECTRUM VALUE

Chroma can easily be reduced, but once reduced in pigment mixing, it is more difficult to increase except with more intense pigments. With this idea in mind, the most intense chromas available are pigments such as gouache, tempera, and acrylic. Several reds may be available, but the intensity of each of them will vary in value. A bright yellow is usually found at a high value; a bright red near the middle or just below middle gray; and an intense blue will have a fairly dark value. It is useful to know the value at which a given hue reflects its strongest chroma, called the spectrum value.

The spectrum values of the different pigments can be seen if swatches are created for each of the intense pigments at their own value. This is significant because it demonstrates each value at which pigments can achieve their highest chroma. It is also useful to a demonstration of the value level of the constant hue chart, which follows in this study and is basic to an awareness of the sources and uses of each pigment (plate 6).

The Constant-hue Chart. The constant-hue chart is a vertical cross section of the color tree. It is a convenient means for visualizing the value and chroma range of an individual hue. Figure 4–8 shows the constant hues for yellow and purple-blue. The vertical band in the center of the chart represents the zero of the chroma scale and is a value scale in neutrals. The outer point of the triangular configuration for yellow falls at a value of 8 and a chroma of 12, which indicates the highest chroma of yellow. At this point there is only one value possible. The first vertical column to the right of the neutral center axis represents the potential value range for yellow at a low chroma.

The Constant-value Chart. This chart provides a look at a horizontal cross section of the color tree. It includes 10 hues that radiate around a neutral central core and depicts a range of chroma that extends outward toward maximum intensity at the value level of 5/. Each color in the spectrum reaches its maximum intensity at different levels of value. Therefore only a few colors are indicated on this particular cross section at value level 5/ (fig. 4–9).

The Constant-chroma Chart. The constant-chroma chart is a cylindrical cross section of the color tree, flattened out to

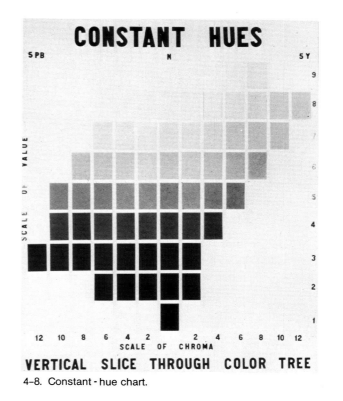

4–8. Constant - hue chart.

form a scale. The scale includes 5R at both sides to suggest that it is a continuous ring and can be shaped into a cylindrical form. The reason one does not see a neutral gray core in the chart in figure 10 is because the chroma band lies beyond the neutral vertical axis and follows a circumferential path throughout the interior leaves of the color tree. At chroma /6, it becomes more apparent how intense each of the hues appear at a similar point away from the neutral core. Notice that several colors vary in intensity at this point (/6) away from the core.

Each pigment reaches its brightest and most intense hue at various points of extension away from the neutral center. The color solid, defined by Munsell, is therefore irregular in overall exterior shape and conforms to the absolute limits of reflecting materials (fig. 4–10).

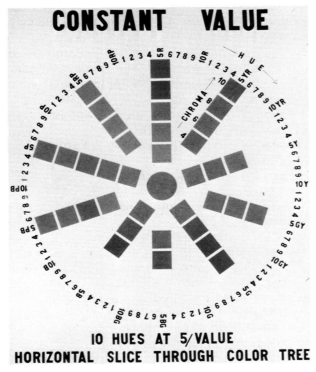

4-9. Constant-value chart.

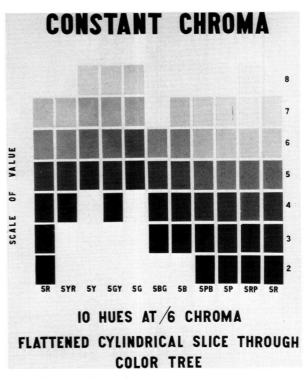

4-10. Constant-chroma chart.

The present Munsell color standards consist of opaque pigmented films on glossy paper for over 1,500 Munsell notations. Each of the samples are subjected to spectrophotometric measurement and visual checks at the time of production and periodically thereafter.

BASIC CONCEPTS OF COLOR AND COMPOSITION

THE GRAY SCALE

Gray can be defined as a mixture of white and black. The percentage of white and black content determines the relative value of gray. The central vertical axis, or gray scale, of the color solid is made up of visually equal steps calculated on the basis of the work of two German scientists, Wilhelm Eduard Weber (1804–91) and Gustave Theodor Fechner (1801–87).

Their calculations in logarithmic progressions, within the limits of high and low saturation, reveal that the visual perception of an equally spaced progression of values depends on a physical mixture in geometric proportions. The Weber-Fechner Law points out the relationship between perception and physical fact, thus permitting an in-depth understanding of a gray scale of visually equal steps (fig. 4–11).

COLOR RELATIVITY

Our perception of related colors—simultaneous contrast—is affected by contrasting relationships of color and value.

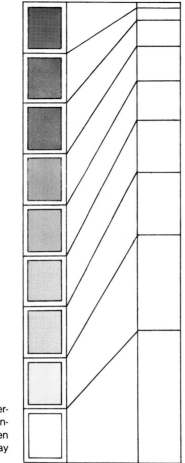

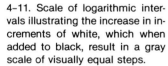

4-11. Scale of logarithmic intervals illustrating the increase in increments of white, which when added to black, result in a gray scale of visually equal steps.

known book *Interaction of Color:* "Recognizing this, one is able to 'push' light and/or hue, by the use of contrasts, away from their first appearance toward the opposite qualities."

Any color related to others will undergo modifications that make it appear different. Some of these changes are quite drastic, while others are subtle. Red, for instance, will change in the following manner (plate 7):

1. Placed in contact with blue, red appears lighter with a yellow temperature shift.
2. Placed in contact with yellow, red appears darker with a blue temperature shift.
3. Placed in contact with green, red appears brighter and more pure.
4. Placed in contact with black, red appears lighter and duller.
5. Placed in contact with white, red appears grayish and duller.
6. Placed in contact with a middle gray, red appears brighter.

The color being modified is pushed as if by a physical force in the opposite direction of the modifying color. Purity of color is desirable in an experiment of this nature and will be valuable to repeat in gouache, tempera, or color papers.

For similar reasons, one can also subtract those qualities not desired to achieve a new color. Experimenting with adjacent colors shows that any ground subtracts its own hue, as well as light, from the color it carries and therefore influences (plate 8).

VALUE KEYS

The visual blending of color can be enhanced if the colors used in a design are brought closer together by using different "keys." Figure 4-12 shows the gray scale segmented into three parts. Value steps 1 to 3 are labeled high key because of the relative brightness found in this range. Value steps 4 to 6 are middle key, and steps 7 to 9 are low key. Figure 4-13 shows a basic design segmented into these three keys. There is an apparent change in mood in each of the segments of this design. High key has a light and airy quality, while low key has a somber effect on us. Middle key contains qualities of both high and low key. When working with a full scale but using only a few steps to complete a

The fact that two samples of a similar color placed against different backgrounds can appear different is evident. A more interesting experiment can be performed by making two different colors look alike. Simultaneous contrast suggests that the greater the difference between the ground and sample colors, the stronger the sense of change experienced. These differences are caused by two factors—hue and value—and in many cases, by both at the same time. As Josef Albers pointed out in his well-

4-12. Gray scales can be separated into thirds to illustrate the ranges of high, middle, and low keys.

4-13. A basic pattern separated into high, middle, and low key areas.

basic geometric design, care is needed to keep the interval between the steps equal. Otherwise, the effect of harmony will be upset and the design will appear erratic in visual sequence and interval. This exercise in color interval is also analogous to the use of octaves in musical tones. We hear many songs in either a high, middle, or low register, and we can create color tones in like manner. Designers should practice the concept of color interval in a discriminating way and understand its wide scope of application to the feeling and control they wish to communicate with color.

VISUAL EQUALITY

Color relationships of visually equal steps can be termed a color "run." In order to have a color run, at least three colors must be used to establish direction and interval. For example, if it is said that yellow is like orange in the same way that orange is like red, a direction has been established and a point of origin can be referred to. One has also established an interval that can continue around the hue circle without breaking or changing direction. Color runs can be made in any of the keys described under Value Keys or in any combination of keys. Plate 9 is designed in combined keys.

THE MODES OF COLOR APPEARANCE

The sensation and appearance of color is encoded through the structure of the eye and in the visual centers of the brain. A particular color may appear solid and opaque like a painted wall, transparent like a glass window, lustrous like the glaze of a ceramic vase, metallic like a holiday ornament, luminous like the beacon of a lighthouse, and voluminous like a bottle of colored ink. The experience of seeing colors is enhanced by our ability to distinguish between three modes of appearance: surface color, film color, and volume color. Through an understanding of this phenomenon, designers can extend their visual vocabulary and explore new and creative modes of color expression.

Surface Color. Opaque surface color is a common and dominant factor in our visual perception of objects in the environment. Many natural and artificial objects—such as paper, wood, stone, or cloth—are examples that communicate an impression

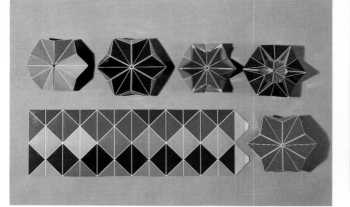

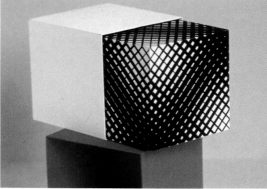

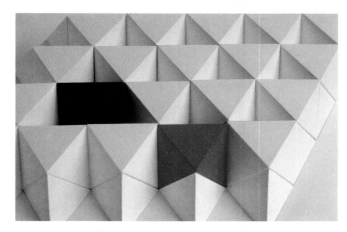

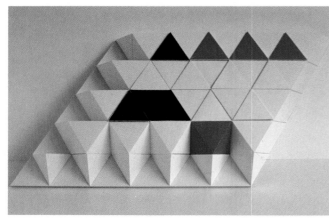

Chapter 3

Plate 1. <u>Upper left</u>: IsoAxis designed by Wallace Walker, unfolded with five rotations.

Plate 2. <u>Center left</u>: Surface color, used as an anomaly within the overall pattern of solids, influences perception of form by decreasing (on the black solids) or maintaining (on the red and white solids) levels of highlight and shadow contrast. (Courtesy of Franz Zeier)

Plate 3. <u>Lower left</u>: The overall shape of the group of black triangles is first perceived as a unit form (trapezoid) defined by levels of color contrast from surrounding forms. (Courtesy of Franz Zeier)

Plate 4. <u>Upper right</u>: A graphic pattern applied to the surface of a solid can influence perception of the form's edges, vertices, and faces. (Courtesy of Franz Zeier)

Chapter 4

Plate 5. <u>Center right</u>: Simultaneous contrast: The effect of this phenomenon exaggerates color differences in areas of adjacent or overlapping hues.

Plate 6. Upper near right: Spectrum value: Swatches showing hues of varying intensity are related to a gray scale in accord with their inherent level of value.

Plate 7. Lower near right: Color relativity: Related colors undergo modifications that can be drastic or subtle.

Plate 8. Upper far right: Subtraction of color: A background color subtracts its own hue and value from the color that it carries.

Plate 9. Center far right: Visual equality: Color runs are formed through the establishment of intervals of visually equal steps.

Plate 10. Lower far right: Film color: A transparent experience of color results from a clear definition of overlapping form and a visual mixture of the color.

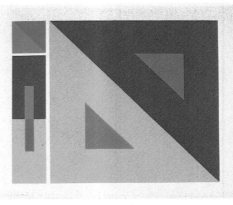

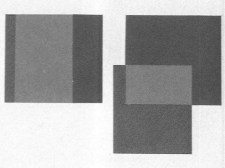

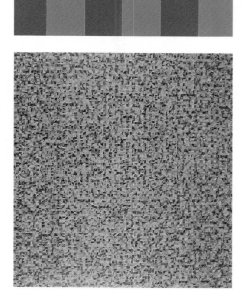

Plate 11. <u>Upper left:</u> Volume color: The properties of volume color can be demonstrated in many organized color ranges, including scales of value.

Plate 12. <u>Center left:</u> Vibration: Complementary or near complementary colors of great intensity and close similarity in value give the strongest impression of vibration.

Plate 13. <u>Lower left:</u> *ZEPHYR* (acrylic) © Harold Linton, Grace Hokin Gallery, Palm Beach and Bay Harbor Islands, Florida. (Collection of Shirley and Nathan Schlafer)

Plate 14. <u>Upper right:</u> Temperature change and luminosity: left, light to dark; center, bright to bright to dull; right, warm to cool.

Plate 15. <u>Center right:</u> Visual mixing and scale.

Plate 16. <u>Upper near right:</u> *Vector 1* (oil on canvas) by Charles N. Smith.

Plate 17. <u>Center near right:</u> *Infrared* (oil on canvas) by Charles N. Smith.

Plate 18. <u>Lower near right:</u> Arrangement of color and shape that achieves symmetrical balance.

Plate 19. <u>Upper far right:</u> Arrangement of color and shape that achieves asymmetrical balance.

Plate 20. <u>Lower far right:</u> Axonometric study in color, form, and space (collage of color paper and magazine clippings).

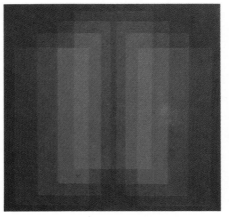

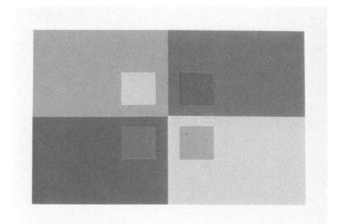

of surface color under ordinary conditions of viewing. In *World of Colour* David Katz contrasts the appearance of a color of spectral light with the surface of colored paper "One feels that one can penetrate more or less deeply into the spectral colour, whereas when one looks at the colour of a paper the surface presents a barrier beyond which the eye cannot pass. It is as though the colour of the paper offered resistance to the eye."

An optimum impression of surface color is given from light reflected in a diffused manner from dull-surfaced objects. Surface colors are perceived on solid objects that possess a clearly defined surface character. Figure 4–14 demonstrates several planes in an overlapping configuration. Our awareness of these shapes as overlapping planes is strengthened by the repetition and sequence of their form. Charles N. Smith writes in the *Student Handbook of Color:* "In any visual situation, our eye tends to complete the simplest form and it is easy to be convinced that we see four squares even though these squares are opaque and the color lies on the surface." The experience of surface color is perceived almost entirely on objects with the infrequent exception of clouds of smoke or steam.

Film Color. The distinctive qualities of film color differ in character from those of surface color. Film color is transparent color that appears as a representation of light and, in this sense, does not fully obscure the dimension of background as does a surface color. Faber Birren mentions in *Color, Form and Space* that the transparency of a film is not necessarily a physical attribute. It can be and often is an interpretation that occurs within the mind. The experience of film color is characterized by a visual mixture of the color of the film itself and the color of the background against which it is seen. Katz confirms that a film color remains between an observer and the background and maintains a frontal parallel appearance in most viewing conditions. By holding a sheet of colored acetate at arm's length between your eyes and the pages of this book, you will notice that at any angle the acetate will always appear flat and parallel to your eyes. This experience is possible only when your vision is focused on the book rather than on the acetate.

The creation of an illusion of transparency with opaque color requires clearly defined and overlapping forms. A distinct comparison is made in plate 10 between the interpretation of film color and surface color. Plate 10 (right) shows two planes over-

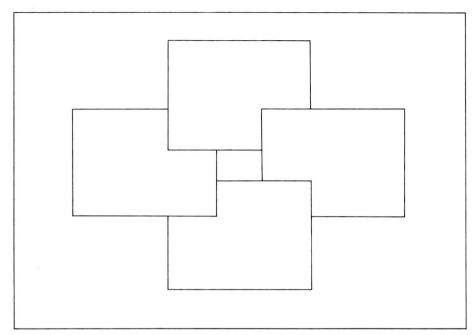

4–14. Four planes perceived in an overlapping relationship because of the strong continuation of form.

lapping. The middle area formed by the overlapping planes is a combination of the colors of the two planes. Both the strong definition of overlapping form and the visual mixture of color make the planes appear transparent. Although the same colors are used in the forms on the left in plate 10, the appearance of form remains opaque because the two planes are only partially overlapped with one line used to distinguish two forms. The illusion of transparent color has decreased because three opaque forms are equally apparent as two transparent planes.

Volume Color. In a variety of natural and man-made conditions, the eye can penetrate the surface and see into a color. This condition is present in nature when looking across to the horizon on a misty day, through the filmy gray fog to objects beyond, or when viewing objects through a transparent colored liquid. On a misty day or beneath the surface of a body of water in a swimming pool, objects at a distance blend into the color of the elements in their environment until they eventually disappear altogether. The illusion of this effect of volume color can be created by the use of visually equal steps observed in simultaneous contrast. The designer may select a color on one end of a scale for the color of the object, and a color on the opposite end of the scale for the color of the volume in which the object is placed. The object may then be repeated in gradually diminished size with a progressive change in color to result in an organized filling of a three-dimensional space. The properties of volume color can be demonstrated in many organized color ranges, including scales of value. Plate 11 is a chromatic example of the properties of volume color.

An increasing interest in color leads to an awareness of visual phenomena that occur when certain colors are used in combination. Some effects are either psychological in origin and relate to one's experience, imagination, and previous education, while others result from physical changes that take place in the body chemistry. Although the color phenomena described in the following sections have little effect at the scale of the built environment, the process of environmental design that occurs on the drawing board is in the same scale at which these phenomena are readily observed.

VIBRATION

A diagram of a cross section of the human eye is shown in figure 4-15, which indicates the position of the lens and the retina. Similar to the lens of a camera, the lens of the eye is transparent and admits light rays (and screens out ultraviolet light) and transmits them to the retina. The retina is composed of millions of microscopic sensitive cells called rods and cones. The rods are sensitive to light and dark and can only transmit achromatic color. The cones transmit chromatic color and are composed of three basic types: red-, green-, and blue-sensitive.

The structure of the eye is so complicated that it is astonishing that a brief glance at an object actually consists of hundreds of repeated visual impressions. Plate 12 illustrates two colors that vibrate. When contiguous color-shape relationships are perceived, the eye will focus alternately on one and then the other in rapid succession. Color pairs that are complementary or near complements of strong chroma and similar value give the strongest impression of vibration.

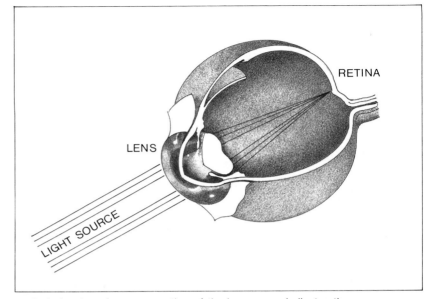

4-15. A drawing of a cross section of the human eye indicates the position of the lens, which receives light rays and transmits them to the retina.

VISUAL MIXING

When two vibrating colors are repeated in a pattern of small shapes—for example, dots, squares, or stripes—on a background that is darker in value than the vibrating colors, the eye's rapid change of focus causes an impression received in the brain to appear as a mixture of the two colors, similar in character to that of two overlapping lights. The color impression will be of an intensity that could not be achieved through the basic mixture of pigments alone.

Today, most color printed material is produced through a four-color printing process that conveys an image made from tiny dots of colored inks. The image is first separated into three positive images, each of which contains one of the subtractive primary colors—yellow, magenta, and cyan. Each of these are translated into three separate plates—with black as a fourth positive plate—and recombined on the press to form the original image.

With the combinations of yellow and magenta, many other colors are produced, but the full range is not perceptible until cyan is introduced. The addition of black results in a correct density to areas that were unsatisfactorily shaded with mixtures of the three primaries. Figures 4-16 and 4-17 illustrate the impact of visually mixed color in the form of a printed poster viewed from two different distances. These halftones reflect an impression of solid

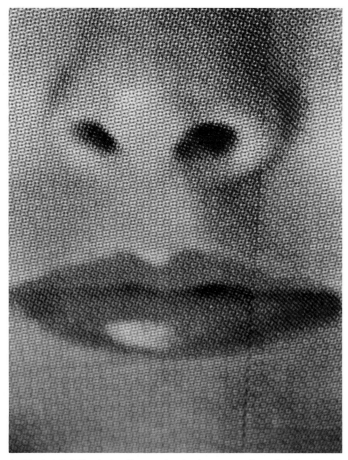

4-17. A detail illustrates the mechanical process of small dots of color that mix optically to appear as facial tones in the portrait. (Courtesy of the Detroit Science Center)

4-16. Poster graphics are produced with small dots of color, which when viewed from a distance combine in our field of vision to form an image. (Courtesy of the Detroit Science Center)

color, but at closer observation, as figure 4-17 reveals, they are composed of dots. The dots are mixed by the eye of the observer, similar to the principle used in Georges Seurat's neoimpressionist paintings.

TEMPERATURE CHANGE AND LUMINOSITY

The perceived temperature of color in the Western tradition has long been accepted as strongly related to the natural environment; blue appears cool and the adjacent group, yellow-orange-red, appears warm. Aside from associations such as red as having an ability to raise the blood pressure or excite the nervous system, yellow and orange being related to the sun and suggesting cheerfulness, and the blue-greens suggesting calm and spacious coolness, any temperature can be read higher or lower in comparison with others. Therefore, within a range of blues and reds, there are also warm blues and cool reds possible, making the usefulness of a warm-cool principle in design highly relative.

Temperature changes can be effective in design, however, when used in the context of a change in key. In plate 13 two ranges of color temperature are incorporated, each of which are organized in progressive changes of keys. Changes in temperature can be enhanced by the addition of the quality of luminosity. Figure 4–18 and plate 14 illustrate a student exercise composed of three color scales: value, chroma, and temperature. As a study in the relative nature of color, this project is useful to help define the differences between value, chroma, and temperature

changes. In order to understand the variables of color mixing, it is important that none of the three following exercises be so "colored" that they can be mistaken for one another. They should be approached as a consecutive series. Gouache or tempera on three-ply white bristol board give a mat finish result and make color judgment easier than do glossy pigments.

A basic composition, such as a mosaic of squares or triangles, is first established, enabling the construction of a color progression from the center of each design outward in all directions. In figure 4–18A the center area has been made light (tinted with the addition of white), and a progression is made in visually equal steps toward a dark outer band by the addition of black and/or the spectrum color (Plate 14 (left)). In figure 4–18B, the center areas are made bright (intense), progressing unit by unit, toward a dull perimeter. The sequence of mixing is controlled in order to create visually equal steps from the center outward in all directions. By mixing any bright color with its complement, a chromatic scale is created that progresses toward a neutral gray at the outside of the design (plate 14 (center)). In figure 4–18C, the center area is filled with warm-temperature hues. A progression toward a cool-temperature band is achieved by mixing relatively cool hues with the warmer hues, which may include complements

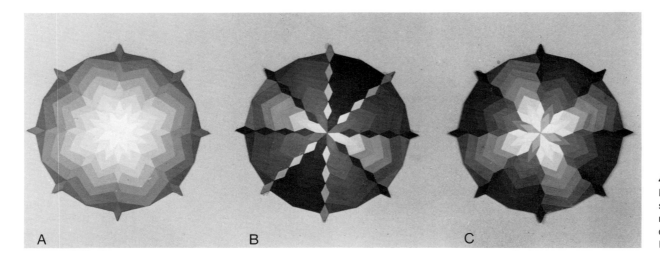

A   B   C

4–18. Temperature change and luminosity: Each of the three designs is produced with a distinct range of color: *A.* From light to dark. *B.* From bright to dull. *C.* From warm to cool.

and analogous colors, to create visually equal steps through the neutral range and into a cool temperature outer band (plate 14 (right)).

VISUAL MIXING AND SCALE

The studies in figures 4-19 and 4-20 concern the concept of visual mixing in the creation of a color scale. They strive to achieve equal steps of visually mixed color as a result of pigment mixing and the influence of a common color paper background on each step in a progression (figs. 4-19 and 4-20).

The design field (10″ × 10″) is subdivided, with a ¾″ square grid for the location of one ⅝″-diameter, one ⅜″-diameter, one and ¼″-diameter ring at each point of intersection formed by the lines of the grid. Designer's gouache can be used along with a ruling attachment for a compass to create the colored rings. A plan for the sequence of value, hue, or chroma dominance may be extended in virtually any direction across the composition. A different set of variations for advancing and receding color relationships may also be planned as a counterpoint within the pattern of outside, intermediate, or central rings across the design.

In these exercises, students were asked to avoid sudden or abrupt changes in the sequence of visual steps, but certainly, a planned shift from light to dark, or from bright to dull along a diagonal, vertical, or horizontal direction will dramatize the optical quality of the mixing experience (plate 15).

OPTICAL ILLUSIONS

The creation of a three-dimensional illusion on a two-dimensional plane is a useful exercise that aids in the development of sensitivity to form and space. The optical juxtaposition of planes is perhaps nothing more complex than a visual puzzle but has the added value of lending interest to surface color. The ability to quickly interpret the manner in which the forms are used to construct an illusion will also be helpful to an understanding of the creative thinking involved in the following studies, where the illusion of transparent, three-dimensional solids is created on a

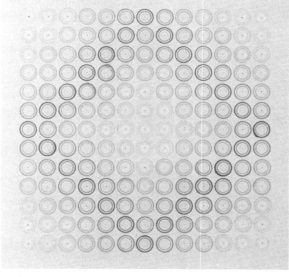

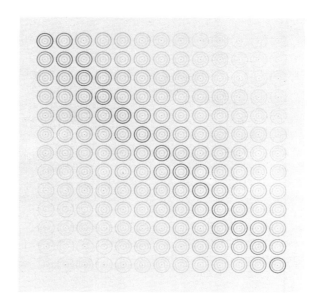

4-19 and 4-20. Visual mixing and scale: The principle of optical mix, along with careful alterations of hue, value, and chroma, can produce subtle gradations and effects of depth.

4-19

4-20

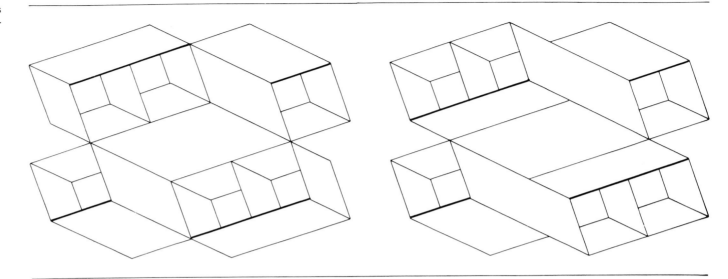

4-21. Optical illusion of volumes and solids by Josef Albers. (Courtesy of M.I.T. Press)

two-dimensional surface. Figure 4-21 is a reproduction of one of Josef Albers's well-known illusions from a book by François Busher, entitled *Josef Albers: Despite Straight Lines.* A survey of illusions is also available in *Optical Illusions and the Visual Arts,* by Jacqueline B. Thurston and Ronald G. Carraher.

Illusions of Transparency. The original designs shown in fig. 4-22 are from *The Interaction of Color* by Josef Albers and were silk-screened and printed in subtle shades of lavender and violet. In A the overlapping rectangles on a light ground are subtractive and appear transparent, while the overlapping rectangles in B on a dark ground are additive and appear as projected areas of light. Film color is a mixture of the color of the film itself and the color of the background against which it is seen. The background is as important as the film in the creation of a transparent illusion. There are three distinctly different types of mixtures that rely in part on the condition of an existing background to reflect their special attributes. These mixtures include additive or light mixture, subtractive or pigment mixture, and optical or visual mixture.

Additive color mixture is a descriptive term for the mixture of light. Figure 4-23 shows a dark field with two imaginary lights

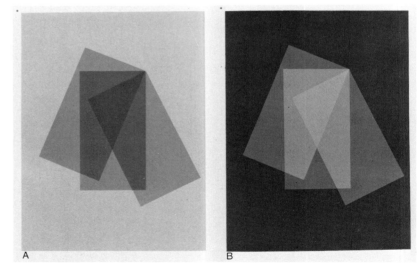

A   B

4-22A-B. The interaction of color: In *A* overlapping rectangles on a light ground are subtractive and appear transparent. In *B* the overlapping rectangles on a dark ground are additive and appear as projected areas of light. The originals of these illustrations are silkscreened in shades of lavender and violet. (From *The Interaction of Color* by Josef Albers)

4–23. Additive color mixture.

overlapping. It is easily perceived that the brightness increases where the overlap occurs. The effect of the combined "candle-power" of both lights is greater than that of a single light. This addition of light may continue until a point of saturation is reached, and the addition of more light will not make an appreciable difference in the effect of brightness. A similar experience can be produced by overlapping sheets of tracing paper on a black ground. Figure 4–24 illustrates additive films progressing toward a lighter plane as they overlap on a dark ground. The selection of visually equal steps illustrated in simultaneous contrast and value keys, together with a strong continuation of form, are both important in the creation of a successful illusion of transparency. A similar effect of brightness can be achieved in chromatic color as long as the relationship to the background is clearly perceived.

Subtractive color mixing, as discussed earlier in conjunction with the pigment mixing circle, results in the darkening of a new color, giving it a greater amount of gray content. Subtractive color might be described as the psychological opposite of ad-

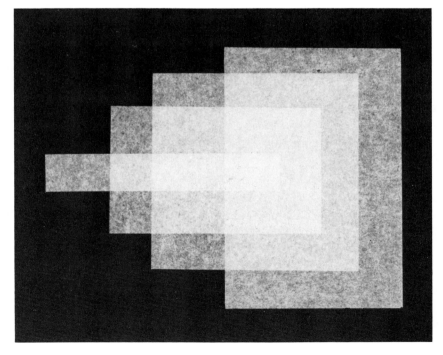

4–24. Overlapping sheets of tracing paper increase in lightness toward a point of maximum saturation in the center of the design.

ditive color. A piece of tracing paper placed on a white ground or in front of a light source will darken, subtracting the light.

CONCEPTUAL COLOR

The additive or subtractive potential of a film color experience depends on the background against which it is seen. The combination of additive and subtractive film colors in the same visual field requires careful planning and thoughtful color judgment. The structural logic required is a natural outgrowth of the previous experiences and exercises with color. The role of the background will have two visual purposes: It will be darker than the additive films and lighter than the subtractive films. Therefore, a color of middle value will be needed and a color run of visually equal steps must be created to cover the complete range of the design.

An additive film placed against a middle value background and overlapped with a subtractive film will cancel one another out and return to the background color where the two films overlap. Figure 4–25 illustrates the structural relationship of the background to additive and subtractive films. Additive films are numbered 1, 2, and 3, respectively, and subtractive films are numbered −1, −2, and −3. The background is numbered 0.

Compare A and B with C in figure 4–25 to see how a combined film illusion differs from an additive or a subtractive one alone. In *The World of Colour* David Katz further discusses three-dimensional transparent objects: "It is noteworthy that the transition from surface colour to film colour is more easily induced than is the reverse change." As we move into a more involved exploration of the effects of light upon pigment, the appreciation and understanding of the structural logic of color and form depend upon past learning and clear color judgment.

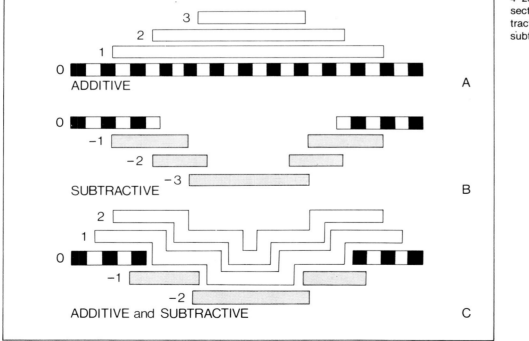

4–25. Three-dimensional cross section diagram of additive, subtractive, and combined additive-subtractive mixing.

Charles N. Smith has contributed a great deal to the growing awareness and use of color through his work as an artist, author, and design consultant. His paintings follow the modern tradition of formal chromatic abstraction called chromatic structuralism. The American arm of this tradition progresses from the synchromist painters Stanton MacDonald-Wright and Morgan Russell. Smith's *Vector 1* (plate 16) provides a clear example of the use of a conceptual color run that appears additive and subtractive in the same plane, while *Infrared* (plate 17) shows a straight additive film color run.

In his *Student Handbook of Color,* Smith has wisely suggested that, "If you interpret understanding of color to mean understanding the structural logic of color, I am sure the picture will be greatly clarified." Color relationships and three-dimensional illusions can represent complete conceptual thinking in which all the action of form and color takes place in the mind of the observer. The three-dimensional forms are forced to appear as two-dimensional objects, and the level of tension and apparent movement can yield an exciting visual sensation (figs. 4–26 and 4–27).

The development of one's powers to use color effectively to achieve an illusion of space relies not only on a plan for color key and order but includes the principles of composition, such as contrast and balance. The remaining sections of this chapter discuss the importance of these factors, some general guides that contribute to the achievement of illusions of depth, and a final project in two-dimensional design that explores the illusory power of "color-space."

PRINCIPLES OF CONTRAST AND BALANCE

The importance of the role of contrast in the perception of all forms of composition cannot be ignored. Richard L. Gregory in

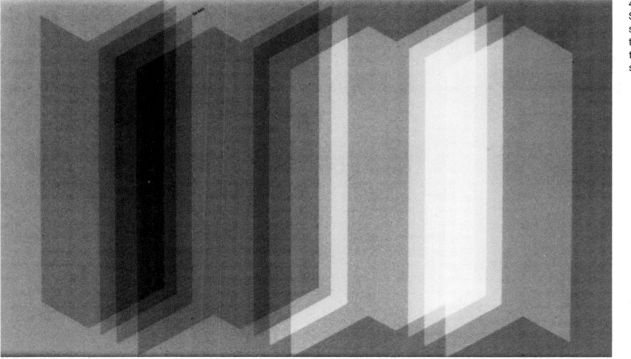

4–26. *Evolution* by Charles N. Smith illustrates both additive and subtractive film color, as well as the combination of additive-subtractive color in a nine-step gray scale.

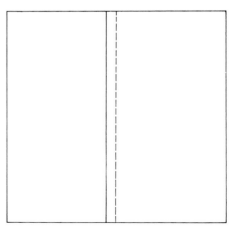

4-27. *White Divided* by Charles N. Smith illustrates the illusion of additive and subtractive layers totally dependent on light and shadow to define form.

our weight against it. If, however, it is not entirely shaky, but not completely upright either, then we are confronted with circumstances of visual information that are not clear. The pattern or visual information is inconclusive, and the need for additional methods of assessing the strength of the post are required. A visual example in abstract terms consists of a line drawn through a square very close to dead center and yet just off it (fig. 4-28). The line is just enough off center to make its unbalanced position distinct. An effective use of visual perception is to position or identify visual clues as balanced or unbalanced, strong or threateningly weak. The Gestalt psychologists deal with this need by describing the two opposite visual states as leveled or sharpened. Kurt Koffka, in *Principles of Gestalt Psychology,* defines sharpening as "an increase or exaggeration" and leveling as a "weakening or toning down of a peculiarity of a pattern." In the language of visual design, sharpening can be associated with contrast (fig. 4-29A), while leveling can be related to harmony (fig. 4-29B). Regardless, however, of the terminology used to describe these polarities, they both are excellent tools for structuring a visual composition with a clear point of view, and applying them in a well-crafted manner avoids confusion for the designer and the viewer. Recognizing the value of these two visual techniques, Gestalt psychologists have established through research that the eye and the human brain constantly seek resolution and closure in the sensory data they perceive. The Gestalt Theory, developed

The Intelligent Eye states, "In this sense 'patterns' are very different from 'objects.' By a pattern we mean some set of inputs, in space or time, at the receptor." The process of seeing necessitates a discernment or sorting out of patterns, with the goal of understanding or recognition. To this end, ambiguity is a natural enemy and is to be avoided if these processes are to function properly. We observe a fence post in the outdoors. If it appears vertical and solid, we know we can lean against it. If, on the other hand, it appears angular and loose, we would probably not trust

4-28. A line just off center, but not so much so as to make its imbalance apparent.

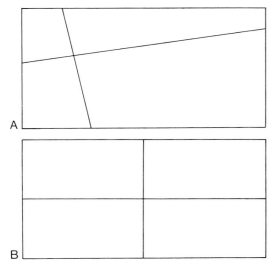

A

B

4-29A-B. Sharpening in *A* is an exaggeration of the peculiar nature of a pattern of shape. Leveling in *B* is a weakening or toning down of the unique attributes of shape in a design.

by Max Wertheimer, introduced the principle that controls this hypothesis and called it the law of Prägnanz, which he defined as follows: "psychological organization will always be as 'good' as the prevailing conditions allow." What is meant by the term *good* is not completely clear; his suggestion, however, regards resolution in terms of regularity, symmetry, and simplicity. Those forces that apply to design include the need to finish off or connect an unfinished line (fig. 4-30A), as in closure, or to match like shapes, as in the "principle of similarity" (fig. 4-30B). Therefore, finishing the lines or grouping like shapes is a step toward simplification of the inevitable operation of the mechanics of perception in the human organism. The question might be asked if this regularity is as desirable as the physiological pull toward it would indicate.

Certainly, absolute regularity can be refined and controlled so that it approaches a perfect visual appearance, as in the example of the Greeks' harmonious designs of temples such as the Parthenon. In addition to the use of the formula of the Golden Mean—the mathematically determined proportion—the Greeks made complete use of axial or symmetrical balance and anticipation of the elements of perception through design and construction, with results as close to perfection as is humanly possible. Knowing that the eye bends a straight line into a slightly concave curve (fig. 4-31A) as it focuses on it from a distance, the Greek architects designed the column of the temple facade with a slight, almost imperceptible convexity (fig. 4-31B) to compensate for the

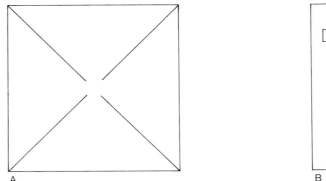

A

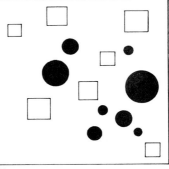

B

4-30A-B. The need to connect an unfinished line in *A* or to match like shapes in *B* is a step toward simplification and a natural psychological pull in the mechanics of perception in human beings.

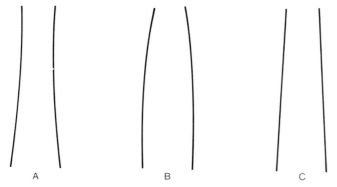

4-31A-C. Anticipation of perceptual phenomena has been useful to many artists and designers. The eye bends a straight line into a concave curve slightly as it is seen from a distance (*A*). Greek architects designed the columns of temple facades with a slight convexity (*B*) to compensate for this phenomenon and produce an apparent straight line (*C*).

perceptual phenomenon and produce an apparently perfect straight line (figs. 4-31C and 4-32).

The act of seeing involves the process of visual acuity and judgment. Figure 4-33A appears completely and indisputably balanced with a similar and quick response to figure 4-33B predicted from the viewer. The structure of the visual elements is not symmetrical in the latter figure and it does not balance in the obvious sense that the elements in figure 4-33A do. Balance, however, need not take the form of symmetry, and the weight of the design elements can be arranged asymmetrically. By imposing additional forces within the order or arrangement of shape, the design is moved away from simplicity, with the final effect of balance structured by weight and counterweight, action and counteraction. It is the same human perceptual ability that establishes symmetrical balance which can quickly measure and respond to asymmetrical balance. Because this process is not as easily demonstrated nor defined, it often seems intuitive rather than physical. In the case of color, we not only take into account the role of value as weight and counterweight, and the relation-

4-32. Greek temple facade.

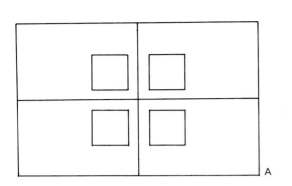 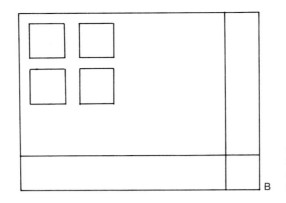

4-33A–B. Symmetrical arrangement of shape in balance (A); asymmetrical arrangement of shape in balance (B).

ships between shapes or forms as action and counteraction, but also the effect of chroma, which extends from intense to dull. Plates 18 and 19 show the line drawings in figures 4–33A and 4–33B with color added to illustrate, respectively, how chroma affects the measure of balance through an arrangement of opposing bright and dull shapes and their respective measures of action and counteraction.

COLLAGE AND SPACE

Basic color concepts of afterimage, simultaneous contrast, and so forth, form the basis of well-known studio exercises that relate to the development of perception and an increased sensitivity to color relationships. The following study helps to both summarize the preceding experiences and to extend the role of color study to include further experiments with color, form, and space.

The reader will discover in this project that dimensional effects are possible through the application of the following principles of color and design:

1. The contrast of bright against dark, with the exception of black.
2. The contrast of pure colors or black and white against grayed colors.
3. The contrast of warm colors against cool colors.
4. The contrast of detail, texture, and microstructure against a plain or film surface.
5. The use of perspective to distinguish near from far distances.
6. The implied use of background design elements behind foreground feature elements.
7. The use of highlights and cast shadows.
8. The use of easily recognized objects, which, because of familiarity and relative size, will give mental cues to their spatial positions.

The purpose of this project is to introduce the concept of collage and color-space into the visual vocabulary. The study begins with a collage of a fixed dimension (4″ × 3″ in 1″ squares) from color papers and images found in advertising, such as magazines, posters, and newspapers (fig. 4–34). The mosaic of one-inch color-texture squares is then used as the subject in the following transformations.

First, a contour line drawing is made directly from the original collage color study (fig. 4–35). This drawing becomes a

4-34. Collage of magazine clippings in a mosaic design of 1″ squares.

4-35. Contour drawing derived from the collage in figure 4-34.

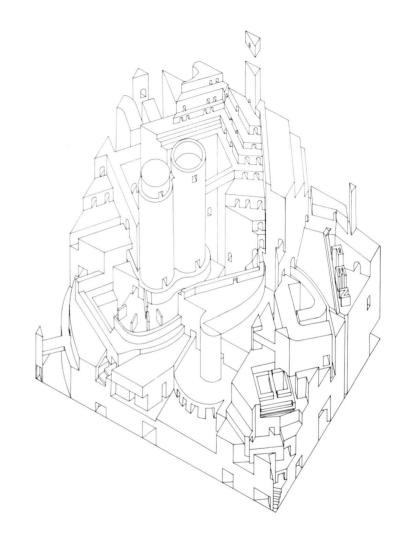

4-36. Axonometric drawing based on the plan drawing in fig. 4-35.

"floor plan" for the axonometric drawing (again in contour line) of an imaginary labyrinth (fig. 4–36). The axonometric contour drawing is used as a vehicle to reexplore the relationship of collage (which itself explores the nature of juxtaposition) to a visual environment and to the consequent architectural environment through an imaginary labyrinth that begins and ends with the colors and images found in magazines, newspapers, and posters (plate 20).

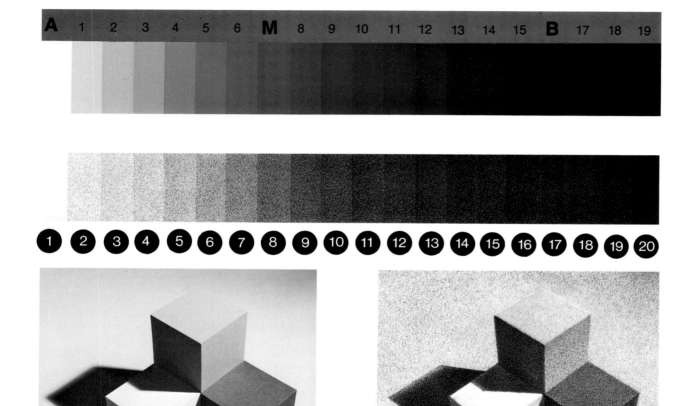

5-1. Standard value scales: A photographic value scale can be compared to a carefully matched "homemade" version. The value delineation numbering system from 1 to 20 on the homemade scale increases with darkness, which typically corresponds with a buildup of an applied drawing medium. The photographic value scale utilizes a similar numbering system; in this case, however, the least applied medium results in black and the medium applied in the greatest amount results in white. (See Minor White's *Zone System Manual.*) The light, middle, and dark value cube groups— a photograph of normal contrast on the left and an illustration matched to the photograph on the right—can be compared with one another and with each of the value scales above. The values represented in the photograph can be found in the photographic value scale and those in the drawing can be found in the homemade version. Both scales can also be used to find a correspondence with values in either of the cube group studies. (Photographic Gray Scale © Eastman Kodak Company, 1977)

5 The Response of Form and Pigment to Light

Many designers and architects have developed the ability to visualize shapes and forms as if they existed in open space. They are able to use their imaginations to create a sense of space that gives reality to what the eye sees. Many designers and architects are also aware that a conception that has looked very good "on paper" has suffered when constructed in the reality of the world itself, and many a form, originally conceived without reference to the environment, has required either alteration or correction to make it appropriate to its location.

In addition, it is equally common for many designers and architects to deal with forms as if they were colorless. Their main emphasis is on line, mass, or proportion as an object or thing unto itself. It is nevertheless true that what is seen by the eye cannot be colorless and that color is an integral dimension of form and cannot be separated from it. White, gray, and black are more than neutrals. In association with shape and form, they communicate visual and emotional messages that are far from neutral. White may be "airy" and stark, gray may appear "formal" or sober, and black may appear "heavy" and ominous. Faber Birren points out an analogy to history by noting that ". . . the spiritual beauty of Gothic Architecture is complemented by the sympathetic mood of gray stone and marble. It would be most difficult to express moods of levity or sensuous pleasure with gray—regardless of how amusing or whimsical the artist attempted to be with design factors alone." In the broadest view regarding perception itself, James J. Gibson, author of *The Perception of the Visual World,* observes that the visual world "is extended in distance and modeled in depth; it is upright, stable, and without boundaries; it is colored, shadowed, illuminated and textured; it is composed of surfaces, edges, shapes and interspaces; and most important of all, it is filled with things which have meaning."

VALUE PLANNING FOR ILLUMINATED FORM

Although we are aware of the general qualities of light, most often we perceive differences associated with the material or surface characteristics of objects. It is important to note, however, that we are only able to perceive form because of the light reflected from it. A profound psychological difference occurs when our awareness is centered on the object rather than the light. The quality of a light source and the reflecting characteristics of surfaces and objects all contribute to the differences we usually experience. In considering the reflecting characteristics of surface and materials, the quality of tone or pigmentation and visual texture are of prime importance.

PERCEPTION OF REFLECTING SURFACES

Our tonal experience incorporates our perception of light and also our awareness of light differences as qualities of objects. Within each of these experiences, there are two groups of tones, chromatic and achromatic. Table 3 illustrates the corresponding dimensions of these experiences.

In addition to tonal differences, visual texture serves as another form of contrast in our visual field. We respond both to the amount and kind of light that surfaces and objects reflect and also to the way in which the light is reflected. This idea is closely related to the tactile quality of a surface. Terms used to describe the character of a visual texture are adapted from our sense of touch—rough, smooth, hard, soft. Other words related to this idea

Table 3. Color and Light Vocabulary

	Light	Tonal Qualities in Pigmentation
Achromatic	Brightness	Value
Chromatic	Brightness	Value
	Hue	Hue
	Saturation	Intensity or chroma

have a visual metaphor—dull, shiny, opaque, transparent, metallic, iridescent.

VISUAL ACUITY

The judgment of color mixing or selection is obviously influenced by the source of illumination under which decisions are made. The designer should undertake pure color judgment only in daylight or under color-balanced illumination. An awareness of the combined effects of the colors of physical light and pigment contribute to an ability to work in all of the dimensions of a design problem that include the perception of color, light, form, and space. Defining form and space through the use of color relies on a plan for the use of contrasting colors with special emphasis placed on their contrasts of value (brightness).

Our eyes have varying degrees of sensitivity under different conditions of illumination. In the light-adapted eye, the spectrum is brightest at the yellow hue. In the dark-adapted eye, the spectrum is brightest at the blue-green hue range, and red dissolves into darkness. In regard to color sources of illumination, many authorities agree that yellow is the region of maximum selectivity and the brightest region of the spectrum. They place yellow at the top of the list because it allows good visibility, with orange-yellow second, followed by yellow-green and green. Deep red, blue, and violet are the least desirable color sources for good visibility.

COLOR UNDER ELECTRIC LIGHT

The creation of designs using colored light, for example, stage settings, window displays, and so forth, involve both the

pigment response to light and the mixtures of light itself. As noted in chapter 4, light and pigments behave differently in mixtures.

Specifically, differences exist in what are known as the primaries, or the hues from which all other hues may be derived yet by themselves cannot be produced by mixture. Mixtures of the pigment primaries, red, yellow, and blue, will yield the intermediates orange, green, and purple. The mixture of the light primaries, red, green, and blue, however, will result in the intermediates yellow, magenta (bluish-red), and cyan (greenish-blue). Figure 4–7A and 4–7B show both a light and pigment circle, with their respective primaries indicated. The light mixtures of the primaries red and blue will produce magenta; green and blue will produce cyan; and the mixture of red and green light will yield yellow light.

Pigments used in the creation of painted stage scenery, fabrics, and costumes all receive light from electric (colored) light sources. These surfaces will behave as do all pigments, which can only reflect their own kind of light. A pigment can only appear as its true color when it receives the vibrations that are inherent to its substance. They may be extracted from white light, but in man-made conditions of light, pigmented gelatins over a light source may subtract part of the vibrant range of the spectrum resulting in a surface unable to receive its own kind of light. In such situations, pigments cannot reflect vibrant energy foreign to their nature and therefore appear as neutral areas. These effects are easily simulated with colored gelatins, lights, and papers and are readily observed in architectural, theatrical, and commercial lighting displays.

VALUE PLANNING

In order to understand the relationship of light and form and apply it effectively, it is necessary to know at least a few basics about the physical behavior of light and the processes of visual perception. The following study, originally performed by Paul Stevenson Oles in *Architectural Illustration: The Value Delineation Process,* has been recreated to demonstrate that our perception of form is not only dependent on the qualities of the materials at hand and the brightness and direction of the source of illumination, but that our response to light as a necessary element for our ability of sight has a significant role in both graphic and three-dimensional representation. As mentioned throughout this book, the act of seeing involves both a response to light and to value contrast. Nature is perceived by the eye as areas of color contrast in many patterns of incredible complexity, which are received and interpreted with great speed and precision by the eye and brain. The eye and brain seek visual cues to the definition of form in design in much the same way as they do in nature. In order to delineate in three dimensions, we must observe, dissect, and analyze the patterns that comprise the visual world. This requires that we recall and apply the principles that govern our perception of value patterns in the real world to a problem during its conception, in order to predict as accurately as possible the image that a particular environment will project to a future viewer.

The eye perceives a specific form principally by its edges or contours, which are defined by the foil or the difference in intensity of adjacent values. The values that provide this are a product of two factors. The first is the inherent light-reflecting property of a surface. More specifically, the inherent lightness or darkness (reflectance) of a surface may be referred to as the intrinsic value of the material. Second, the intensity or concentration of the incident light (incoming light falling on a surface) that strikes a material is of importance. The combination of both factors, intrinsic value and incident light, results in the perceived value, which may be referred to simply as the overall perceived value or apparent brightness characteristic of a material or form under a given lighting condition. Gray scales can be established for objectively measuring a material's perceived value in both photography and drawing. A comparison between a normal photograph of a cube model in a given lighting scheme with a standard Kodak scale of gray values provides an objective measure of a material's perceived value (fig. 5–1). Figure 5–1 also shows a comparison between a rendering of a cube model and the artist's gray scale. A number can be indicated to signify a specific gray value and thereby define the perceived value of this object.

Incident light varies drastically in intensity from one set of circumstances to another. With exterior views in sunlight, parallel rays and equivalent incident light intensity across the complete format of a design construction can be assumed. A major variable in incident light concentration in this situation would be the angle at which its rays meet a surface. Naturally, without light rays present on a surface, the result is shade or deep shadow. Incident light is the most concentrated and therefore appears the brightest that is possible for a particular material and situation. Light falling onto a surface at an angle of less than 90 degrees becomes progressively less concentrated and therefore appears less bright. Incident light that falls in a nearly parallel angle to a surface—often called raking or grazing light—is perceived as approximating the shade range, assuming there are consistent intrinsic values on all surfaces of the forms (fig. 5–2).

The sky is more than 1,000 times brighter than the shaded side of a building. Within interior spaces where designers work, however, the reduced levels of illumination used in conjunction with design materials rarely yield contrast ratios greater than 15 or 20 to 1; specifically, the intrinsic value of the lightest material will be only 20 times greater than the darkest material. This assumption is based on the concept that the whitest white reflects about 80 percent and the blackest black is capable of reflecting about 4 or 5 percent of light.

In drawing, painting, or illustration, the artist usually is concerned with the representation of an object at one point in space and time, or in one context. In three-dimensional design, the designer may be concerned with one or more views of an object or environment taken from different points across the physical dimensions of a form or its orientation to our line of sight. In addition, observation and study of the altered effects from a light source moved to various positions around a subject provides a basic lesson in understanding the contrast of highlight and shadow similar in purpose to the east-to-west movement of the sun. In a scale block model or study model, a designer would be interested in the dynamic simulation of color along five "dimensions": hue, value (brightness), chroma (saturation), time (movement), and angle of view.

SHADOW VALUE

When working toward a scheme for color representation in either two-dimensional, bas-relief, or three-dimensional forms, there are a few familiar rules concerning the relative darkness of shade and shadow. Perhaps the most general rule is that shadow (the dark patch on the ground) is usually darker than shade. This

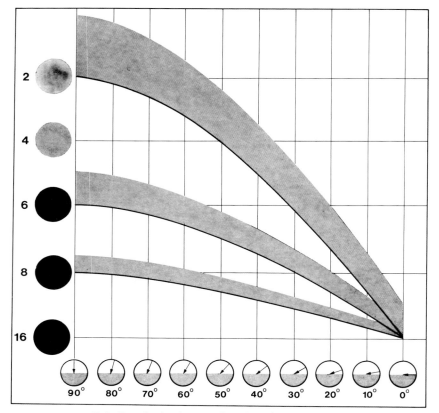

5-2. Perceived value as a function of incident light angle: This graph illustrates three curves: The top curve represents the perceived value or luminance of a mat surface of light gray intrinsic value; the middle curve a medium gray; and the bottom curve that of a dark material. The extreme left vertical column of the graph indicates perceived values resulting from perpendicular incident light, which produces the greatest luminance possible. The extreme right side indicates values produced by raking light, representing the lesser brightnesses for a given material and context. The hard-line curves that converge at 0 degrees and 0 brightness (or value number 16) are the result of experimentation in a controlled environment with no "free" or diffuse light, and as such would be analogous to a moonscape or "black sky" context. The gray zones of the curves begin to suggest more natural and useful contexts in which a certain amount of diffuse light is present. (Graph courtesy of Paul Stevenson Oles)

appears to be true in a comparison of the shade and shadow in the lightest cube shown in figure 5-3. In the situation of a shadow from a dark object on a light ground plane, however, this is not the case, as is shown by the darkest cube in the same figure. Here, the typical distribution of values is reversed, resulting in the shade side of the object being darker than the shadow side. Where identical materials are very light and the shadow is narrow, the shade will tend to be lighter because of an increased quality of diffused light reflected from the adjacent and ground planes (fig. 5-4). The most important aspect of the plan for shade and shadow requires some value difference between adjacent shade and shadow surfaces, which is necessary to distinguish them.

The cube studies in figure 5-5 reflect certain consistencies in value. Materials that have an identical intrinsic value and are on parallel plane surfaces illuminated by parallel incident light rays (sunlight) reflect an identical perceived value throughout the format with the exception of local reflections, which occasionally contribute slight variations. In this series of cube studies, which appear under variable lighting conditions, the perceived values are predictable and approximate a similar level of gray on their visible planes. A high sun has produced cubes with lighter tops in the group on the right than those in which the sun is lower because the light falls from a nearly perpendicular angle to their planes.

The intrinsic values of various materials can have a substantial effect on the darkness of a shadow that falls across them. A designer's perception and ability to creatively adapt the effects of light are enhanced by an awareness of their role as form givers in the natural environment. A fence post shadow lying across a light cement walkway bordered by a medium gray paved road and a dark green lawn would appear to have three values rather than one. Each of the perceived shadows would be darker than the particular material surface in light. However, the lightest shadow value for the sidewalk may appear equal or lighter in value than the darkest surface (green lawn) in bright sunlight. These relationships are illustrated for drawing and photography in figure 5-6. It is also important to add that the perception of textural consistency from sunlit to shaded portions of each material surface aids in the identification of dark areas as shadow and not simply as a change in the actual material (fig. 5-7).

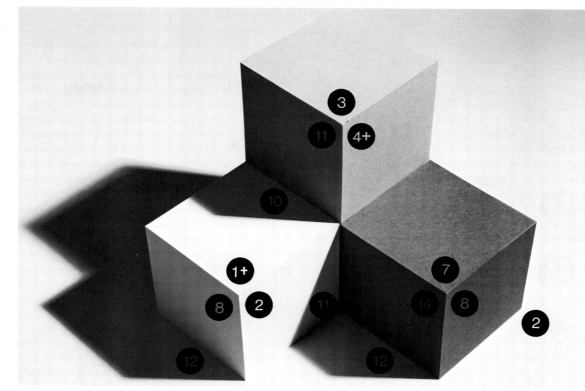

5–3. Three value cubes: This normal contrast photograph shows three mat surface cubes of intrinsic values 1, 3, and 16 in direct light. Perceived values are quantified and indicated in relation to the standard value scale. Reflected or "bounced" light can locally modify value readings slightly, especially in the case of lighter surfaces.

VALUE ALGEBRA

To cultivate an awareness of the visual patterns of highlights, shade, and shadow that accompany the organization of three-dimensional forms, the perceived difference in one level of light on a form to either a higher or lower level of light can be understood as a concept of "light quantity." In figure 5–3, the value difference of the light side to the dark side of the lightest cube will remain constant over (normal) daylight conditions. Light in extreme high or low quantities, however, will result in these differences increasing or decreasing.

REFLECTIVE VALUES

It is worthwhile to remember that however useful these studies may be in the plan of a construction, they apply only to opaque/mat surfaces such as paper, cardboard, and wood and not to opaque/reflective surfaces such as glossy papers and boards, films, plastics, glass, or reflective metals. Highly reflective materials have little if any intrinsic value of their own. Figure 5–8 shows how reflective materials borrow perceived value from their neighbors and thereby substantially alter the perceived value patterns even when conditions of light are constant. Mater-

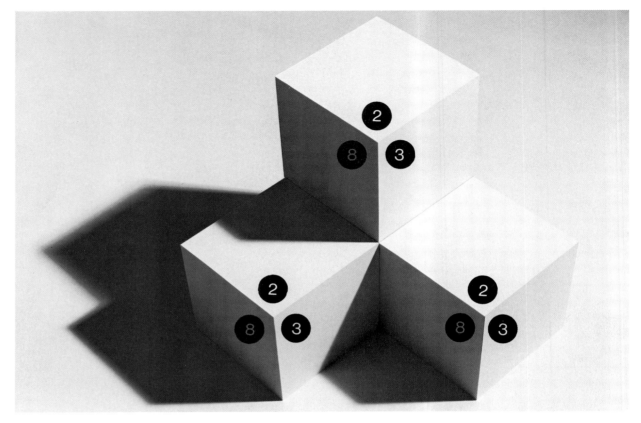

5-4. Gray cubes: This normal contrast photograph shows three cubes of a mat, middle-gray surface on a base plane of approximately similar value. The actual, or intrinsic, value of the material determined by its direct comparison with the standard value scale is 3. The apparent or perceived value numbers indicated on the highlighted, raked, and shaded sides of the cubes are determined by comparing the tones of those sides in the photograph with the standard value scale. The numbers suggest that for a given intrinsic value, perceived values of similarly lighted parallel planes are identical within a given context.

ials used for design and model construction have the general characteristics of surface finish similar to architectural and design product materials, for example, mat; semigloss; glossy, or specular.

Dull metal surfaces and semigloss paints exhibit characteristics of both mat and partly glossy finishes. The behavior of shade, shadow, and reflection on these hybrid materials can be analyzed through isolating their separate value characteristics and then recombining them to observe their patterns. The series of cubes in figure 5-9 includes a comparison of two-value forms made of semigloss opaque acrylic sheet. The dark surface of the

5-5. Variably lighted gray cubes: The series shows the gray cube group from figure 5-4 in nine different angles of incident light originating at the extreme right. The central row (D,E,F) shows lighting parallel to the picture plane, with F being the typical angle of lighting used in most of the cube series photographs. The top row (A,B,C) shows right front lighting, and the lower row (G,H,I) shows right rear lighting. The left vertical row (A,D,G) shows low lighting angles, and the right vertical row (C,F,I) shows high sun angles. Note that all sunlit and shaded parallel planes are of virtually equal value within each picture. A subjective rating of the lighting angles in terms of effective form definition might list F as one of the best in relation to the greatest range of perceived value; while E and G would be considered geometrically interesting and graphically the simplest (having in effect two values).

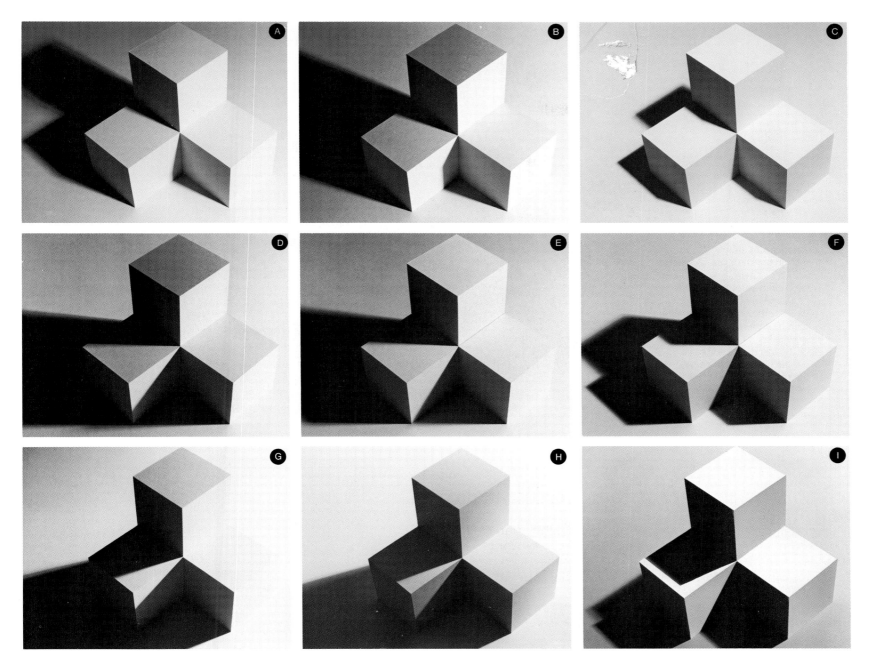

5-6. Perceived value in shadow: This median exposure, normal-contrast photograph shows three samples of mat board with actual, or intrinsic, values of 1+, 3, and 8 located in direct light coming from the right with an object casting its shadow across the three. The indicated perceived values, determined by a comparison of the photograph with the standard value scale, shows a typical set of relationships of sunlit to shadowed surfaces under a deep blue sky.

forms is noticeably more reflective than the white. This is due in part to the contrast of the two values but primarily to the intrinsic value of a light color semigloss surface, which tends to simply veil or wash out the reflected image. Images that are reflected in material surfaces are actually darker than the perceived value of the object itself, with the exception of those objects that borrow brightness from other sources (such as a transparent surface with a light source visible inside or seen from a source beyond).

KEY

A basic lesson relates to the important value concept of key discussed in regard to color theory in chapter four. Key refers to a range and interval of value spacing, as well as to the degree of contrast observed in a scene, photograph, or drawing (figs. 5-10A and 5-10B). A Photostat print and Kodalith print are both examples of extremely high-key graphic devices. The chromatic definition of key is analogous to white and black: High key may include saturated chroma, whereas low key is characterized by less intense, neutral hues.

The dimension of key can be a highly useful tool in design, either to suggest mood or—along with selectivity—to emphasize near or important objects. High-key effects in design tend to be stark and simplified, giving high visual impact and drama to a relationship of form and space. The application of low-key effects can be useful for a subtle definition of form groups and often results in a quiet, soft, or sometimes atmospheric effect.

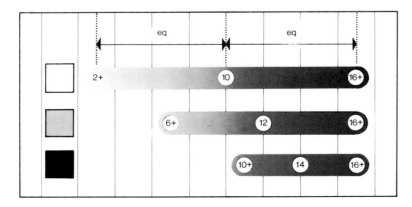

5-7. Perceived value relationships of sunlit and shaded surfaces: This graph shows three value bars; the upper bar represents a material of light intrinsic value, the center bar a medium value, and the lower bar a dark value material. The number on each bar at the left indicates perceived value in direct sunlight, and the midpoint number on each bar represents the shade or shadow value of that material in a typical "blue sky" context. The righthand number is the maximum value possible in a given photograph or drawing format. In the case of a deep blue sky context (less diffuse skylight), the shadows will darken, increasing the middle numbers and moving them proportionately to the right of the midpoint. A simple rule-of-thumb for both drawing and the plan of values for mat surface materials in three-dimensional design is that values will be strong and appear at the middle to dark value range when lighting is direct or the sky is blue. (Graph courtesy of Paul Stevenson Oles)

5–8. Reflective cube series: This series of four photographs begins with a light-middle-dark value cube group in *A* (upper left) and substitutes one cube per frame until all three cubes are mirror reflective. The base plane remains a mat gray (intrinsic and perceived value) of 2 throughout the series. In *B* (upper right) the shade side of the top cube has been replaced with a reflection of its own shadow. In *C* (lower left) the deflected light and reflected image of the top cube results in a two-value shadow on the white cube. Light deflection is now obvious on the base plane beneath the right side of the left cube along with its reflection in that face. In *D* (lower right) all shade and shadow on the left cube disappears. Parts of three deflections (one from the right face of each cube excluding the top cube) are seen on the mat base plane, on which the shadows of all cubes also remain intact.

5–9. Reflective cube series with "hybrid" surfaces: In this series the first cube type has a "hybrid" or semigloss surface made of black-and-white acrylic sheet with two highly contrasting intrinsic values. The second cube is transparent/reflective and the third is opaque/reflective. Notice in *A* (upper left) that the shade value across the left side of the top cube is affected by the intrinsic value, appearing darker in the black zone than in the white. On the base plane in *B* (upper right) the partial deflection of the transparent/reflective cube is naturally weaker than that of the opaque/reflective cube but is more geometrically exact because of the greater precision of the transparent cube surfaces. In *C* (lower left) notice a deflection from the right face of the right cube onto the base plane and back onto its face. Note the slight loss of linearity in the reflected shadow image in the left face of the mirrored cube. In *D* (lower right) a variety of subtle and pronounced alterations of value and few if any surprises are shown.

5-10A. High key in nature (sunny day): This photograph of the Buell Management Building at Lawrence Institute of Technology was taken in the morning of a bright fall day. Notice the sharpness of the corner foil in each of the sunlit building forms.

5-10B. Low key in nature (cloudy day): This photograph shows the same building as figure 5-10A but was taken on an overcast day. The contrast, definition of form, and the key have all been greatly reduced in diffuse light.

A range of value keys may be useful in three-dimensional design to manipulate the visual elements from one orientation of form to another. As one moves through one interior space to another, the key range may be altered in many ways—for example, middle to either high or low (fig. 5-11). As one moves in relation to the changing views of exterior form, exterior spaces are subject to dynamic changes in key due to quantity and direction of natural light. Similar to the sculptor who creates a statue to be viewed outdoors, a "dynamic key" suggests that the study of an object include the relationships of quantity, direction, and temperature of light source.

HUE AND VALUE SELECTION

Once the selection of an appropriate single value key or a dynamic set of keys for a design is made, a determination of an array of colors to be applied is possible. The qualitative process for making reasonably accurate and relatively consistent value pre-

dictions for a color scheme relies on the careful selection of the value factor in color materials (the range of natural light to dark quality in a hue), the effects of color interaction in adjacent relationships on a surface, and the interrelated conditions of incident light and perceived value. The following guidelines for the prediction of value patterns serve as a frame of reference to the designer and presupposes that the designer begins planning with three-dimensional studies.

For opaque/mat materials:
1. Create a basic study model.
2. Determine the intrinsic values for all of the project materials on the model. Use available means of observation, memory, and intuition, and design notebook resources, or a table of material reflectance if appropriate.
3. Consider all incident angles of lighting with material surfaces, and determine the relative intensities of natural or artificial lighting.

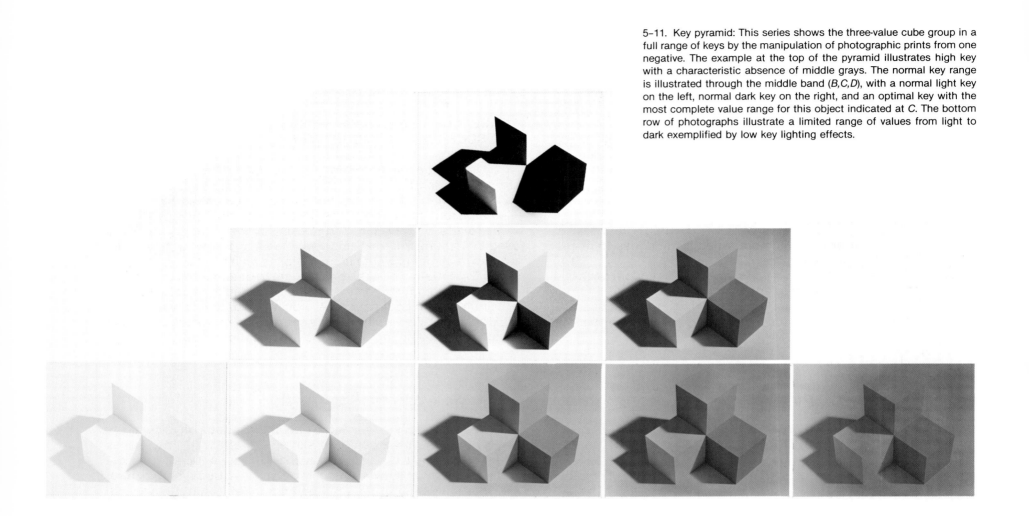

5–11. Key pyramid: This series shows the three-value cube group in a full range of keys by the manipulation of photographic prints from one negative. The example at the top of the pyramid illustrates high key with a characteristic absence of middle grays. The normal key range is illustrated through the middle band (B,C,D), with a normal light key on the left, normal dark key on the right, and an optimal key with the most complete value range for this object indicated at C. The bottom row of photographs illustrate a limited range of values from light to dark exemplified by low key lighting effects.

4. Establish the range for both key and contrast. (Photographs, sketches, and notes from observation or study forms are all useful aids.) The application of color may then be related to the evolving patterns, forms and qualities of light viewed within or around a three-dimensional structure.

For opaque/reflective materials (hybrids):
1. Create a basic study model.
2. Determine the intrinsic values.
3. Determine the qualitative intrinsic reflectivity of each material surface—or how physically smooth and fine it is.

4. Determine the perceived reflectivity—or how glossy or shiny the material appears (dependent on the angle of incident view and the angle of incident light).
5. Determine the perceived values of reflected objects, noting that reflected images appear somewhat darker than the objects reflected.
6. Establish the range for both key and contrast. The application of color may then be related to the evolving patterns, forms, and qualities of light viewed within or around a three-dimensional structure.

For transparent/reflective materials:
1. Create a basic study model.
2. Determine the intrinsic reflectivity versus transparency. Mirror glass is more reflective and less transparent than clear glass.
3. Determine the perceived reflectivity dependent on incident viewing angle and incident light.
4. Determine the perceived values of objects seen through the material—brightness of interior surfaces and lighting.
5. Establish the cause for both key and contrast. The application of color may then be related to the evolving patterns, forms and qualities of light viewed within or around a three-dimensional structure.

MUNSELL NOTATION FOR BAINBRIDGE ALPHAMAT AND CRESCENT MUSEUM RAG MAT BOARDS

As an aid for the designer who wishes to systematically select colored mat boards and relate them to value and chroma scales, the notations from the Munsell Book of Colors in Appendix 1 have been coordinated and matched to the Alphamat rag boards, made by Bainbridge, and the Crescent Cardboard Company's museum-quality colored rag boards. This listing was compiled under daylight conditions (a typical clear day), using manufacturer's samples and keying each sample to a matched color chip from the Munsell Book of Colors. In cases where a manufacturer's color sample does not appear identical to a Munsell color chip, two notations are given that indicate the position of a manufacturer's sample within the Munsell System.

The manufacturer's samples have been listed according to the code numbers found in each company's brochure, and they have been further distinguished by groupings in related hue ranges, such as gray values, warm tertiaries, red and orange, and green and blue (see Appendix 1).

CORRELATIONS BETWEEN DESIGN MEDIA AND SOURCES OF ILLUMINATION

The Munsell charts for judging the luminous reflectance factors of colored walls and other surfaces have been developed for three standard illumination sources established by the CIE (Commission International de l'Eclairage, the official French name for the International Commission on Illumination). They are used by lighting and television engineers and architects and designers in all fields where illumination is an important factor (fig. 5–12). Essentially, they serve as a guide to determining the degree of change in reflectance that may be expected for a color sample with a change in light source. A wide range of colors helps to approximately match a particular surface with minimum influence of hue and chroma factors on the judgment of value.

COLOR ILLUMINATION AND FORM

As this book has pointed out, color is not a physical property of the things we see: it is simply the effect of light waves bouncing off or passing through the various materials and objects. The color of a given object is determined by several factors: the characteristics of the light source under which it is viewed; and the way the object absorbs, transmits, or reflects the light waves that strike it. The environment of color (or surrounding colors) also influences the mind and determines color, as does the physical condition of the viewer's eyes. Only those light waves entering the eye from the object, however, are technically responsible for what color is seen.

Color associated with objects can be changed in many ways—by changing the light source (such as from incandescent to fluorescent lamps), by adding light filters (such as wearing sunglasses), as well as by physically altering the object itself. For ex-

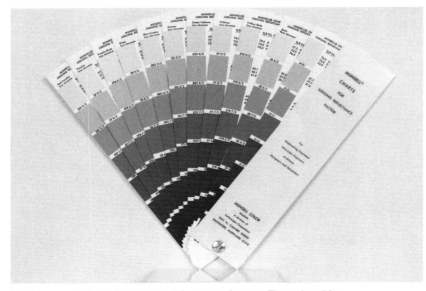

5-12. Munsell charts for judging reflectance factors: The color chips of these charts are mounted at the edges of narrow cards so that each chip can be placed directly next to the surface in question. Also provided are masking devices in gray, white, and black papers for the control of contrast between the comparison of a color chip and a sample under consideration. There are 11 cards, each displaying one of the ten principal and intermediate Munsell hues and one card of neutrals ranging in Munsell value from 2 to 9.5 in steps of 0.5, all applicable for tasks illuminated by daylight or its equivalent.

ample, to change an automobile color from red to blue, a different paint pigment is used—one that will reflect blue light waves while absorbing other colors of light waves.

If you have ever seen a red car parked under a clear mercury street lamp at night, you might have easily mistaken the car for brown in color, for the clear mercury lamp, while very powerful in producing light, is practically devoid of red energy. Therefore, few red light waves were available to reach the eye. Since light and color are such integral parts of our everyday lives, the lamp design engineer must design not only lamps that give light to see by, but more important, he or she must design lamps that simultaneously appear white and render naturally the color appearance of familiar objects.

LIGHT SOURCE AND PERCEPTION (COLOR CONSTANCY)

The sun and electric lamps are considered light sources because they transform energy from another form into the radiant energy wavelengths that we call light. These light sources also emit useful energy at wavelengths both shorter and longer than light waves. Ultraviolet energy is valuable for its germ-killing, suntanning, and photochemical properties and has wavelengths shorter than light waves. Infrared energy waves often referred to as heat waves are longer than light waves. All radiant energy, when absorbed, can be transformed into heat. It is now apparent that without light there can be no colors, for colors are simply names that describe the various mixtures of electromagnetic energy that exists only in the transient state of radiation. The term *color* describes an imbalance of visible radiant energy reaching the eye from light sources and objects (imbalance can be defined as any deviation from the average amount of energy at all wavelengths). The possibilities for deviation or imbalance, which are almost infinite, account for there being so many names to describe the various "mixes" or combinations of visible energy.

We call tomatoes *red*, lemons *yellow*, and pine trees *green*. In fact, we have assigned color names to almost everything we come in contact with in our lives. That these objects appear to be the same colors under all conditions of lighting is called *color constancy*, which means that those objects consistently appear to reflect or transmit light waves only in a particular, narrow color range while absorbing all others. Water does not have color constancy because it reflects and transmits all light waves and therefore appears to be whatever color is dominant in its surroundings.

Within our visual experience of lightness, darkness, color, and space, color constancy is a curious and remarkable phenomenon of perception. In the *World of Colour*, David Katz writes, "The way in which we see the color of a surface is in large measure independent of the intensity and wavelength of the light it reflects, and at the same time definitely dependent upon the nature and intensity of the illumination in which it appears." The key to explaining this rather abstract statement lies in the distinction that Katz makes between light and illumination. A white card taken outside on a clear day reflects 1,000 units of light; viewed under an overcast sky, the card might only reflect 500 units. If it began to rain, and the card were then viewed indoors, it might reflect only 1 unit. In all cases, the card would still appear white, confirming what Katz has stated, that "The color of a surface is in large measure independent of the intensity . . . of the light it reflects." However, if the same card were isolated from its environment and viewed through a narrow hole in a dark screen, its color constancy of white might be lost or confused. In order for the eye to hold constancy of color, it must be able to see the whole environment. According to Katz, the phenomenon is "definitely dependent upon the nature and intensity of the illumination in which it (the color) appears." Therefore, the eye is able to make color judgments in terms of the general illumination in which it is seen and does not respond in terms of light energy alone, as a photoelectric cell does, a process involving both visual and mental interpretation.

Faber Birren also envisions the significance of this sense of illumination—which at the same time involves a sense of space—in two ways by noting, "First, an understanding of it will help to explain many natural phenomena and sharpen the artist's powers of observation. Second, it may be turned to new expressions in architecture and design. Nature's own processes may be repeated under controlled conditions and applied in many original and creative ways."

The following simple experiment is derived from the work of Ewald Hering (fig. 5-13). Place a white card (1) on a window sill. Stand inside a room and face the light holding a second white card (2), which has a hole in it and look through the hole at the first card. If cards 1 and 2 are held on the same horizontal planes, both whites will have a similar brightness. If the second card is tipped toward the light, it will reflect more daylight and become brighter, and at the same time the first card will appear deeper and grayer in color. On the other hand, if the second card is tipped back to reflect less light, the first will appear to increase in brightness.

One notices that card 2 maintains a white appearance even though it reflects different intensities of light as it is tilted toward and away from the window. Card 1, however, which remains parallel to the windowsill and always reflects the same volume of light, changes in brightness from light to dark. Card 2, which is tipped at various angles, tends to look the same, while card 1, which is stationary, will appear in different shades.

Color constancy relates to the observable fact that the colors of the world hold a normal and uniform appearance under

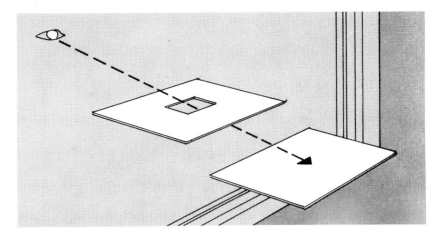

5-13. Ewald Hering's experiment.

conspicuous changes in the intensity of light. If the sensations of color (and brightness) were dependent on reactions to visual stimuli alone, a white surface would appear gray and flowers in a garden would darken when a cloud moved in front of the sun. This suggests that what occurs in the world of light is independent of what transpires in human perception.

COLOR IN OBJECTS

There are two fundamental ways in which objects and media modify the colors of light: transmission and reflection. As discussed in chapter 4, objects and media are usually selective in how much energy and at which wavelengths they will transmit or reflect light. Just how much the color and intensity of transmitted light is modified depends on the molecular composition of the materials through which the light passes. For example, in some colored lamps coatings of colored pigments and dyes are used to selectively absorb unwanted wavelengths or colors and transmit the desired wavelengths. In other cases the glass or medium itself is colored to achieve the same effect. When light is played evenly on a diffuse (mat) surface, light waves are reflected in all directions, but only after they have been modified by the absorption qualities of the surface. The resulting effect is a surface that appears to have a color all to its own, different from the color of the light source. This is because the surface has absorbed varying amounts of different wavelengths of spectral energy. A coat of paint on an object is a basic example of a surface that has relatively even spectral absorption properties and therefore will evenly reflect the colors that are not absorbed by the paint.

It is important to restate that since all light waves are modified in some way by all physical objects, the color appearance of an object is determined by the mix and energy of light waves, which remain intact to reach our eyes. Objects have a characteristic color only because of the manner by which they selectively reflect or transmit or otherwise modify various wavelengths of light.

As shown in the reflectance chart in figure 5–14, butter appears yellow because it absorbs blue light and reflects a high percentage of all other colors. The resultant combination, or dominant wavelength, is yellow. Similarly, lettuce reflects light with wavelengths primarily in the 500 to 600 nanometer (green) range and absorbs most of the energy at other wavelengths. (A nanometer is the millionth part of a millimeter.) A tomato, then, is red only because it reflects radiant energy at 610 to 780 nanometers while absorbing most of the energy at other wavelengths. Equally important to the apparent color of objects is the character of light waves being radiated onto the objects by the light source.

COLOR IN LIGHT SOURCES

Colored light sources emit energy in selective wavelength bands, and "white" light sources generally emit energy in all visible wavelengths. But some light sources actually are deficient in energy at various wavelengths and still emit what is considered "white" light (fig. 5–15). This deficiency affects the perception of object colors (color rendition) and color differences, making some colors appear gray and others more vivid.

"Warm" sources, such as most incandescent and some fluorescent lamps, produce white light that tends to be strong in the red, orange, or yellow wavelengths. Conversely, "cool" sources, such as clear mercury lamps, some metal halide, and some fluorescent sources, produce white light that is strong in blue and green. Lighting a surface alternately with warm and cool

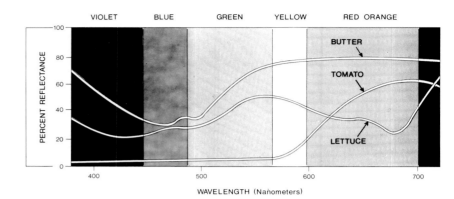

5–14. The color appearance of an object is determined by the mix and energy of the light waves that remain intact to reach our eyes. Objects have a characteristic color only because of the way they selectively reflect or transmit or otherwise modify various wavelengths of light. (Courtesy of the General Electric Company)

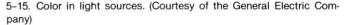

5–15. Color in light sources. (Courtesy of the General Electric Company)

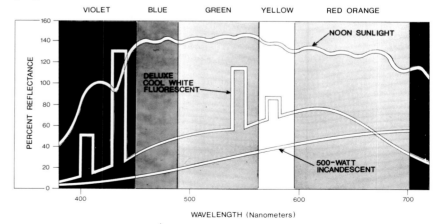

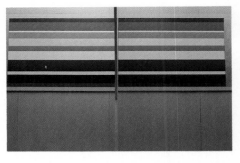

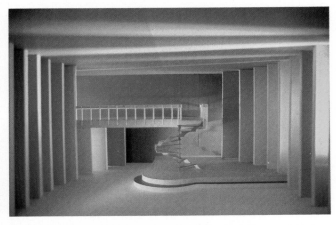

Chapter 5

Plate 21. <u>Upper left:</u> The effects of an incandescent light (left) and cool fluorescent light (right) on similar spectrum bands of pigment colors. Incandescent light neutralizes cool hues and heightens warm hues, while cool fluorescent light neutralizes warm hues and heightens cool hues. (Courtesy of General Electric Lighting Institute, photograph by Stan Tracy)

Plate 22. <u>Center left:</u> The effects of a warm fluorescent light (left) and a cool fluorescent light (right) on similar spectrum bands of pigment colors. (Courtesy of General Electric Lighting Institute, photograph by Stan Tracy)

Plates 23A–B. <u>Lower left and upper right:</u> Several kinds of light sources are incorporated into full-scale living spaces at the General Electric Lighting Institute in Cleveland to demonstrate the effects of various light sources on residential furnishing colors and textures. In plate 23A the vertical blinds behind the sofa are illuminated with a cool fluorescent light and the brick wall with incandescent lights. In plate 23B a warm fluorescent light is used to blend effectively with the existing incandescent sources over the fireplace. (Courtesy of General Electric Lighting Institute, photograph by Stan Tracy)

Plate 24. <u>Center right:</u> Yellow-pink illumination. (Courtesy of Robert Preusser)

Plate 25. <u>Lower right:</u> Yellow-orange illumination. (Courtesy of Robert Preusser)

Plate 26. <u>Upper near right</u>: Red-blue illumination. (Courtesy of Robert Preusser)

Plate 27. <u>Center near right</u>: Shirley Avenue Plaza Project. The special spotlighting is activated by push buttons on the poles that initiate automatically timed fading of selected spotlights and highlights the supergraphics in a dynamic fashion. The Schnadelbach Braun Partnership, Landscape Architects; J. Ritchie Smith, Jr., Landscape Architect, Project Designer; Constance Dee, Landscape Architect, Construction Supervisor; Dick Dunlop, Lighting Designer, Chesapeake Lighting Associates, Inc. (Reprinted by permission from *Landscape Architecture,* Louisville, Kentucky, May/June 1983)

Chapter 6

Plate 28. <u>Lower near right</u>: View from above color chamber where linear elements are grouped together at the widest portion of the chamber.

Plate 29. <u>Upper far right</u>: Gray paper isolates the first layer from the remaining elements behind it to demonstrate the plan for color and value gradation on the first layer.

Plate 30. <u>Center far right</u>: Gray paper is moved behind the second layer of elements to demonstrate the coordination of color planning across two layers of linear elements.

Plate 31. <u>Lower far right</u>: Gray paper is removed to demonstrate the full plan of a color run defining a volumetric form.

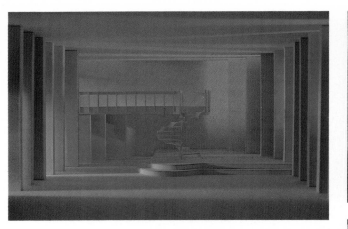

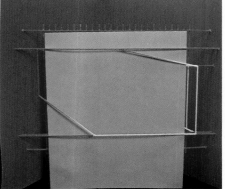

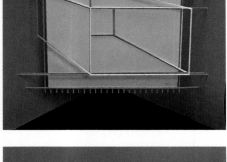

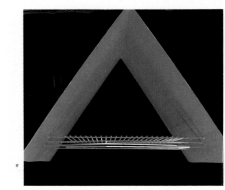

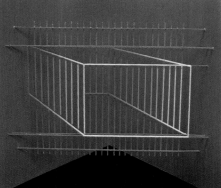

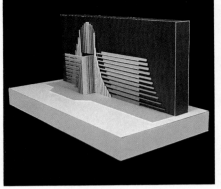

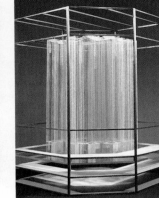

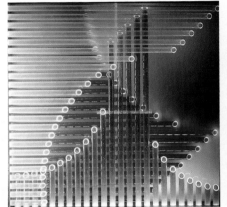

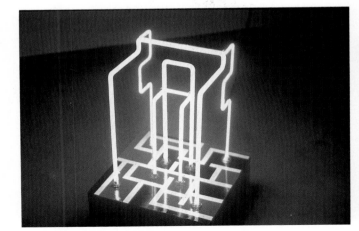

Plate 32. <u>Upper left:</u> Entryway made from mat board, balsa wood, and designer's gouache.

Plate 33. <u>Center left:</u> Linear design created in transparent acrylic tubing and illuminated with fluorescent light from each side.

Plate 34. <u>Lower left:</u> Linear design in neon light.

Plate 35. <u>Upper right:</u> Project model for *International Square* by Gerhardt Knodel. (Courtesy of the artist)

Plate 36. <u>Center right:</u> Detail of project model for *Grand Exchange,* Cincinnati Bell Atrium, by Gerhardt Knodel. (Courtesy of the artist)

Plate 37. <u>Lower right:</u> View of *Grand Exchange* installed in the Cincinnati Bell Atrium by Gerhardt Knodel. (Courtesy of the artist)

Plate 38. <u>Upper near right:</u> *Neon* (8′ × 30′) by Stephen Antonakos. (Courtesy of the artist, photograph by Roy M. Elkind)

Plate 39. <u>Center near right:</u> *Four Walls for Atlanta* by Stephen Antonakos. (Courtesy of the artist)

Plate 40. <u>Lower near right:</u> Proposed exterior neon design for Tacoma Dome by Stephen Antonakos. (Courtesy of the artist)

Plate 41. <u>Upper far right:</u> *Night Drawing* installed on the front facade of the Memphis Academy of Art by Quentin Moseley. (Courtesy of the artist)

Plate 42. <u>Center far right:</u> Detail of *Night Drawing* by Quentin Moseley. (Courtesy of the artist)

Plate 43. <u>Lower far right:</u> *Venezuela Square* by Carlos Cruz-Diez. (Courtesy of the artist)

lamps, then, will produce an apparent change in the perceived color of that surface, despite the fact that, in both cases, so-called white sources are used. This effect is most pronounced if the changes are rapid and the observer does not have time to adapt to the difference in whiteness.

Some light sources, of course, are deliberately made with only one color predominant to achieve a specifically desired effect. For example, if a wall that appears white under a white light receives a light source that is predominantly red, the wall will appear red because only red wavelengths of visible energy are present to be reflected from the wall to the observer's eye. And as seen in figure 5–14, lighting the red surface of a tomato with a "white" light source will make the surface appear red because only red wavelengths of light are reflected toward the observer's eye and all other wavelengths are absorbed.

Before further discussing color in sources of illumination, it is appropriate to consider day and night vision and color deficiencies in vision. Many theories offer explanations of the phenomenon of color vision. The most easily understood is Young's Three-Component Theory, which assumes three kinds of light-sensitive elements (cones), each receptive to one of the primary colors of light—red, blue, and green (fig. 5–16). The cones in each eye number about seven million. They are located primarily in the control portion of the retina called the fovea and are highly sensitive to color. People can resolve fine details with these cones largely because each one is connected to its own nerve end. Muscles controlling the eye always rotate the eyeball until the image of the object of our interest falls on the fovea. Cone vision is known as photopic or daytime vision. Other light receptors, called rods, are also present in the eye, but they are not involved in color vision. Rods give a general overall picture of the field of view, and are receptive only to the quantity of light waves entering the eye. Several rods are connected to a single nerve end: thus they cannot resolve fine detail. Rods are sensitive to low levels of illumination and enable the eye to see at night or under extremely low lighting conditions. Therefore, objects that appear brightly colored in daylight when seen by the color-sensitive cones appear only as colorless forms by moonlight because only rods are stimulated. This is known as scotopic or night vision.

As the spectral sensitivity curves show in figure 5–17, the

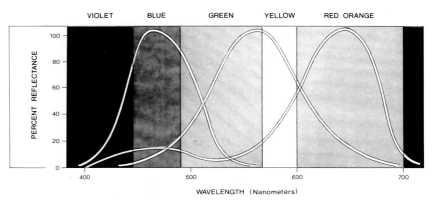

5–16. The human eye is sensitive to each of the primary colors of light—red, green, and blue. When combined, these colors of light form white light as postulated in Young's theory. (Courtesy of the General Electric Company)

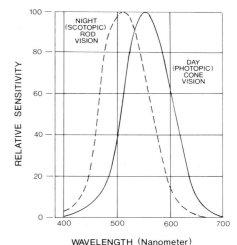

5–17. The Purkinje effect. (Courtesy of the General Electric Company)

eye is not equally sensitive to all wavelengths. In dim light particularly, there is a definite shift in the apparent brightness of different colors. This was discovered by Johannes von Purkinje, who, while walking in the fields at dawn one day, observed that blue flowers appeared brighter than red, while in full daylight the red flowers were brighter than the blue. This is now called the Purkinje effect and is particularly important in photometry, the measurement of light.

The totally color-blind person cannot distinguish between color and quantity because the cones are either partially or totally impaired and only the rods are functioning. This person's eyes are only sensitive to luminance, or quantity of light. As a result, light sources appear "brighter or dimmer," and objects appear "lighter or darker." A completely color-blind person has full appreciation of his surroundings, but in values of gray, much as a person with normal color vision has full appreciation of a color program viewed on a black and white television set.

The most prominent type of color deficiency is known as deuteranopia, or red-green blindness. This person sees yellows and blues normally, but has trouble differentiating reds and greens. Only about five percent of the male population has this deficiency, and only 0.38 percent of the females. An even smaller number of people, approximately .003 percent of the males and .002 percent of the females, are totally color-blind.

WHITE LIGHT SOURCES

The types of white light sources in use today vary greatly. Fluorescent, incandescent, and high-intensity discharge lamps, as well as daylight, are all thought of as sources of white light. But as discussed previously in this chapter, white lights are seldom what they seem, each varying significantly from others in spectral energy content, and all appearing white to the observer because of color constancy.

The goal of lamp designers has been to achieve good commercial sources of white light. The three criteria or requirements for effective commercial white light are efficiency, or the most light per dollar; color rendering, or the ability to make objects appear in their most familiar colors; and whiteness, or absence of color tints. Continual research and development with

light source materials has produced remarkable improvement in today's light sources, but as yet the perfectly balanced lamp has not been achieved. The best lamps are the results of compromises among the three main criteria. The most efficient light sources known are deficient in color rendering capabilities. To improve color rendering, filters and coatings must be added, but they reduce the efficiency. And obtaining a lamp that "appears" white can only be achieved by affecting both efficiency and color rendition. Each type of light source, however, has special advantages that are useful and important in different types of applications.

TYPES OF LIGHTING

The three basic types of lighting used today are incandescent, fluorescent, and high-intensity discharge lamps. Incandescent lamps produce light by electrically heating high-resistance tungsten filaments to intense brightness. Fluorescent lamps produce light by establishing an arc between two electrodes in an atmosphere of very low-pressure mercury vapor in a chamber (a glass tube). This low-pressure discharge produces ultraviolet radiation at wavelengths that excite crystals of phosphor (a white powder) lining the tube wall. The phosphor fluoresces, converting ultraviolet energy into visible energy—light. Types of high-intensity discharge lamps include mercury, metal halide, and high-pressure sodium lamps. An arc of electricity spanning the gap between the electrodes generates heat and pressure much higher than that found in fluorescent lamps, high enough to vaporize the atoms of various metallic elements contained within the arc tube. This vaporization causes the atoms to emit large amounts of electromagnetic energy in the visible range. As will be shown throughout the latter chapters of this book, many artists, architects, and designers have become increasingly interested in the potential of a formal plan that reflects a coordination between the overall use of the elements of color, texture, and form and the careful selection of a particular light source.

COLOR EFFECTS OF WHITE LIGHT SOURCES

Selecting a white light source on the basis of its color appearance or its color-rendering properties alone is rarely done for overall lighting. The term *color rendering* with reference to light sources is a measure of the degree to which the perceived colors of objects illuminated by various light sources will match the perceived colors of the same object when illuminated by standard light sources for specialized viewing conditions. (These conditions include an observer with normal color vision who has adapted to the environment illuminated by each source in turn.) Often, efficacy (lumen output per watt consumed) is a major consideration. Ease of shielding and direction control, as well as maintenance and overall system economics also must be considered. Incandescent lamps generally are considered slightly superior to other lamps in color rendering, not for their ability to render colors more naturally but because through decades of usage they have come to be considered the norm. This point is relevant to both the previous discussion of color constancy and is of foremost importance to designers who wish to create a particular visual appearance or feeling of light, form, and space as opposed to those who only use lighting to solve functional and task-oriented problems.

Good rendition is generally interpreted to mean the familiar appearance of familiar objects. Objects assume familiar colors only by being seen frequently under certain types of light sources (daylight or incandescent light). If fluorescent lamps had come into wide usage before incandescents, it is possible that object colors would appear most familiar under them, instead of under incandescents. Color and color rendition are as much functions of individual preferences as they are functions of light sources. People are familiar with the color effects of daylight, which emphasize cool colors, and equally familiar with the color effects of incandescent lamps, which accentuate warm colors. This obviously incongruous situation is compounded by the effects of memory, atmosphere, environment, and personal color preferences to the point where true colors and true color rendition are subjective at best. The choice of which lamp to use for a particular situation always will vary according to personal preference. The color-rendering properties of different kinds of lamps described in table 4, may be of considerable aid, however, in pointing out to lamp users the relative color effects of white light sources.

Some lamps tend to "flatter" object colors, or emphasize the dominant color of the object while deemphasizing complementary colors. For example, warm white and deluxe warm white fluorescents and all incandescent lamps will bring out warm object tones; the more efficient warm white fluorescents lack the capacity to bring out reds, but they do emphasize other warm tones. Warm colored lamps are usually recommended for homes, social settings, where illumination will be fairly low, and other applications where a warm visual environment is preferred.

On the other hand, when a cooler atmosphere is desired, cool white metal halide, cool white, and deluxe cool white fluorescent lamps are frequently used, resulting in a crisper atmosphere.

Mercury lamps are completely satisfactory in their rendering of blacks, whites, and grays, but the scarcity of red and the concentration of blue, green, and yellow in a few narrow bands make them poor sources for producing the familiar appearances of warm colors. In recent years, improved color in mercury lamps has been achieved by the addition of phosphor coatings.

LAMP SELECTION GUIDE

Table 4 illustrates the general range of color-rendering properties for commercial lamps on the atmosphere, people, and objects. Plates 21 and 22 illustrate the effects of several of these lamps on spectrum bands of pigment (paint) colors; plates 23A and 23B show the effects of lamps under conditions simulating interior residential lighting. These tests were performed at the General Electric Lighting Institute at Nela Park in Cleveland, Ohio, in color-controlled environments to redemonstrate the effects of color light sources on mat surface pigments and the effects of color light sources on the textures of fabrics, brick, and wall paneling.

COLOR MATCHING AND GRADING

Color matching is, as the term implies, a process by which fabrics or other colored materials are matched with other fabrics or with completely different materials. It is usually desirable to match such materials under lighting conditions identical to those under which the products are to be used or displayed.

Color matching is done in various ways. An artist may begin with a pure pigment colorant, adding white, black, or other colors. A printer, on the other hand, may alter the size of the half-

Table 4 Lamp Selection Guide
Fluorescent Lamps

Types of Lamps	Cool* white	Deluxe* cool white	Warm** white	Deluxe** warm white	Daylight	White	Soft white/natural
Efficacy (lumens/watt)	High	Medium	High	Medium	Medium-high	High	Medium
Lamp appearance effect on neutral surfaces	White	White	Yellowish white	Yellowish white	Bluish white	Pale yellowish white	Purplish white
Effect on "atmosphere"	Neutral to moderately cool	Neutral to moderately cool	Warm	Warm	Very cool	Moderately warm	Warm pinkish
Colors grayed	Red	None appreciably	Red, green, blue	Blue	Red, orange	Red, green, blue	Green, blue
Effect on complexions	Pale pink	Most natural	Sallow	Ruddy	Grayed	Pale	Ruddy pink
Remarks	Blends with natural daylight; good color acceptance	Best overall color rendition; simulates natural daylight	Blends with incandescent light; poor color acceptance	Good color rendition; simulates incandescent light	Usually replaceable with cool white	Usually replaceable with cool white or warm white	Tinted source; usually replaceable with deluxe cool white or deluxe warm white

* Greater preference at higher levels.   ** Greater preference at lower levels.

tone dots to change the ink color tone in which the picture is printed or add an additional dot pattern (screen) in a different color to change the final color.

Color grading and shading are processes by which materials are divided into groups of colors or tints and shades. For example, batches of white chinaware may vary slightly in whiteness as a result of the firing process in the kiln. A trained color shader can separate the products into several dozen different shades of white. This is important in the ceramics industry, since complete table settings must be well matched.

Some object colors may appear to be the same colors under a particular light source, while they are actually different in spectral reflectance characteristics. These colors are called metameric. If the light source is changed, however, the object color differences may be readily noticeable. Only color samples that have the same spectral energy distribution curves (S.E.D. Curves) will continue to match under all light sources. Color matching of metameric colors is also dependent on the eyes of the observer, since people differ considerably in the way they see colors. In the past, the ideal light sources for color matching were thought to be the sun and sky, particularly because of their presumed temperature balance. Actually, sunlight varies from about 1800 degrees on the Kelvin scale (K) at sunrise to 5300K at noon. Skylight ranges from 7000K (uniform overcast) to 28000K for an extremely blue clear northwest sky. Because of these variations, skylight and sunlight are not the best color matching sources.

Types of Lamps	Incandescent Lamps	High-Intensity Discharge Lamps			
	Filament**	Clear mercury	Deluxe white* mercury	Multi-vapor*	Lucalox**
Efficacy (lumens/watt)	Low	Medium	Medium	High	High
Lamp appearance effect on neutral surfaces	Yellowish white	Greenish blue-white	Purplish white	Greenish white	Yellowish
Effect on "atmosphere"	Warm	Very cool, greenish	Warm, purplish	Moderately cool, greenish	Warm, yellowish
Colors grayed	Blue	Red, orange	Green	Red	Red, blue
Effect on complexions	Ruddiest	Greenish	Ruddy	Grayed	Yellowish
Remarks	Good color rendering	Very poor color rendering	Color acceptance similar to cool white fluorescent	Color acceptance similar to cool white fluorescent	Color acceptance approaches that of warm white fluorescent

When the specific light under which materials are to be seen is unknown, or when the materials are suspected of being metameric, two light sources should be used—one at a time—to study the samples. One of the two light sources should be predominantly blue in its spectral characteristics, such as a daylight fluorescent lamp; the other should be predominantly red, such as a tungsten filament lamp.

If it is not feasible to use two light sources, one good light source available today is the deluxe cool white fluorescent lamp, as this lamp has a relatively balanced amount of energy in all portions of the spectrum. This means that all colors receive about the same treatment without undue emphasis on one portion of the visible spectrum.

Color matching booths provide the controlled environment necessary for critical observations of many objects. The interior is often a neutral color in a mat surface finish for objects having diffuse surfaces and black for objects having specular or polished surfaces. In all cases, the neutral tones have little or no influence on the color of the object.

For color grading and matching in critical or extremely subtle situations, it is desirable to position the light source so that the reflections of the source are directed away from the observer. With three-dimensional objects, however, elimination of all reflected images of the source may not be possible. Therefore, a luminaire relatively large in area and uniform in brightness is the best choice for this application.

COLORED LIGHT SOURCES

The colors of light are commonly discussed according to the terms, *hue, saturation,* and *brightness.* Hue refers to a particular quality of color such as red or green. In everyday language, the word color is often used to describe hue. In the C.I.E. color system, hue describes the dominant wavelength. Saturation, like Munsell's chroma, and C.I.E. purity, refers to the amount by which the light appears to differ from white—the strength or depth of the color. A deep red light, for example, is said to be of high saturation. Brightness is related to the apparent quantity of light, without regard to hue or saturation.

Most colored light sources, even those that appear highly saturated, are not truly monochromatic—that is, they emit a fairly wide band of wavelengths, often including small amounts of energy in other hue regions. The less saturated the color, the greater the content of other hues. Yellow light is unusual in that a strong sensation of yellow may be produced either by monochromatic light of about a 580 to 600 nanometer wavelength, or by mixture of red and green light covering about two-thirds of the spectrum.

COLORED LAMPS

Colored light can be produced by starting with white light and filtering out or subtracting the undesired portion of the spectrum. A colored or filtered incandescent lamp uses this principle. Colored light can also be produced by a light source that generates only the desired portion of the spectrum, such as fluorescent lamps, in which varying kinds of phosphor produce varying colors of light.

So-called natural-colored incandescent lamps have bulbs of transparent colored glass. The bulbs of most colored sign and decorative lamps, however, begin as clear glass; they then are coated with finely ground colored glass (vitreous glass enamel) and fired to fuse the coating into a hard, colored enamel finish. The coatings contain a white pigment, as well as colored ones, for better diffusion of light. Fluorescent lamps produce colored light by the use of special phosphors. These interior coatings convert the ultraviolet energy generated within the lamp to visible light of the desired wavelengths. In two colors (deep blue and red), col-

ored filtering materials are added to the outside bulb wall to produce more saturated colors than can be produced by the phosphors. The gold fluorescent lamp achieves its color by pigmentation within the glass tube, since no phosphors emit primarily yellow light. A yellow filter coating on the inside of the tube absorbs the unwanted wavelengths from a warm white phosphor.

Blacklight fluorescent lamps utilize a special phosphor that emits primarily near-ultraviolet energy with a small amount of visible blue light. But for many blacklight effects, even a small amount of visible light is undesirable. For these situations, a black light bulb made of a special dark filter glass transmits the near-ultraviolet energy but absorbs all of the visible energy.

EFFICACY OF COLORED LIGHT SOURCES

Luminous efficacy is reduced whenever filtering techniques are used. To obtain any strong color with filament lamps, it is necessary to remove most of the light emitted by the filament. The more saturated the color, the lower the efficacy of the source-plus-filter combinations. Because it is necessary to remove the greatest amount of energy to obtain the correct hue, cool-color lamps, such as blue, have the lowest efficacy of the filament lamps. In the case of fluorescent lamps, the phosphors are usually selected to generate the desired hue—a substantially more efficient process.

STUDIES WITH COLORED LIGHT AND PIGMENT

The work of Robert Preusser and his students at the Massachusetts Institute of Technology, Department of Architecture, reflects a great deal of interest and involvement concerning design investigations with color, light, and space. As part of his course, Environmental Light and Color, architectural experiments are performed with colored light articulated in both interior and exterior space. Preusser, whose long association with Gyorgy Kepes is well known, believes that the built environment would benefit from a wider application of more strongly colored illumination. Writing in *Color for Architecture,* Preusser suggests that "Although colored artificial lighting has been exploited in outdoor advertising, theatrical production, expositions, bars, discotheques, etc., its potential for enhancing an expanded range of man-made environments has yet to be explored."

Preusser's students have explored many transformations in model forms of interior spaces articulated with colored planes. In figure 5-18, experiments with colored illumination (fluorescent) on stripes of color (acrylic paint) in opposite corners provide two distinct alterations. Baffles are used successfully to confine the light of each colored source (green, red) to its intended area of influence.

Plates 24 to 26 show the effects of colored light sources on the plan of a stage set model. The model is constructed from foam core board and colored with sheets of color-aid papers. Theatrical gelatin filters (transparent colored acetate) have been mounted over incandescent floodlights on a "barn door" attachment to enable the direction, quantity, and number of colored light sources reflected into the model to be modified. The model itself is designed with vertical louvers to allow light to enter only from stage left and stage right and not from above or below. In figure 5-19 the plan of colored paper surfaces and forms is apparent under an incandescent (white) floodlight without the use of colored gelatin filters. The examples in plates 24 to 26 of the combined sources of yellow-pink, yellow-orange, and red-blue, respectively, transform each view of the model into a distinct mood and pattern of spatial organization.

In other interior model projects, combined sources of illumination located within the model as a point light source (a fixed light source with a focused beam of light) and outside the model as a source of general illumination are used to further explore the role of color and light as a form-giving and space-defining element of design. Figure 5-20 illustrates the multiple arrangement of light sources with a 1,000-watt photographer's spot lamp above the model for overall illumination. Figure 5-21 illustrates a number of materials and colored surfaces placed into the model to explore the effects of level of illumination, contrast, and color reflectance throughout a variety of locations within the interior model space.

The ability to control the effect of colored light on pigment can be applied successfully to the design of both interior and exterior environments, especially where the needs and requirements of the users are served. The Shirley Avenue Plaza Proj-

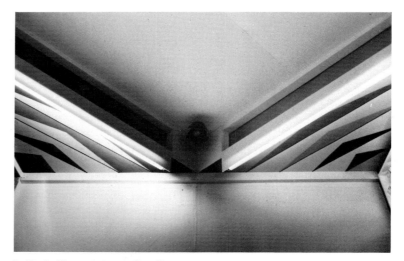

5-18. Baffles act to confine the influence of different colored light sources.

5-19. Stage set model constructed with vertical louvers to allow light to enter from only left and right.

ect is a rather special example of how several professional design offices and civic organizations worked together to coordinate and resolve both the technical and visual issues of the interaction of light and pigment for an outdoor environment.

A successful example of the potential of colored lighting in the outdoor environment, the Shirley Avenue Plaza Project is the collaborative effort of several design consultants in lighting, electrical engineering, landscape design, and civic planning with the City of Baltimore, Maryland Department of Parks and Recreation and the citizen organizations of the Shirley Avenue Block Group and the Park Heights Community Corporation. Shirley Avenue Plaza is dominated by a massive, west-facing brick wall at the end of a row house block (fig. 5–22). Throughout the afternoon, the wall is bathed in sunlight; at sunset, the glow softens to vermilion and orange. It was this daily light show that inspired the park's

5–20. Interior model with lighting equipment for experimentation and study. (Courtesy of Robert Preusser, M.I.T.)

5–21. Testing of various colored materials and their effects under different qualities of light. (Courtesy of Robert Preusser, M.I.T.)

5–22. Shirley Avenue Plaza Project. The Schnadelbach Partnership, Landscape Architects: Ritchie Smith, Landscape Architect, Project Designer; Constance Dee, Landscape Architect, Construction Supervisor. (Reprinted by permission from Landscape Architecture, May/June 1983)

design. Two bands of "light"—diagonal, spectrumlike graph-ics—project down the row-house wall in a matrix of overlapping color (fig. 5-23). This pattern continues in the plaza paving to com-plete a single composition of wall and floor. A series of pole-mounted 100-watt spotlights, each a slightly different shade of red or orange, extends the color and light display until 10:00 P.M. each evening, as determined by the residents of the area (plate 27). Moreover, the light show may be readily controlled by any passerby. A button such as those used for crosswalks on each of the four light standards increases the intensity of lighting for three to ten seconds. When none of the manual spotlights are in use, two other spotlights engage automatically on a random timed circuit. Therefore, whether on manual or automatic opera-tion, the effect is seldom the same twice. The many afternoon and evening activities, both scheduled and spontaneous, that occur at Shirley Avenue Plaza attest to the success of the design. The plaza is usually attended on warm summer evenings by a number of people "at the controls"; the space's stagelike qualities are often put to good use for impromptu concerts and street theater.

5-23. A closer view of the graphic design shows the application of outdoor paint creates a transpar-ent illusion across the wall and ground plane.

6 Principles of Color and Design

The preceding chapters, have concentrated on the basic elements of design, identifying the three qualities of color: hue, value, and chroma. Each is a distinct visual stimulus with an established range of variability. An approach to the problems of combining these qualities for artistic and design purposes should include the achievement of two important goals: Color must first convey an expressive meaning that is appropriate to the specific project for which a color solution is sought; and color and form must be presented to the observer in a manner that achieves visual unity. Quite clearly, both phases of the problem require knowledge and technical insight.

Richard G. Ellinger in *Color Structure and Design* describes the structural order underlying effective color expression based on the laws and principles of design. His writings have been influential on those who work creatively with color and to those who require a sound understanding of the resources, expressive potential, and the means and techniques of ordering color to convey personal expression in the most effective form. His influence and approach to the creative problems of color in design have played an important role within the organization of material for this study of color and light in three-dimensional design. Ellinger writes, ". . . the complex manifestation which we call color must first be clarified to reveal its three separate ranges of variability, each of which will be found to be an elemental factor of form and separately subject to the principles of order."

An understanding of structural and organizational requirements are necessary in order to pursue the techniques involved in the expressive dimensions of a design problem. The goal of visual unity is a constant for all designers in the arts. Each individual strives to control the visual qualities of form so that the end result may be perceived as a unified resolution by the observer.

A FUNDAMENTAL THEORY OF COLOR AND DESIGN

Visual form encompasses the various elements of line, shape, texture, mass, and the qualities that define color. These aspects of form are commonly considered the elements of form, or the elements of design. It is also significant to note that each of the three dimensions of color are representative of the basic aspects of form. Because each design element presents a distinct and separate visual stimulus and has innumerable variations, the designer should exercise a degree of restraint in the interest of order and visual clarity. Because the impact of all the elements is received visually, the emotions are directly involved. The observer's impressions and response to stimuli become the mediator of the designer's accomplishment. The problem of theory is to uncover the circumstances through which the emotional responses are freely receptive and affirmative. The theory of design is founded on the supposition that we require a certain kind of order in the presentation of the visual stimuli.

LACK OF A COMMON TERMINOLOGY

Design concepts have been proposed that encompass the creation of order necessary for visual unity. They are often referred to as principles of order or principles of design, but writers in design fields, unfortunately, are susceptible to inventing their own terminology, so that in spite of widespread agreement in concepts, the names assigned to them vary greatly.

The principle that deals with the presentation of opposing forces is referred to variously as balance, opposition, contrast, or symmetry. The principle regarding movement is discussed as rhythm, sequence, repetition, gradation, or transition. The principle that deals with the resolution of conflict is referred to as dominance, subordination, or harmony. All these principles are a means to unity. (Some books present unity as a principle, which is misleading and confuses the concepts of means and ends.)

There is also much discussion of the design principles in relation to elements of line, shape, plane, volume, and texture without consideration of their application to color, usually treated as a unique element, too involved and complex for design principles to handle. Yet, when color is perceived as the sum of hue, value, and chroma, the relevancy of design principles to color is apparent.

THE NEED FOR A THEORY OF COLOR AND DESIGN

Although it is too early to imagine a universal terminology accepted by all artists and designers, a need for clarity in the organization of design elements, and perhaps a philosophy, is desirable. If the problem is examined from a broad point of view, the existence of visual stimuli provided by the elements as well as the perceptive human dimension that is receptive to stimuli and responds to them with emotion must be acknowledged. Basic human needs underscore the proposed following principles and establish a rational basis for the requirements of organization and theory of design.

Limitation. We are surrounded with a world of visual stimuli and have feelings and responses to both order and disorder. Because disorder along with unrestrained diversity can result in emotional reactions of repulsion, we have a limited tolerance for diversity. Therefore, we must place limitations on the ranges of diversity if we seek order and an affirmative emotional response.

Balance. The second human demand is related to our emotional response to tedium or monotony. We are often in search of variety in our lives and enjoy the play of opposing forces. This human need is included in the principle of design called balance.

Dominance. In the principle of balance, there is a need for the play of opposing forces. The opposition of equal forces can result in tension or dichotomy, and preclude the resolution of a sense of oneness. To include the emotional dimension, we require that an outcome be demonstrated that is favorable to one of the elements or forces. The embodiment of this demand for a resolution of conflict is called dominance.

Continuity. Discussed in depth in chapters 7, 8, and 9, continuity reflects the need for ease of passage throughout a presentation. It is a summing up of the whole, touching on visual elements such as rhythm and an overriding sense of some singular aspect in the principles of organization and order.

The foregoing principles suggest ways in which laymen and designers respond emotionally to sensory stimuli. The finest presentations of the use of color in design visually reflect the attributes of the order embodied in these principles.

If we analyze outstanding color work from previous ages and the work of the modern masters we find evidence of such an ordered presentation. The windows of the thirteenth-century cathedral, Sainte Chapelle in Paris, France, suggest a space transformed by the effects of stained glass windows. Once inside, moving color and light completely dominate the atmosphere; the viewer is completely unaware of the physical structure that supports the glass panels.

Another example is the ceiling frescoes by Giovanni Battista Tiepolo in the eighteenth-century Prince Bishop Residence in Würzburg, Germany. Light extending across the main staircase animates the internal light source of Tiepolo's allegorical ceiling frescoes of the four continents. As the visitor climbs the main staircase, the combination of light, space, and color imparts a feeling of being uplifted, attributable to the vast physical space, the light entering the space, and an internal light source painted in the fresco, giving it an apparent life of its own.

APPLICATION OF DESIGN PRINCIPLES

The principles of limitation, balance, dominance, and continuity owe their validity to a basic emotional need for order in the presentation of visual stimuli. The four design principles indicate characteristics of color essential to visual unity and thus propose a structure for designing with color. The principle of limitation suggests restrictions to the range of variability in one or more dimensions of color. It is an important means of suggesting order through color, while still allowing for visual interest through the selective use of limitation. A color plan with a restricted range of hue might very satisfactorily incorporate wide ranges of value and chroma to maintain interest.

The principle of balance supports the need for opposing color groups within a range of variability and implies the use of opposing groups of hues, values, and chromas in the field of vision. The nature of the opposing color forces must not be made ambiguous by the inclusion of intermediates that cancel the perception and drama of difference. The principle of dominance presumes that a need for the resolution of conflict between opposing forces is identified and that the outcome is favorable to one of the forces, granting it greater total area in the field of view. Dominance is established for hue, value, and chroma by emphasizing a chosen group of each of these color qualities. The amount of the total area necessary to achieve the main or dominant character of a scheme relies on each of the color variables being clearly stated.

THE CONTROL OF COLOR PRINCIPLES

The preceding principles of design suggest ways of imposing order on the three dimensions of color experience. Each of these color principles—limitation, balance, and dominance—has application to each of the dimensions of color—hue, value, and chroma—making possible nine distinct ways of governing the use of color in design.

Limitation of Hue. As the range of hues is restricted by the designer, order is imposed on the color statement. Hue limitation, therefore, may encompass a single hue and neutrals; two adjacent hues on the hue circle (yellow and orange) and neutrals; and complementary hues and neutrals. The principle of limitation, while restricting the range of color in a design, should allow for oppositional groups of hues to be identified.

Balance of Hue. The concept of balance of hue refers to the grouping of colors on one side of the design field in balance with those on the other side. Perhaps the most obvious form of hue balance concerns the opposition of complements on either side of a design field. Neutrals, however, can also serve to balance a single hue or a group of adjacent hues. A group of three or more hues achieves balance when it opposes a similar group of hues across the design field.

Dominance of Hue. Dominance of hue suggests the concept that one hue or group of hues is given the major portion of the total area of the design. An important factor in dominance regards the strength of a color, or its chroma, as a means to achieve dominance over relative hues elsewhere in the design field or in relation to a group of neutrals.

Limitation of Value. The concept of limitation concerns restriction placed on the range of value. Any abbreviation of the range of value establishes limitation and serves the purpose of order. An entire value range from white to black is virtually unlimited. The restriction of the use of part of a value range should not impose the problem of identifying opposing value groups.

Balance of Value. This principle provides for opposing groups in all of the visual elements. The main purpose is to ensure that a range of values away from the dominant value scale of a design is present and in opposition or relief to the value dominance of the design. In the case of value dominance between light and dark values in the design field, both groups of contrasting values share the role of value balance, and their combined areas must remain separate and subordinate when judging areas of value dominance.

Dominance of Value. The concept of value dominance is achieved through the allotment of a major portion of the design to a chosen group of values. The relative amounts of area assigned to the dominant and subordinate groups permit effects of strong or weak contrast. As discussed in chapter 5, the use of strong contrast aids in our visual perception of form, while weak contrast tends to dissolve the apparent dimensions of a solid. This statement can be further modified by adding that stark contrast in the case of the extremes, black against white, also flattens the appearance of dimensional form unless a third and intermediate value is present to model the existing relationship. When several closely related values establish the value dominance, it is often desirable to reduce the amounts of some values to emphasize one member of the group.

Limitation of Chroma. As discussed in the section on the Munsell system (see page 64), the range of chroma extends from neutral at the center to the highest chroma at the periphery of the circle. Therefore, the range of chroma extends along any radius of the hue circle. The use of any portion of the chroma range establishes limits. In many applications, however, limitation is often placed on the outer end of the chroma range where each hue is at its maximum intensity.

Balance of Chroma. The concept of balance of chroma requires the presence of opposing groups of chromas. The portions of a design that provide relief to the dominant chroma can be considered areas of chroma balance. Subordinate chromas, like subordinate values, which may lie on either or both sides of a dominant value group, may lie on either or both sides of a subordinate chroma group. Groups of chromas in opposition share the subordinate role, and their combined areas are subordinate to the dominance.

Dominance of Chroma. Chroma dominance requires a major portion of the design to be allotted to a chosen chroma group. Dominance of chroma is established upon a single degree of chroma or upon a group of closely related degrees of chroma. With the exception of color schemes that severely limit the range of hues, many designers have consistently avoided the use of high-chroma dominance because of difficulties with the perception of form that frequently make such an attempt difficult.

BASIC STUDIES

This section explores the organizational problems of the simplest of color schemes—the simplest because it involves a value range from white to black and one color (a monochromatic color range). The forms used will be limited to linear elements that in grouping imply plane, mass, and volume. The designer's problem, therefore, becomes one of using a basic palette of color along with organizing form.

Several factors must be considered in organizing a color scheme. Given only a range of values as provided by the neutrals, white, black and grays, the possibilities for various organizations are nevertheless tremendous. It is possible to work within the confines of a value range including the extremes of white and black. Value dominance may be established on any degree of the value scale or on any group of closely neighboring values. The field of selection is wide and how these choices are placed into a design must also be considered.

Oppositional features in a design often serve as a means of relief or change from dominance and must be placed where there is the greatest need for them. This suggests that they should be included at the heart of the design as opposed to the edges, sides, or corners. It is often advisable to experience the dominant areas as having a central purpose in the design, with subordinate areas being less important. This is not to say that subordinate areas should not appear at the outer limits of a design, but when this occurs, there should normally be a recurrence of a subordinate at the heart of the design.

A sense of consistency in the contrast of character can be achieved if the opposition recurs in several places throughout the design field. In designs that are organized along an axis in a symmetrical manner, it may be possible to locate a single subordinate area somewhere along the central axis.

CONSTRUCTING LINEAR GEOMETRIC FORMS

Chapter 3 explored the construction of solid geometric forms constructed of flat planes of even thickness. This section investigates the construction of open geometric forms defined at their vertices and edges by linear elements. Geometric forms can be reduced to a framework of linear elements. In constructing the frame, edges are thereby transformed into linear elements that indicate the borders of the faces and form the vertices where they join. Balsa wood sticks with square cross sections have been used in the illustrations of linear relationships for this section. These shapes are, in fact, elongated prisms that have faces, edges, and ends.

In using wooden sticks for construction, refer to the discussion of wood joints and adhesives included in chapter 2, Construction Methods. To build a flat frame, the selection of a simple joining technique and an appropriate adhesive for wood (preferably waterproof when dry) are necessary. Also consider the following possibilities for the arrangement of linear elements.

The two ends of the linear element can be shaped in any way desired (fig. 6–1A). They can all be the same length or have

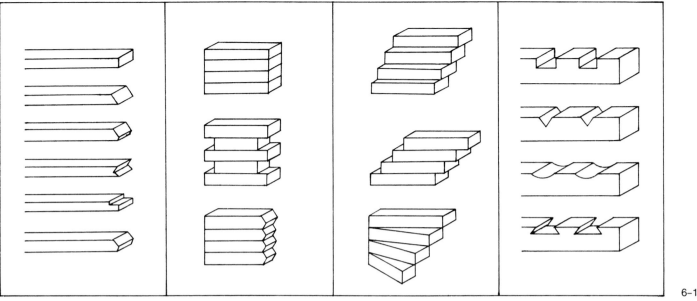

6-1. Variations of layering.

varying lengths (fig. 6-1B). One element can be positioned directly above the next or in gradations of position and direction (fig. 6-1C). The body of a linear element can be specially carved or formed (fig. 6-1D).

There are several possibilities for the gradation of shape if more than one element is used in each level. Two elements can be of the same or different length (fig. 6-2A). They can be joined at one end to form an angle or V-shape, and crossed to form an X-shape (fig. 6-2B). They can also be glued or connected end-to-end or side-to-side (fig. 6-2C). The sequence in figure 6-2D is an example of one method of construction.

PROJECT 1: LINEAR CONSTRUCTIONS IN RELIEF

The three-dimensional project shown in figures 6-3 and 6-4 deals with the use of a single hue and value range from white to black. The mixture of a single hue with neutrals, a monochromatic scheme, is used as a color "run" applied to a sequence of linear elements, which contrasts with the single hue of the supporting background chamber (fig. 6-3A). Stipulated is that the color "run" should follow a geometric pattern of shape and should gradually alter in value toward a higher or lower key as it is applied to each of the linear elements within the chamber (fig. 6-3B). The chamber itself is derived from a polygonal prism with top, bottom, and one face removed for viewing the interior. It is made of one sheet of colored mat board and may be further supported by the addition of foam board from behind so that it is rigid and able to stand upright or on its side on a tabletop (fig. 6-3C).

Think of the chamber as representing a geometric volume of space in one hue and the plan of linear elements as the vertices, edges, and faces of a three-dimensional form defined and distinguished from the background chamber by the application of varying levels of contrast in color and value (fig. 6-4A). Consider

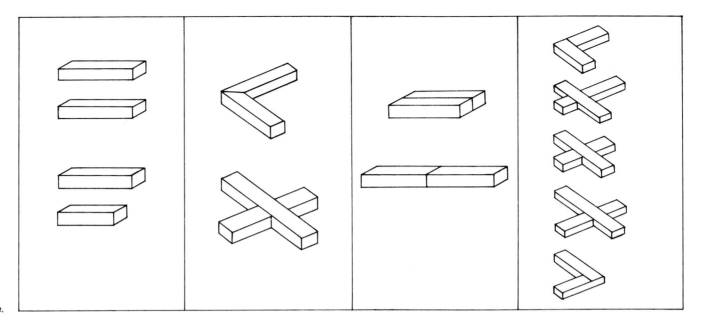

6-2. Gradation of shape.

how a variety of linear elements can be oriented in a few overlapping levels to imply the vertices and edges of a plane or volume (fig. 6-4B). Recall that the path of a plane in motion away from its inherent direction becomes a volume. Along with color, or light and dark value, a point, line, plane, and volume can be subtly or abruptly distinguished from its environment (fig. 6-4C).

A color run can be applied to the organization of several lines of linear elements to appear as an illusion of volumetric form suspended within the chamber's interior space (plate 28). A run across consecutive linear elements also serves to create the following visual effects and illusions.

1. It may distinguish geometric shape and volume from the hue of the background (plate 29).
2. It may imply an artificial light source within the chamber and on a point, line, plane, or volume that is either completely distinct from the hue of the background or is subtly graded in value to blend into the hue of the background (plate 30).

3. It may imply a transparent illusion of overlapping geometric planes or intersecting volumes (plate 31).

The effect of both the shape of the chamber and the spatial organization of colored linear elements can be observed through a fixed point of view. The focal length or viewing distance from the observer to the various levels of the linear elements should be great enough so that the viewer does not perceive a spatial shift in orientation, which disrupts the linear composition. The location of two or more fixed points of view at the open face of the chamber and the use of a variety of color runs on consecutive levels of the linear frames can imply multiple illusions. Diffuse or general lighting from a ceiling fixture will produce limited contrast of shade and shadow within the interior walls of the chamber. A light source from above directed at one of the walls, however, will brighten and thereby create heightened contrast behind the design of linear elements. Conditions of lighting, however incidental, can influence the plan of color and illusion within the chamber.

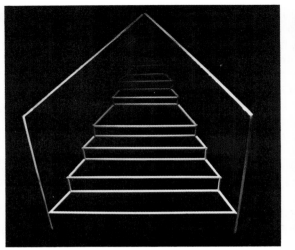

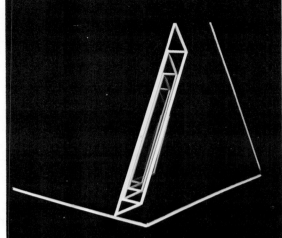

6-3A. Linear elements within a chamber are grouped into a "ladder" sequence and ordered into a value scale.

6-3B. View of chamber from above.

6-3C. Chamber rests on one face to allow for the view of linear elements through the hollow interior spaces created.

PROJECT 2: LAYERS AND TRANSFORMATIONS

The preceding project concerned an arrangement of linear elements in overlapping planes and the perception of their color-form from a fixed point of view (or a set of fixed points of view). This exercise in linear elements introduces the concept of an evolution of mass through the creation of a sequence of progressive transformations. In this project the patterns of the occurrence, variation, and the elevation of linear form, culminating in an evolution of mass, are important. The palette should be limited initially to the neutrals, after which this and the preceding study can be followed with a color application that combines an understanding of both the design concepts and color principles experienced.

This project begins with preliminary black-and-white line drawings of progressive spacing and asymmetric arrangement within a basic shape. One sketch is chosen for a model on the

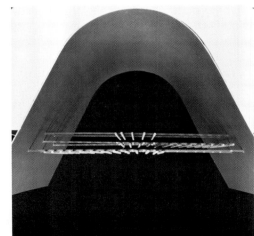

6-4A. Chamber viewed from above shows linear elements grouped in consecutive layers.

basis of interest in rhythmic interval, implied shape, and the potential for imaginative spatial relationships when layers of linear elements are added. Working objectives include the exploration of a number of principles of organization, such as spatial closure, implied plane, and the spatial grouping of elements. The construction of successive layers and the transformation of the original pattern drawing imply that two points of view must be considered during the design process. First, a sequential plan is required for the progressive alteration of the pattern viewed from directly above. Second, the use of an innovative plan for the concepts of layering and the principles of organization is necessary to the achievement of an evolution of mass with imaginative spatial relationships.

A selection of one of fifteen scales of elevation from table 5 will indicate how many elements can be layered in each of the stages of transformation. Within one or more areas of the composition of each stage, layered elements must reach but not surpass the number of layers indicated in the table.

Every stage can generate a new direction in the development of composition and thereby offer multiple suggestions of exploration for the stage to come. Liberal experimentation with the possibilities of layering and organization provides one with an important exercise in seeing and therefore planning the evolution of an experience of multiple visual relationships (figs. 6–5 to 6–8).

Table 5. Suggested Layered Elevation Ratios

Layer	1	2	3	4	5		1	2	3	4	5
A	1	2	4	6	8	I	1	3	8	14	20
B	1	2	5	8	12	J	1	3	9	15	22
C	1	2	5	9	14	K	1	4	8	14	20
D	1	2	6	10	16	L	1	4	10	18	24
E	1	2	6	10	18	M	1	4	12	18	28
F	1	3	5	7	9	N	1	5	10	15	20
G	1	3	6	9	12	O	1	6	16	28	42
H	1	3	7	12	18						

6–4B. Chamber viewed from the front: A sheet of gray paper is inserted between layers to isolate a part of the color run and to demonstrate the process of planning for each consecutive level.

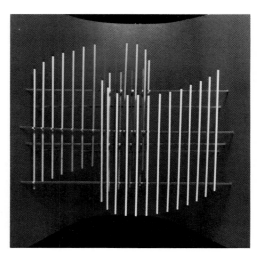

6–4C. The alignment of linear elements in the field of view defines a volumetric form according to the organization of the elements and the contrast in their hue and value to the color of the interior walls of the chamber.

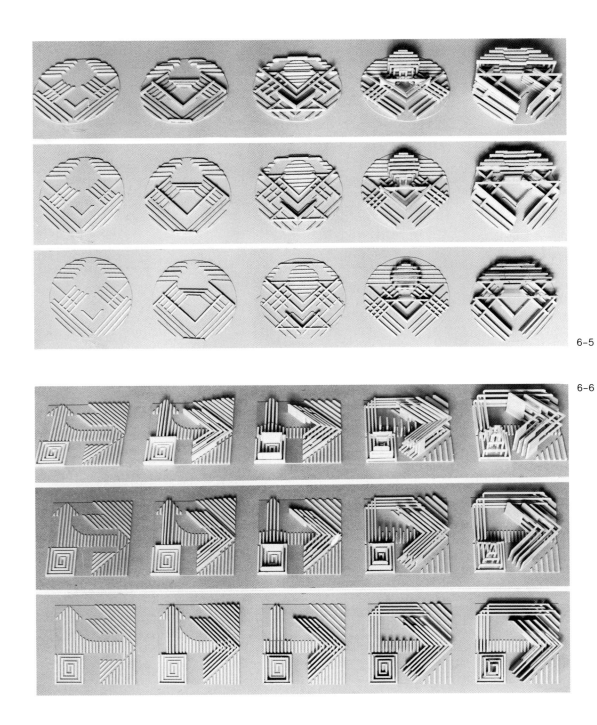

6-5

6-6

6-5 to 6-8. In each project, notice how the flat shapes are continually transformed with each stage and evolve into unique conditions of mass.

116

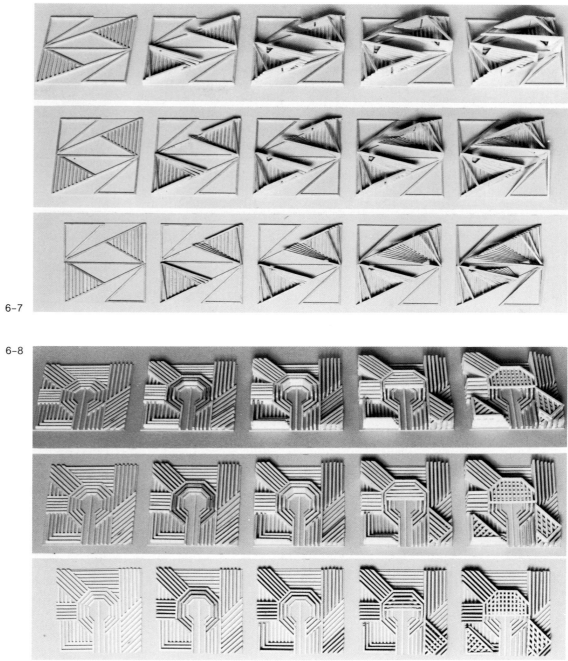

6–7

6–8

117

PROJECT 3: ENTRYWAY

A third project adopts the theme of entry or place of passage from one space to another. This can have several connotations that suggest entry to a public or commercial space, a separation between private and public space, or a simple pathway to a room, hallway, or staircase. The purpose and kind of entryway have been left to the interpretation and the imagination of the designer; the organization of color and form is of primary relevance to this project. The visual significance of an entryway draws attention through its appearance and organization of design elements, and therefore serves as a point of reference and place of departure for the application of design principles.

Figure 6–9 illustrates the use of concepts of layering discovered in the previous project, as well as the color principles learned from the first of the linear projects, Linear Constructions in Relief. Each layer is a simple frame with sticks, transformed by variations in the layering of a linear element; for example, sticks with ends that have been shaped; sticks with similar and varying length; and sticks positioned above others in gradation of size and spacing, producing an implied shape. Figure 6–10 is a rendering of the student project in figure 6–9: it transforms the concept into an actual entryway to a civic center and adds a sense of scale and proportion and the specific context of an urban environment.

Aspects of the construction and form are also significant to the plan of color shown in plate 32. The choice of palette for the linear elements has widened to include several hues mixed with white as tints and in sequences as monochromatic color runs. Unlike the color runs in the first project, which were graded in value to blend into the walls of a background chamber, the color runs in this example contrast with a dark background, drawing sharp and dramatic attention to the relief structure and internal relationships of color and form. Red and green monochromatic color runs have been juxtaposed on overlapping layers of sticks, which yields a third mixture and the appearance of an implied color form. The implied wall plane formed by the joining of light blue elements closest to one's view attracts and holds the attention through the contrast of a cool hue to the apparent warm hues of yellow and orange behind, and the additional contrast in directions of the horizontal elements in the front to the vertical

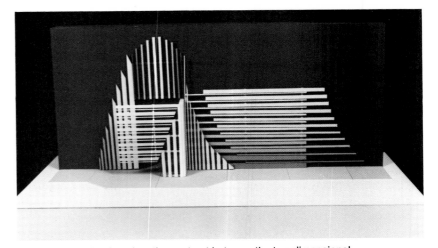

6–9. Emphasis is placed on the contrast between the two-dimensional graphic relationships of linear form and a solid background.

6–10. Perspective view illustrates the graphic qualities of the entryway form proposed as a large facade for the Gene Baker Theater. (Rendering by Richard Rochon)

elements behind. Unity in this design is found in thematic contrasts, but also in the thick-to-thin layers of sequential elements and spacing found in the implied light blue wall plane and repeated to the left in the red and green color runs. Finally, notice that the use of contrasts in color and form are located at the viewer's eye level and color runs in white to black in the vertical layers above the entryway are graded in value to blend into the color of the supporting background wall.

An example of an entryway composition with a different emphasis in the organization of design elements and principles is illustrated in figure 6–11. This model has been constructed with an unobstructed passageway, contrasting with the use of layered elements in Project 2. It has also been planned in the "round" as a freestanding partition with views to the opposite side through the use of spaces between individual and groups of linear elements. The dual purpose of an entryway as a place of physical and visual passage is clear in the organization of elements. The linear elements appear in vertical and horizontal directions, creating rhythmic sequences of plane and mass when viewed from the side and rhythmic intervals of line, space, and implied mass when viewed from the front.

The concepts of both a freestanding partition, viewed in context with the man-made environment, and the principles discovered in Project 1 result in this project in the selection of warm tertiary hues and whites in monochromatic color runs. The principles of design in this example incorporate principles of organization explored in Layers and Transformations, while the principles of color and form found in the previous entryway model incorporate principles of organization explored in the first linear project, Linear Constructions in Relief. The models in figures 6–9 to 6–11 demonstrate the use of elements discovered in both of the previous projects; however, each draws a different correlation between the purpose for an entryway and the organization of design elements and color principles to communicate a decorative and functional form.

LINEAR ELEMENTS AND LIGHT

This study with layered frames concerns the application of linear elements made from transparent (acrylic) hollow tubes

6–11. Emphasis is placed on mass as a freestanding form with intervals of open spaces.

and illuminated by fluorescent fixtures. Figure 6–12 illustrates a series of clear acrylic tubes treated on the inside with transparent color dyes (acrylic monomer-based dyes) made especially for color tinting sheets, rods, and related acrylic products. The tubes are arranged in layers of overlapping hues, with their visible ends cut at a 45-degree angle and their opposite ends concealed within an enclosed chamber at the perimeter of the design. The chamber acts as a baffle containing all the light except for a portion that passes through holes drilled for the acrylic tubes and enters the visible field of the design. Within the enclosed chambers, the ends of the tubes are close to the fluorescent fixtures; however, an open space or gap is provided to avoid direct contact of the tube ends and the light source. (An incandescent light source produces more heat than a fluorescent light and would eventually cause burning or melting of the acrylic.)

In plate 33, fluorescent fixtures illuminate the colored tubing and produce a transparent mixture through the levels of overlapping tubes. The visible ends of the tubes directly in front of the design have not been tinted and appear as circular shapes il-

6-12. Design in colored acrylic tubes without illumination.

gas and phosphorous coating on the interior wall of the glass tube. The selection of either neon or argon gas and a colored phosphor are largely responsible for the type of color produced; however, without an electric current, all phosphor coatings within glass appear white. This particular project involves two widely used gases in lighting—neon and argon—and interior coatings of white phosphor in both sections of tubing.

There are several colors of phosphor used in combination with a few gases to produce the color range of neon light. The two most prevalent are neon and argon. In combination with a white phosphor, neon (red-colored gas) produces a pink light; in combination with a blue phosphor, a deep pink light; in combination with a violet phosphor, a pale violet light; in combination with a green phosphor, an orange light; and in combination with a turquoise phosphor, a peach light. Argon (a pale blue-violet colored gas), in combination with a white phosphor, produces a white light; in combination with a blue phosphor, a blue light; in combination with a green phosphor, a green light; in combination with a turquoise phosphor, a blue-green light; and in combination with a violet phosphor, a pale blue-violet light. Yellows are generally produced within transparent yellow-tinted glass tubes with argon, although a slight coating of white phosphor is often added to help light diffusion.

The outside diameter of glass tubing in this form of lighting varies somewhat, with .511 to .590 inches being a common size. In addition, the brightness of a color can be increased when smaller-diameter tubes are used. The amperage of a transformer necessary to ignite the gas inside also contributes to the level of brightness achievable. Recently, European tinted glass tubes have become increasingly available in this country and are used by artists and designers whose work is housed indoors. These tinted transparent tubes produce rich and vivid colors and extend the range of possibilities for highly saturated hues in lighting design.

luminated only by a white fluorescent light source. The back plane of this design has no direct illumination other than that reflected from the length and ends of the acrylic tubes. In the following chapters a variety of ways of lighting clear, tinted, and opaque acrylic materials and additional methods of treating their surfaces for controlled visual effects will be examined.

An additional study with light and transparent tubing is illustrated in plate 34. Each of the hues—pink and white—are created inside separate sections of glass tubing formed through the process of neon sign fabrication. The color of the light itself is created by the interaction of an electric current with a specific

PROFESSIONAL PROJECTS

This section of the chapter concerns the use of linear elements primarily from an approach to the models and completed projects of professional artists and designers. The intention is to extend previous discussion of the principles of color and organization to encompass a broad range of possibilities of line, form, and space.

FIBER AS A LINEAR FORM

The work of Gerhardt Knodel, professor of art and chairman of the Fiber Department at the Cranbrook Academy of Art, has not only been influenced by his surroundings but also by his study of the history of fabric. In his utilization of light, color, surface, space, and so forth, he creates an art that conveys the richness of his travels and collections, studies of past traditions, and an appreciation of theatrical illusion. The sequence of models entitled *International Square* (figs. 6–13 to 6–15 and plate 35) is conceived for a 12-story office building occupying a full city block in Washington, D.C. At the center of the complex is a huge atrium, the hub of activity in the building. The building is on a pedestrian path leading from the subway station located at one corner of the block. The audience for the "piece" is composed mostly of people on the move—people going from the subway home, to work, to shop, and to the many offices that look out onto the open space from each of the 12 floors. Knodel's objective includes the creation of an environmental sculpture for people who are not seeking art and to take them for a moment to a place where they did not intend to be. In a catalogue of his work Knodel states, "Up, down, in or through. Lead them to consider what's up there, or if they're up there, lead them to consider what's down." There are some familiar elements of line, color, gradation, and overlapping plane. In this concept, however, the effect is of an increased scale, created by metal rods, linear fiber panels, and implied volumes that span the vertical composition. Familiar elements or keys make it clear that the space is for human use. Ladders—to the rooftop, in swimming pools, or to nowhere—are an example of such visual metaphor. These ladder shapes, in keeping with the overall linear family of form, extend a visual invitation to look through, into, and out of a suspended linear chamber of color, form, and space. They also suggest interiors and exteriors and allow the viewer to feel inside and outside simultaneously. The entire sculpture first appears to be surrounded by cords. But as one descends the stairs to the lowest level of the building and looks up, an inner channel of unoccupied space appears to lead to the sky.

In each of Knodel's works a relationship is constantly sought between an imaginary world and a real one, and among size, material, color, and light and those elements present in the surrounding environment. These ideas are especially evident in his project, *Grand Exchange,* for the Cincinnati Bell Atrium. In this corporate structure, a four-story atrium provides a contrast to the more intimate office spaces and is usually accessible from the corridors surrounding it on several levels. The main floor of the atrium is the employees' restaurant (figs. 6–16, 6–17).

The project's objective was to create a visual parallel to the communications activity at Cincinnati Bell, which is the heart of a grand relay system. The project title *Grand Exchange* refers to the reciprocal movement occurring between the dominant impulses of form and space in the architecture of the atrium and in Gerhardt Knodel's sculpture. On every level, the view extends on the open space of the atrium, where suspended fabric planes suggest stairs, steps, planes of landscape, clouds, or geometric constructions occurring in space beyond the practical limits of reality (fig. 6–18 and plates 36 and 37).

Viewed from the main floor, the suspended construction creates a cloudlike atmosphere, except for a few places where the fabric dips down into a canopy, an implied shelter. This atmosphere is enhanced by the use of the fabric to provide shade from the intense sunlight that occasionally penetrates the four-story window at one end of the room. A parallel between the objectives in the design of *Grand Exchange* and the work of Eero Saarinen can be found in lessons recalled by Eero of design experience with his father, Eliel Saarinen, "Every object, small or large, has a relationship to its neighbors. Perhaps the most important thing I learned from my father was that in any design problem one should seek the solution in terms of the next largest thing. If the problem is an ashtray, then the way it relates to a table will influence its design."

LIGHT AS A LINEAR FORM

The application of linear elements of light to full-scale interior and exterior environments also requires a sensitivity to the relationships of color, form, and space to the work of art and its

6-13

6-14

6-13. The model for *International Square* by Gerhardt Knodel is set inside a steel frame that suggests the overall shape of the building and supports the interior model forms. The horizontal floor planes toward the bottom of the model are all made from Formica. The suspended sculpture combines pressure-sensitive color tapes (for vertical line elements) with square acrylic sheet columns to suggest a hanging fabric. (Courtesy of the artist)

6-14. In this detail of figure 6-13 the "ladders" at the top and bottom, as well as the curved panels, were made from colored papers.

6-15. Additional details for figure 6-13 were made from handwoven fabric and applied directly to the acrylic sheet panels.

6-15

placement in an environment. Stephen Antonakos of New York City is an example of one artist whose work involves the exploration of these relationships with neon light. The use of neon in his vocabulary of design includes a melding of aspects of painting, sculpture, and architecture. Antonakos's interests and sensitivities for materials and their properties took root in his early experiments with collage, assemblage, and constructed forms of art.

Early on, Antonakos used neon tubing in severe forms—circles, squares, and parallel lines—making "ribbons" of colored light. The linearity and great flexibility of the tubes, combined with neon's intensity, give the medium its appeal and have little to do with the common use of the material in signs or with its commercial connotations. His abilities to use the medium of light for creations of precise, controlled, and refined forms have led him through an in-depth exploration of its qualities and to many exhibitions and public commissions.

One of Antonakos's consistent themes involves the use of neon forms on colored walls. A beautiful example combines incomplete squares and circles along with straight and wavy lines, all in light blue on a strong red ground (plate 38). Some of the forms project beyond the wall's edges, while a part of one form

6-16. The model for *Grand Exchange* at Cincinnati Bell Atrium by Gerhardt Knodel utilizes steel, Formica, Plexiglas, pressure-sensitive color tapes, handwoven wool, and Mylar. (Courtesy of the artist)

rests exactly along part of one edge. The bold dynamism, the command of the vocabulary, and the impression of complete rhythmic balance are all dominant qualities within many of his projects.

The installation piece *Four Walls for Atlanta* (plate 39) also illustrates the dynamic use of neon light. Neon tubing is suspended at different heights against a series of four individual solid-colored walls and follow one's descent on the main escalator to the below-ground transportation mall and departure gates at the Hartsfield Atlanta International Airport. In this piece the ar-

tist carries the concept of time and movement along a straight path with a sequence of linear elements, which in turn illuminate the interior wall and ceiling planes of the escalator well and orchestrate the descent with four linear color patterns composed of open geometric shapes.

A domed stadium project planned for Tacoma, Washington (fig. 6-19) illustrates one of many potential applications to exterior environments that Antonakos has found for this medium. The stadium, 530 feet in diameter and 150 feet in height, is painted on top with a blue ground color for the application of a red

6-17. Detail of model for *Grand Exchange*.

6-18. Detail of completed installation of *Grand Exchange*.

6-19. Proposed neon light design for a domed stadium in Tacoma, Washington by Stephen Antonakos. (Courtesy of the artist)

neon design by the artist. Plate 40 shows the project model from the opposite side as well as the painted and raised red elements that suggest the plan for an enormous open scheme of light and space.

Quentin Moseley, professor of art at the Maryland Institute, College of Art, also works in linear elements of colored neon light. Many of his "light drawings" incorporate timing devices called chasers and flashers, which create a structured sequence of linear elements in lively and unpredictable patterns that are constantly in motion.

Mt. Royal Neon, shown in figures 6–20 and 6–21, illustrates a light installation of linear and geometric shapes on the grounds of the Maryland Institute, in which timing devices help to structure a sequence of isolated gestures within an overall pattern of linear composition. A lecturer on the subject of luminous art, Moseley finds a great breadth in the applications of neon

6–20. *Mt. Royal Neon* by Quentin Moseley utilizes a program for timing devices that alter and re-create new patterns of shape. (Courtesy of the artist)

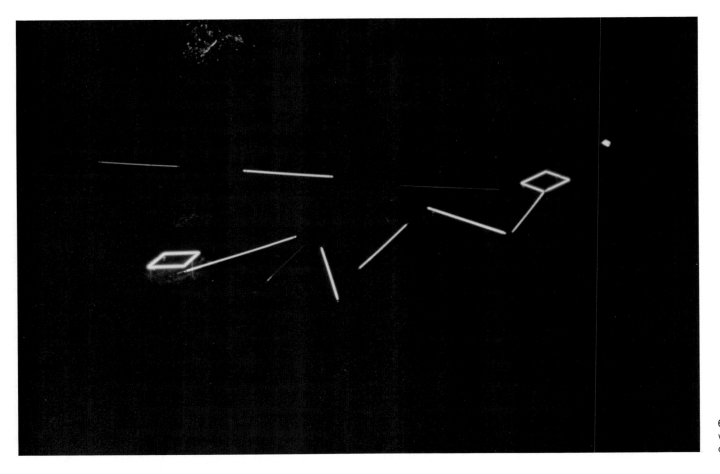

6-21. Detail of *Mt. Royal Neon* with an alteration in the sequence of lights.

forms currently being explored and notes that, "Some artists draw with neon as intuitively as they might draw with paint and brush, while others carve and fill space with light as if it had the physical presence of reflecting steel."

    All light artists and designers, however, must deal successfully with a number of technical considerations that more traditional artists are not confronted with. Glassmaking (or bend-

ing) is one of them; incorporating gas and electricity into a work is another. Size, scale, color, and subject matter are all important considerations. In plates 41 and 42, a very large and exciting commission by Moseley, *Night Drawing,* was installed in December 1982 on the building housing the Memphis Academy of Art. The design uses 20 transformers, more than 200 six-foot tubes and 8 timing devices to animate a pattern of geometric shapes that cover the front of the academy's main three-story building. The installation was designed with horizontal, vertical, and diagonal elements in harmony with the overall form of the architecture. Glass neon tubes are mounted directly on the front edge of the roof line to follow its triangular pattern along the facade. The glass windows and the cement grille of the building reflect the glow of light, which in turn creates a lively and animated expression of the building's architectural forms.

LINEAR ELEMENTS AND WALL PLANES

The Venezuelan artist Carlos Cruz-Diez applies the concept of linear elements directly to wall planes. In the man-made environment, perhaps no other artist has explored a completely visual experience of color and human activity as rigorously as Cruz-Diez. His environmental projects have emerged from the world of Op Art—a formal art that exploits certain characteristics

6-22. *Venezuela Square* by Carlos Cruz-Diez. (Courtesy of the artist)

of visual perception. Much of his effort has centered on plastic research and an attempt to isolate the color experience from other phenomena, extending as well as questioning the teachings of Josef Albers (which clearly concerned color interaction on a single plane) to include the multidimensional nature of space.

Cruz-Diez's fundamental interests regarding the observer-stimulus relationship and basic principles of color vision have led to a variety of environmental projects in his native city of Caracas and abroad. Many of these projects include distinctive patterns of vibrant colors in stripes planned for city surfaces, for example, pedestrian crossings, entire streetscapes, interior and exterior applications to buildings and buses, and several walls of color applied to the pilings of existing roadways and to specially designed relief wall structures in city parks and squares. *Venezuela Square* (figs. 6–22 and 6–23), designed by Cruz-Diez for the city of Paris, France, is a circular area, 60.8 feet in diameter, which produces a chromatic effect when the light and the spectator move. Geometric linear patterns of strong contrasting colors are deployed at an increased size to create an impression that rapidly alters with distance as the colors merge and interact (plate 43).

6–23. Detail of *Venezuela Square*.

Much of Cruz-Diez's work demonstrates the visual modification inherent in the process of color perception: the changing appearance of colors with alteration in the intensity and angles of illumination (natural or electric), coupled with a change in angle and distance of viewing; and changes due to purely optical effects in the perception of certain kinds of color patterns. The work of Cruz-Diez engages the spectator in a repeatable experience of color and light through physical movement, behavior, and successive perceptions. Through the use of simple phenomenal principles and a complete awareness of their order, it is possible to foresee and plan consequences of those principles.

7 Columns, Planes, and Wall Structures in Color and Light

A relief wall structure constructed with forms attached to an established plane, or a freestanding wall structure constructed in open space has qualities of physical stability and extension in height, width, and depth. Whether a structure implies a flat, curvilinear, or irregular plane through an arrangement of repeating unit forms or is constructed as one overall volumetric solid, the qualities that define its structure must also include elements of size, color, texture, and light. Beginning with a basic solid such as a cube, the possibilities of organization, the arrangements of unit forms, and variations in the unit form itself can be defined, after which the related visual elements of size, color, texture, and light can be discussed in a broader sense.

UNIT FORMS AND ARRANGEMENTS

The various possibilities for making wall structures begin with the concept of stacking one form above another to form a column (fig. 7–1). Columns can then be repeated to the left and right to form a wall. The emphasis of this structure is two-dimensional, with cubes repeated first in a vertical direction and then in a horizontal direction. Each unit form in a wall structure, however, has some depth, and each of the unit forms can be made into spatial cells.

FORMS AND CELLS

There are many possibilities for constructing unit forms in wall structures (fig. 7–1A). Bend a thin strip of paper, or glue four pieces of cardboard together to form a cube without the front or rear planes. This is a basic spatial cell that allows one to see through it and place additional unit forms inside. Interior forms may be as simple as a flat plane used repetitively or varied in position and orientation.

A unit form can also be a positive or negative shape or be a combination of positive and negative shapes. They can be used in gradation of shape and size by enlarging or reducing them proportionately, by changing the width only, or by changing the height only. If the unit form is a combination of two smaller shapes, the size of one can be kept constant while the size of the others may vary, or both may vary in different ways.

VARIATIONS OF POSITION IN GROUPING

The general ways in which unit forms can vary in position in relation to the established direction of a frontal plane are illustrated in figure 7–1B. The position of a unit form can be changed by moving the shape forward or backward; by moving the shape up or down; and by moving the shape left or right. The height or width may also be reduced to suggest the feeling of a unit form sinking into an adjoining plane.

VARIATIONS IN DIRECTION OF UNIT FORMS

Within each spatial cell unit forms can be related in many possible directions. The four groups of diagrams in figure 7–1C demonstrate the effects of rotating a square shape. In each group, the first column on the left represents the view from the front; the second column, the view from the side; and the third column, the view from above. Note in group 1 that rotation on the shape's own plane does not change the shape in the front view, and that the side and the top views appear as straight lines. In

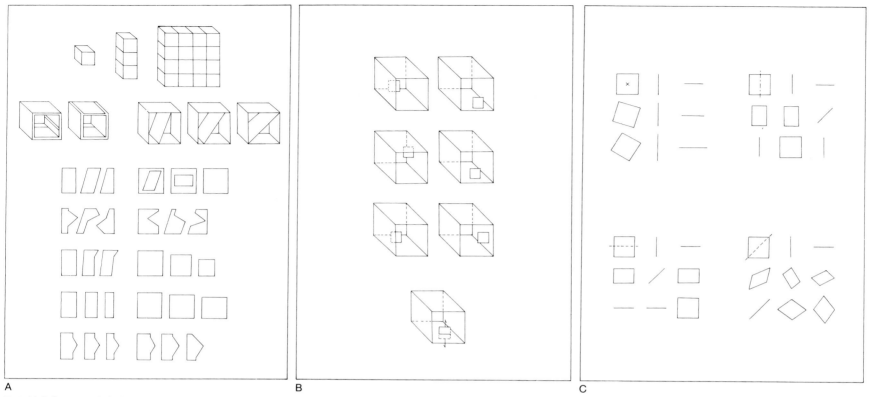

A   B   C

7-1. Unit forms and their arrangements.

groups 2 and 3 rotation along a vertical or horizontal axis narrows the square shape of the front view into a line. In group 4 rotation along a diagonal axis produces more complicated results. The square is transformed into a series of parallelograms in the front view with variations of parallelogram shapes seen from the side and top views.

DISTORTION OF PLANES

There are many ways to produce variation in a flat plane. These include: curling; scoring and bending along one or more straight lines; scoring and bending along one or more curved lines; cutting along with scoring, bending, and/or curving (fig. 7-2A).

A variety of three-dimensional effects are also possible through the modification of spatial cells (fig. 7-2B). When one cell is placed above another, the flat frontal plane can be varied by positional shifts in the depth and direction of the cells. Enclosing planes of the spatial cells can be trimmed to produce front edges that are not perpendicular to the base or side planes. Modifications can be made to produce curvilinear edges constructed so they are not at right angles to one another. Spatial cells can also be constructed as a part of a unit form structure or unit forms can be used to construct a wall structure without the use of spatial cells.

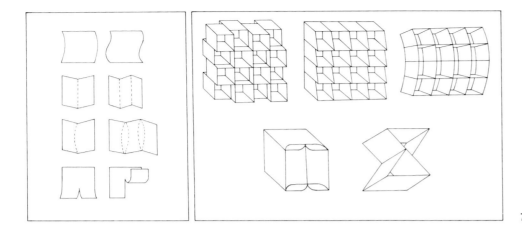

7-2. Variations of position in grouping and direction.

PRISM FORMS AND VARIATIONS

In addition to cubes, many other three-dimensional forms, such as prisms, can be used to create more complex structures by joining multiple forms together. The minimum number of flat planes that can be used for the sides of a prism is three, which results in a solid form with a triangular top and bottom (fig. 7–3A). If the number of sides on a prism is increased, the top and bottom become polygons. The more sides a polygon has, the less angular and more like a circle it becomes. A hexagonal prism is less angular than a triangular prism and approaches a rounder body. Increasing the number of sides of a polygon infinitely results in a circle. In the same sense, increasing the number of sides of a prism infinitely creates a cylinder.

From a basic prism with parallel square ends and rectangular sides that are all perpendicular to the ends, variations can be developed in the plan and construction of new forms (fig. 7–3B). The square ends can be changed to triangular, polygonal, or irregularly shaped ends; they can be nonparallel to one another; they can vary in size, shape, or direction; the ends do not have to be flat planes, nor do the edges have to be perpendicular to the ends; and edges do not have to be parallel to one another and may be curved or bent along with the body of the prism.

7-3. Prism forms and variations.

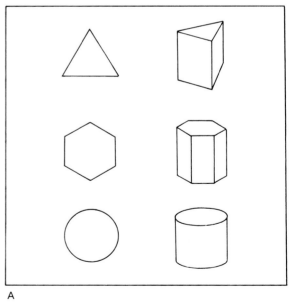

A

If one works with a hollow prism constructed from paper or cardboard, variations can result in even more complex forms (fig. 7–3C). The ends may be partially covered with planes containing negative shapes; the edges or faces near the ends can be cut into many shapes; the ends can be divided into separate sections; and a special shape can be formed on or attached to the ends.

The edges and faces can reflect conditions of nonparallel straight edges, wavy edges, a plan for a circular shape, or intersecting edges (fig. 7–3D). Other treatments might reflect the subtraction or addition of shapes along the edges. It is possible to attach separately made shapes to the edges of cutaway negative shapes and to have lines cut and scored or shapes partially cut along the edges of adjacent faces. These shapes may then be bent inward and/or outward without detaching them to create a play of positive and negative forms. Face treatment follows a similar plan to that of edge treatment. Holes can be made on the faces and additional shapes can be fitted to negative shapes on the faces. Partially cut shapes can remain hinged or folded in and out of the prism.

VARIATIONS WITHIN REPETITIVE STRUCTURES

A three-dimensional structure can be extended forward and backward and not only has a front view but can be seen from all sides. A repetitive structure can be defined as one in which the unit forms or the spatial cells containing them are constructed in regular sequence and pattern so that they relate to one another in the same way (fig. 7–4A).

Repetitive structures may be arranged in layers of spatial cells or unit forms. One example of a basic arrangement is stacking one layer directly above the next. The repeated structures may also shift in position between alternate layers or be arranged in positional gradation of layers. Position and direction of individual cells within a layer are also variables for additional arrangements.

Within each layer, rows can be shifted and gaps created between individual unit forms and/or whole rows (fig. 7–4B). It is also possible to arrange spatial cells or unit forms so that they do not touch one another; adjacent layers are then arranged to help hold the forms of the first layer in position.

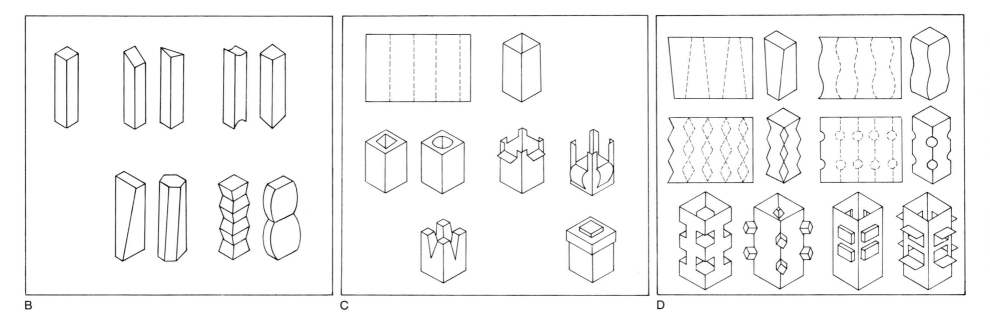

B

C

D

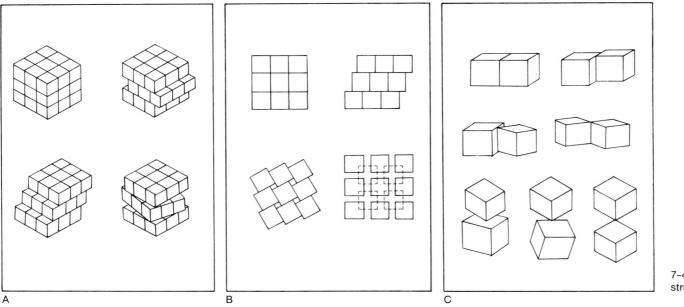

A   B   C

7-4. Variations within repetitive structures.

JOINING UNIT FORMS

A basic method of joining—face-to-face contact—gives the firmest bond, which can be full face contact or partial face contact (fig. 7-4C). Edge-to-face or edge-to-edge contacts will produce weaker joints but may provide desired flexibility between two or more forms. Vertex-to-face, vertex-to-edge, and vertex-to-vertex contacts are the most difficult to control and require a careful plan and precise execution.

JOINING SQUARE PRISMS

Square prisms can be joined in a number of different ways within a design (fig. 7-5A). They can be brought together through faces in contact, edges in contact, and ends in contact. The end of one prism can be joined to the face of another, making a T-shape or L-shape. The ends of two prisms can also be mitered to form an L-shape. They can be designed to interlock or fully cross,

and a number of prisms joined together can form framelike structures or structures with linear continuity.

Unit forms can vary in shape from a cube to many other possible forms. If the unit form or spatial cell is not a cube, the ways in which they can be related and joined increase in complexity. A square prism is used in figure 7-5B to demonstrate the possibilities of how two or more units can be joined. One unit can be stacked directly above another with or without aligning the edges. Two or more prisms can be stacked in many different directions. Three prisms give a wider range of complex combinations, and each combination can also be repeated in a repetitive structure. A basic square prism is actually a form that contains two cubes. Three cubes can be arranged into a right-angle shape to form an L-shape unit form or spatial cell and create challenging possibilities for grouping in repetitive structures (fig. 7-5C). Two or more L-shapes can be combined to form multidirectional structures. These are more complex structures than can be created with a plain cube, a square prism or an L-shape alone. The

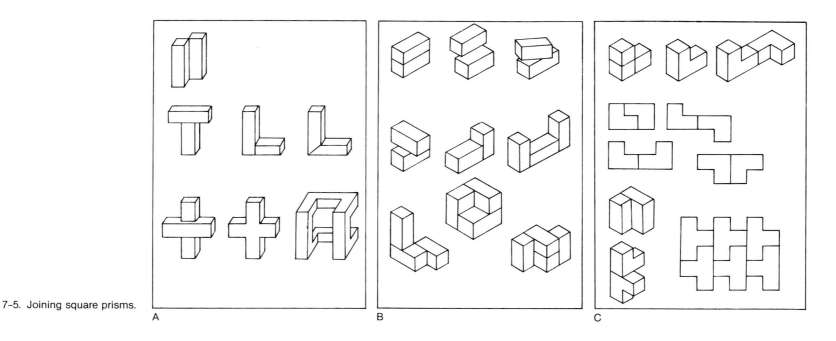

7–5. Joining square prisms.

A   B   C

organization of unit forms in a repetitive structure should include the following general principles: the strength of an overall structure must be taken into account whereby all unit forms are anchored; one view should not dominate or be emphasized over all other views; unit forms should interlock, interpenetrate, and fill space between other unit forms on different layers; and concavity or convexity should be used to complement the joining of two or more forms.

BASIC STUDIES

The first group of wall structures deals with forms attached to background planes as studies in relief. These projects explore the role of color, light, and movement and the organization of both unit form and spatial cell compositions. Aspects of the discussion of linear elements in chapter 6 are also appropriate to the perception and understanding of the forms in this chapter.

WALL STRUCTURES IN RELIEF

Unit forms and spatial cells can be constructed in various dimensions and from many different materials. Their application to a supporting plane requires an awareness of the individual and total weight of the unit forms, their physical strength and that of the background supporting wall plane, and a sturdy method of application. The supporting walls in this series of projects are all constructed with wooden frames (1″ × 2″ furring strip) and covered in an appropriately colored mat board.

The study in figure 7–6 is very basic and serves as a means of demonstrating the application of several white tetrahedrons to a white background wall. The repeating units suggest very little shadow play under general and diffuse lighting conditions. They have been arranged in a sequence of horizontal and parallel rows with one flat face directed toward the floor plane. Diffuse light, largely from above and the sides, provides a minimum amount of shadow contrast on the faces of each tetrahedron and, to a slightly greater degree, on the faces directed toward the floor.

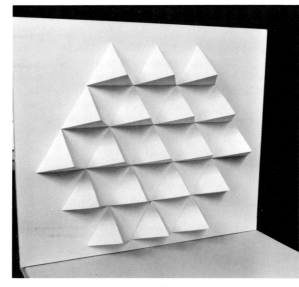

7-6. Bas-relief wall structure with tetrahedron.

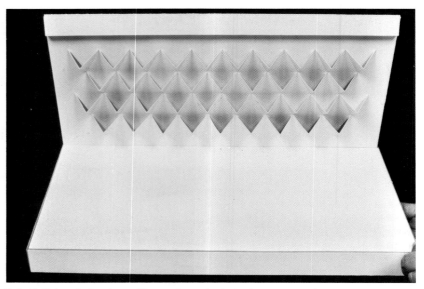

7-7. Relief wall structure with one face of tetrahedrons removed.

If each of the tetrahedrons is inverted to direct one face toward the ceiling and this face and a back face are removed to create a spatial cell within, the possibilities for the play of light and color increase (fig. 7-7). The interior faces of each of the units in this study have been given a distinct hue—yellow, orange, or green (plate 44). Diffuse light reflected from the interior of each unit washes the light background wall with a soft glow of color. When a paper figure is introduced as a concept of scale and the design is viewed from the side, one can better appreciate the effect of reflected color through progressive angles of viewing as they would be seen by a passerby (fig. 7-8). The geometry of the tetrahedron forms are transformed and opened into a structure that is capable of reflecting an atmospheric color effect.

The unit forms in figure 7-9 are also developed from a tetrahedron. In this study, however, they are constructed from silver semireflective mat board (fig. 7-9).

The center portion of each of the unit's four faces is cut and removed to reveal a hollow interior space and a linear

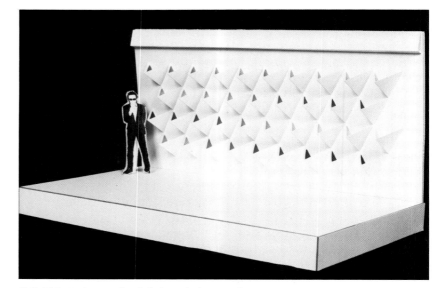

7-8. Tetrahedron wall relief viewed at an angle.

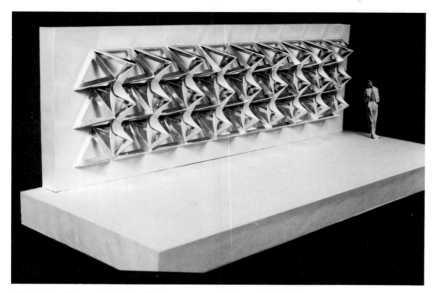

7-9. Reflective wall relief with faces removed from tetrahedron.

tetrahedron frame. The frame is capable of casting a linear shadow pattern on the background wall and creates an additional shadow pattern from a shape placed against or inside each cell. A pattern of concave elliptical shapes in white bristol board, adhered in a crisscross fashion, links the exterior faces of each unit form and offers an element of variation to an otherwise rigid geometric structure. Under diffuse light, the silver mat board surface appears in dark and light reflected tones and in contrast to soft shadows cast behind on the background wall. The white concave shapes along the frontal plane of the wall structure conceal the view of part of each unit and offer a third level of light reflection, shadow, and patterns of shapes across the design.

A relief wall structure recessed within a chamber offers many potential patterns for reflected color and form. In figures 7-10A and 7-10B the transformation of unit forms from octagonal pyramids to octagonal prisms occurs along the horizontal rows of a repetitive structure and within an octagonal necklace (raised grid) of mirrored acetate, which in turn creates spatial cells for each of the solids. Each octagonal solid is constructed with white

bristol board, covered with tints of red, violet, and blue transparent film, and arranged in the progression of a color run across the horizontal rows of the design. The background wall has been colored with an airbrush to create a smooth gradation from light to dark and to suggest an implied light source behind and around the octagonal solids (plate 45).

Up and down the vertical rows of the design, the height of an octagonal prism gradually increases until it becomes an octagonal pyramid and then decreases at the same rate. Because the reflective acetate grid extends outward from the back wall of the design to varying degrees, any view from extreme right and left will produce overlapping reflections of blue-violet and red in the mirrored cell walls. A view from just right or left of direct center will produce reflections of multiple solids along with the pattern of form.

In figures 7-11A and 7-11B, a group of materials similar to those in the previous study are used to produce illusions of color pattern and depth when viewed only from angles directly in front of the structure. This variation employs pleated spiral forms that are suspended in front of a mirrored column background wall structure. The mirrored columns are constructed as square half columns turned at a 45-degree angle to the background plane and covered with mirrored acetate. Because of the relationship created between the angle of the columns and the pleated forms, reflections are only perceived from angles that approximate a line of sight that is perpendicular to the implied front plane of the structure. (Reflections of the pleated forms do not appear from an angle to the extreme right or left of a perpendicular line of sight to the front plane of the structure.) The pleated paper forms, covered in color tints of transparent films, create a pattern of triangular planes that appear in a light and dark sequence under conditions of diffuse light. A color run from blue-green to red and back to blue-green in light values is evident across the repetitive structure of the design. An angle of view perpendicular to the implied frontal plane of the wall structure results in the appearance of overlapping reflections of red and violet; red, violet, and blue; and violet, blue, and blue-green on the mirrored columns. Because of the additional reflection from one mirrored surface to another, however, a different order to the sequence of pleated forms appears behind the actual sequence to create alternating color patterns across the design (plate 46).

7-10A. Relief wall structure with octagonal prisms and mirrored necklace.

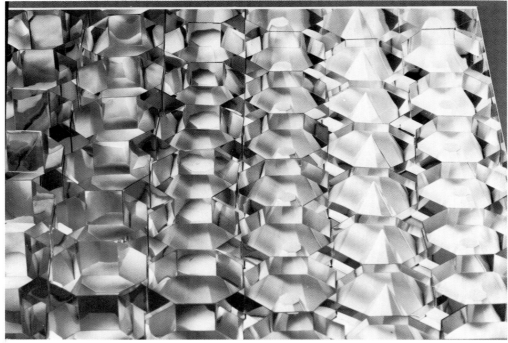

7-10B. Detail shows a series of reflections from the prisms to the mirrored necklace.

140

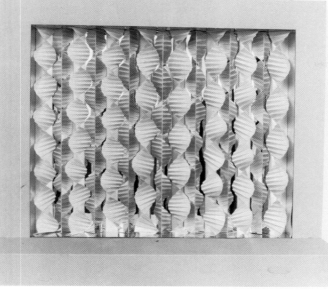

7-11A. Relief wall structures with pleated spiral folds and mirrored columns.

7-11B. The view of the pleated forms at an angle obscures the reflections of form from the mirrored columns.

A   B

FREESTANDING WALL STRUCTURES

The following studies in paper, cardboard, plastic, and acrylic sheet explore the possibilities of grouping unit forms, spatial cells, and columns in repetitive structures to respond to the conditions of diffuse (indirect) or focused (direct) light sources.

A plan for the construction of freestanding wall structures requires consideration of the selection and joining of materials for unit forms and/or spatial cells that can only be supported from below at the floor plane. It is also important to have a plan for the use of the elements of color, form, and light in relation to both the structure itself and to those similar elements found in interior or exterior environments that affect the appearance and potential views of the structure from both sides.

Figure 7-12 illustrates a basic repetitive structure with rhythmic intervals of dark exterior and light interior triangular

faces. It is constructed along a straight path in linked and continuous rows of paper forms stacked one above the next in vertex-to-vertex contact. They are further supported by attachment to clear acrylic tubes in vertical positions in the middle and at the sides.

In figure 7-13 the increasing and decreasing size of rectangular elements viewed at this angle establish and define the overall mass of the structure. From a view directly facing one side of this structure, however, the rhythmic spacing of the elements, along with a reduction in their appearance of mass, is evident. As we experienced in relief wall structures, the possible arrangements of form are capable of visual alteration, depending on one's relation to and view from around the design.

Freestanding wall structures can be designed without space between unit forms for viewing the opposite sides. In many of these forms the ability and resourcefulness of the designer in selecting materials and forms that create interest because of

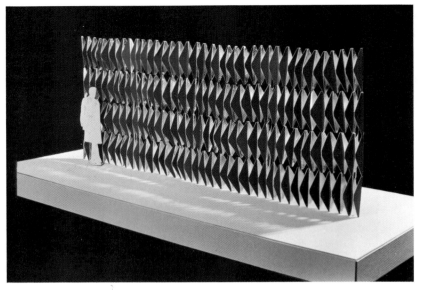

7-12. Wall structure made from light and dark papers.

7-13. Wall structure made from mat board.

their shape, color and texture is an important factor. Figure 7–14 illustrates a freestanding structure that reflects a concept similar to that discussed in recessed wall structure projects on page 139. The use of rhythmic intervals of planar forms (in semireflective mat board), along with color and shadow contrast, creates interest under diffuse lighting. If the path or direction of the unit forms in a wall structure varies from other than a straight line, as illustrated in figure 7–15, the opportunity for viewing changes as the appearance of positive, negative, or a combination of positive and negative form increases. In this type of structure, color from the interior faces of the unit forms can play a dominant or subtle role in attracting the attention of the viewer along with either reflective or mat surface exterior faces.

In figure 7–16, spatial cell and unit form are identical, creating a cubic cell with interior planes that project to a square opening at the implied frontal plane on one side of the cell. The form is covered on the reverse side with semireflective mat board and on the front with colored paper and is used in alternating front and back positions throughout the pattern of a repetitive wall structure. Therefore, both sides of the wall structure appear with the same pattern of diagonal rows of alternating colored and reflective cells (plate 47).

In figure 7–17 unit forms are circular strips cut and folded outward from the side planes of spatial cells. With a direct colored light source from under the base of the design, the interior of the cell walls glow in hues animating the linear pattern of circular shapes.

Transparent materials used in wall structures can create a very subtle and effective play of color and light in the surrounding space. If diffuse light is a constant factor in the plan of form, colored transparent materials may be used to enhance or suggest greater modeling of surfaces. In figure 7–18, clear acrylic sheets have been cut and formed into saddle-shaped units, which overlap in opposite positions with edge-to-face contact. Tints of self-adhesive transparent colored films have been laminated to each unit's surface to imply a gradation of light (or a light source at the base of the design). Diffuse light from above and around the structure passes through the transparent layers of unit forms and helps to blend one level of color and value with the level of color on the surfaces beneath.

In figures 7–19A and 7–19B a triangular piece of clear

7-14

7-14 and 7-15. Columns made from semireflective mat board and colored papers.

7-15

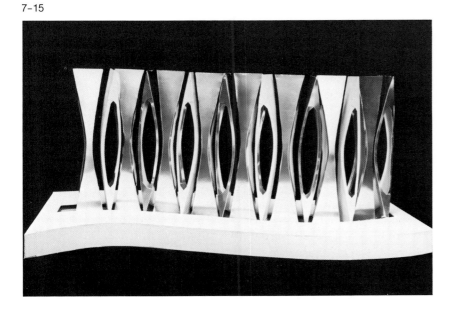

7-16. Unit forms made from semireflective mat board and film overlays.

7-17. Cell structure made from pieces of heavy paper laminated together to form contrast between light interior and dark exterior colors.

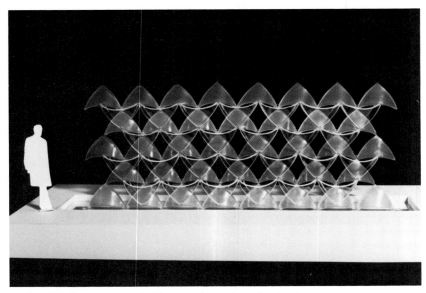

7-19A. Unit forms are created from preformed acrylic sheets.

7-19B. A color run is applied to the center layer of shapes with self-adhesive film overlays.

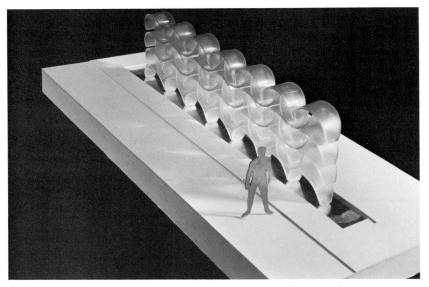

7-18. Elements are cut from acrylic sheets and heated to form curvilinear shapes. An open structure is created from these preformed shapes, and a color run is applied by means of self-adhesive film overlays.

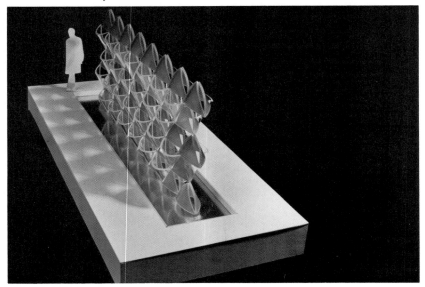

acrylic sheet has been slightly curled to serve as the unit form. The units have been joined in vertex-to-vertex or vertex-to-edge contact to form a necklace of varying degrees of color transparency. Units along the outside layers on both sides of the wall structure are made of clear acrylic sheets, while the layered units in the center have been covered with transparent colored films to produce a gradation from blue along the top row to neutral gray along the middle row to a warm tertiary hue along the bottom row (plate 48). Blending of color is also a factor here, less so, however, than in the previous example, largely because of the greater extremes of hue and value and diffuse lighting. The effect of transparent levels of overlapping rhythmic form is the major source of visual interest from either side and both ends of this structure.

Clear acrylic sheeting can also be modified by sanding its surface (or by using a modified-surface acrylic sheeting) to soften the effects of color, light, and form present in a wall structure. In figures 7-20A and 7-20B compound prism forms are grouped in opposing directions to create a repetitive structure. The top and bottom portions of each prism have been lightly sanded, while the clear (V-shape) portion in the middle of each form has been lined on one interior face with mirrored acetate. The wall structure is designed within a chamber that houses warm white fluorescent lamps, one directly above and one below the structure. Plate 49 illustrates the quality of light diffusion from direct sources within the sanded portion of the hollow prisms. In contrast to this pattern, very little light appears in the clear section, allowing the mirrored surfaces to sharply reflect other form. The glow of light around the wall structure can be modified in color and intensity by the brightness and saturation of the unit forms within the repetitive structure.

An arrangement of unit forms in irregular positions in a

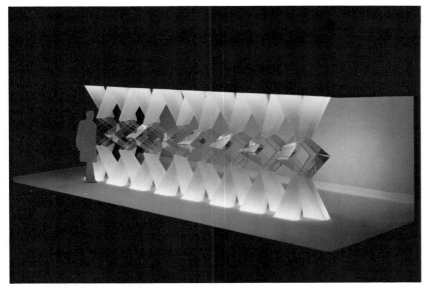

7-20A. The columns shown are compound prism forms made from acrylic sheets. The top and bottom portions of the prisms have been sanded to diffuse the internal light source, while the middle areas remain transparent.

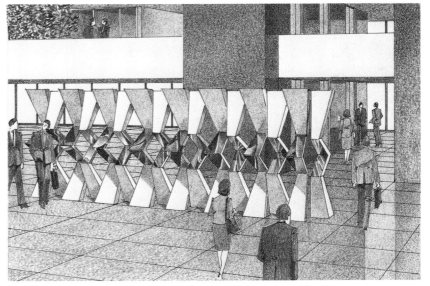

7-20B. Prism wall structure proposed as a sculptural element within a public lobby. (Rendering by Richard Rochon)

wall structure can also produce variation in the play of reflected colored light around the structure. Figures 7-21A and 7-21B illustrate cubes constructed from transparent acrylic sheets in several colors and arranged in random position across the base plane of a model. Direct light from inside the model's base helps to illuminate the colored edges of the transparent cubes, while diffuse light from around the structure creates random patterns of reflected color on the floor plane next to the wall (plate 50).

Figure 7-22 consists of three concentric layers. The innermost layer has the tallest but also the narrowest prism forms, while the outermost layer has the shortest but largest prisms. In plate 51 the intensity of light originating in the base is most strongly seen in the largest prisms, decreasing in brightness and saturation as it illuminates each of the smaller prisms on higher levels. Colored acetate used in the bottom of each prism filters out unwanted portions of the spectrum, producing yellow, orange, and red light within the hollow forms. Notice the red light on the bottom level at the right is a brighter and more saturated hue than the same color at the highest level. Not only do filters affect the saturation of light, but they also act to subtract a portion of a lamp's brightness, especially as the distance from the source to the filter is increased.

PROFESSIONAL PROJECTS

COLUMNS

Franz Zeier is a unique artist whose work reflects the balance of orderly and imaginative forms, surfaces, textures, and their combinations. His publications *Papier* and *Paper Constructions* have been an inspiration for many designs, including the projects described on pages 6 to 9. Zeier's attitude toward his work

7-21A. Wall structure of cubes made from acrylic sheets in transparent colors.

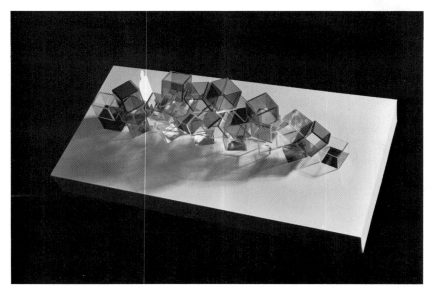

7-21B. Open structure illuminated by a light source within the base and from diffuse light outside the model.

7-22. Hollow prism forms of graduated height, width, and depth arranged in a cylindrical volume.

shows the special creative possibilities of paper. With his students, he consistently encourages experimentation with geometric shapes and the resulting extended structures to accent the special and exciting potential for the transformation of form and to demonstrate that planning and execution are not separate but can be thought of as interwoven activities. Many of his structures, illustrated in figures 7–23 to 7–30, suggest sculptures, buildings, and practical forms that go beyond a state of pure abstraction. These columns and structures can be enjoyed as studies toward utilitarian purposes, for their process of construction, and for their high level of craftsmanship.

COLOR PLANES

The additive, reflective, and subtractive principles of color applied in the relief wall structures of Carlos Cruz-Diez offer a clear understanding of how our perception of wall planes can be altered through a permutation in which the color of a structural element changes. Traditionally, the "reading" of a plan of color has always been made perpendicularly from the spectator to the work. The perceptive impact is direct. The many experiments, color theories, and environmental projects of Cruz-Diez, however, provide insight for the creation of works applied to the built environment that surround and present the viewer with a changing experience (figs. 7–31 and 7–32).

Many of the titles of these experiments describe the interaction and effects of optically mixed color in various structural arrangements. In plates 52 and 53, "chromatokinetic" elements are incorporated in the walls, ceilings, and floors of the Union des Banque Suisses (The Union Bank of Switzerland), in Zurich-Altstetten, Switzerland, in such a manner that people moving in the halls, corridors, and common rooms are captured by an ever-changing play of color and light in a manner both arresting and stimulating. Cruz-Diez defines these as changing structures that project color in space, creating an atmosphere of colored light changing with the intensity and position of the source of illumination and the distance of the viewer. They combine three different conditions of color interactions: additive, reflective, and subtractive color (figure 7–33).

Additive Color: The background is covered by differently colored parallel stripes that merge in the spectator's eye. The color mixture is modified by the distance of the spectator from the wall. This optical fusion creates a new color.

Reflective Color: When light hits the parallel stripes on the background, it rebounds and is projected onto colored perpendicular baffles, carrying with it waves of color that in turn send chromatic waves onto the next baffle. The second process modifies the effect of the first one.

Subtractive Color: When light crosses the transparent colored baffles axially, it modifies the pigment in the multiple

7-24. Transformation from a cube to a tetrahedron in 12 phases by Franz Zeier. (Courtesy of the artist)

7-23. Experiments made from a cube arranged into a wall structure by Franz Zeier. (Courtesy of the artist)

7-26. A high relief wall structure achieved by stacking seven-sided "shell" shapes by Franz Zeier. (Courtesy of the artist)

7-25. A column with cube-to-star transformations by Franz Zeier. (Courtesy of the artist)

7-27. Pattern for a spatial wall structure evolved from one seven-sided "shell" shape by Franz Zeier. (Courtesy of the artist)

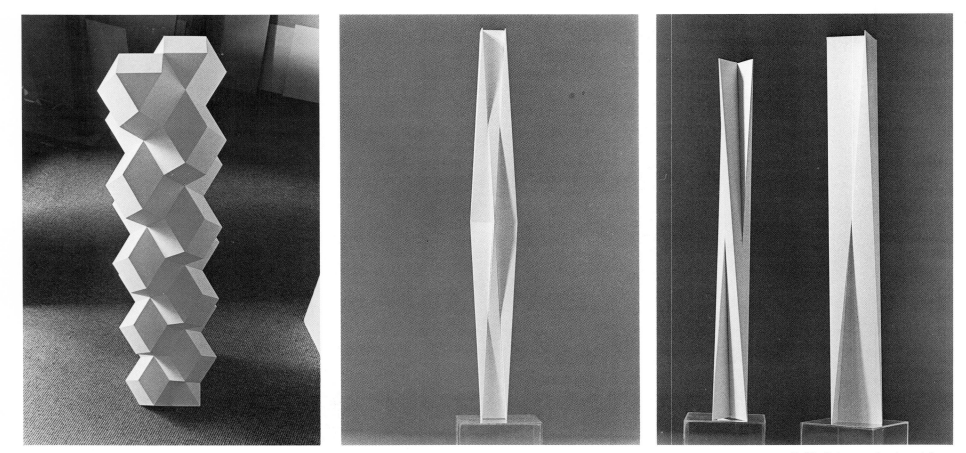

7-28. A connected column built without interruption by Franz Zeier. (Courtesy of the artist)

7-29. Column developed from a tetrahedral pattern by Franz Zeier. (Courtesy of the artist)

7-30. Columns developed from a tetrahedral pattern by Franz Zeier. (Courtesy of the artist)

parallel stripes on the background. If the spectator positions himself diagonally to the work, a different effect is achieved.

Cruz-Diez's progress within kinetics and its developments can only be understood in relation to different environmental situations, which create a series of visual events based on an intense color experience. The effectiveness and "plastic" action of these chromatic events are the main concern of the artist. Cruz-Diez answers the challenge of the visual and the physical, the optical and the real, the sensory and the conceptual. In his work, color is a renewable experience as long as it depends on two

7-31. Installation of "chromatokinetic" element on the ceiling plane of the Union des Banque Suisses by Carlos Cruz-Diez. (Courtesy of the artist)

7-32. Installation of a "chromatokinetic" element on the wall plane at the Union des Banque Suisses. (Courtesy of the artist)

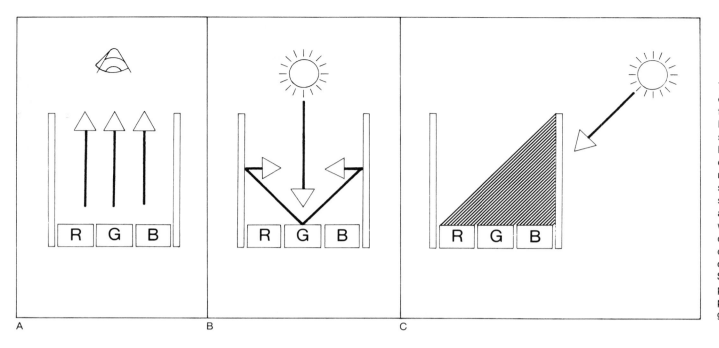

A   B   C

7–33. Color mixed optically: This explanatory diagram is based on the experiments of Carlos Cruz-Diez. *A.* Additive color: an infusion of a multitude of "isolated" hues merge in the eye and fuse to create a new color. Each optical mix will differ when the same stimulus is viewed from different spatial points. *B.* Reflective color: a modification of the color of light waves, which after striking one colored surface, bounce to another to be modified before their chromatic energy is perceived. *C.* Subtractive color: light energy passing through transparent planes of color, such as stained glass, is modified.

aleatory conditions: the movement of the spectator and the use of daylight. In this manner Cruz-Diez avoids saturating the public in a closed environment and creates an open structure (figs. 7–34 and 7–35).

WALLS OF LIGHT

The last professional project to be discussed in this chapter is an installation of fluorescent lighting designed by Dan Flavin in collaboration with Massimo and Lella Vignelli for the Hauserman Showroom at the Pacific Design Center, in Los Angeles.

The Vignellis wanted to project the Hauserman corporate image and the related qualities of Hauserman's major products—demountable partitions and office systems. Their design for the showroom included two important and complementary goals. The first was to focus attention on Hauserman's product line. The second was to emphasize the image of the company as a champion and leader in contemporary design. Sunar in Chicago, a subsidiary of Hauserman, had previously gained recognition for its spectacular showrooms, created by Michael Graves. The Vignellis realized that the key to a successful solution was to use full-scale mock-ups of the various wall systems as a foil for similar luminary constructions designed by Dan Flavin.

Flavin's work is based on increasing our perception of color in space. His work transforms surfaces and dissolves corners through the location of lighting fixtures in a space. The plan model in figure 7–36 illustrates the central portion of the showroom divided into three corridors that have all been oriented at a 45-degree angle. Two of the corridors are barred at midpoint, preventing the viewer from walking through them but allowing views from either end. The central corridor is open from one end to the other. Flavin was commissioned to create three installations to be set into these simple corridors, resulting in exciting il-

7-34. Pedestrian crossings designed by Carlos Cruz-Diez for La Pastora Square in Caracas. (Courtesy of the artist)

7-35. Public lobby design in ceramic tile for Simón Bolívar Airport in Caracas by Carlos Cruz-Diez. The lines narrow optically with distance and perspective and create a vast chromatic scale. (Courtesy of the artist)

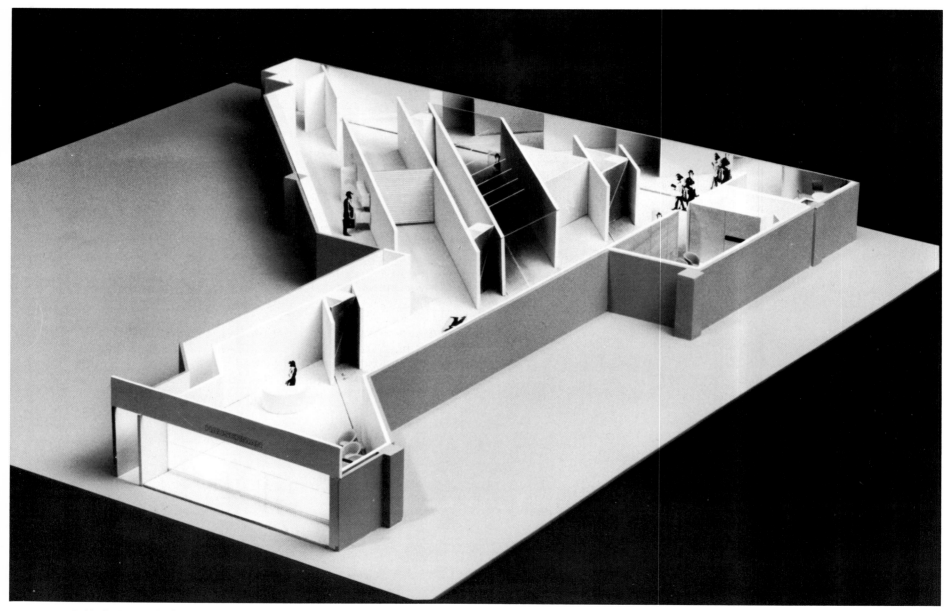

7–36. Project model for the design of the Hauserman Showroom shows the orientation
of corridors and the path of circulation. (Photo courtesy of Sunar Hauserman)

7-37. The visitor entering the showroom is greeted by the project title *The Walls.*

lusions of planes and volumes of light. Each corridor is colored differently. One is yellow and pink fluorescent light, one is green and yellow, and the central corridor is all blue, with fixtures mounted in angled configurations on the wall and ceiling planes. In addition, there are five small alcove spaces that have been illuminated with blue fluorescent lights.

The viewer's perception of the color and space alters and varies greatly in spatial effect, depending on angle of view throughout the network of illuminated corridors. The impression gained from walking around the perimeter corridors is of pastel hues reflected on the corridor walls. Just before one turns the corner to the central corridors, the presence of green light stimulates and increases one's perception of color in these areas. Colors viewed in the corridors after this point are stronger, with more intense hues, and are perceived to envelop the viewer from inside the corridors (plates 54 and 55).

Regardless of the hypnotic effects of moving through pools of ambient light, the prominent features of the walls are also clear. Samples of fabric coverings for the Hauserman wall systems have been slotted, in a spectrum sequence, into the wall next to the reception area. The reception area is a light, neutral color and serves as an introduction to the space with the inscribed reminder, *The Walls* (fig. 7-37). In 1983 this project was recognized by the Illumination Engineering Society, winning both the National Award of Lighting and the prestigious International Award for Lighting Design in the same year. At the close of the exhibit, part of the project was donated to the Museum of Contemporary Art in Los Angeles.

8 Studies of Mass in Color and Light

There are many ways to group volumetric forms. The cross sections and the manner in which a form can be cut at regular intervals to result in a series of planes can be analyzed. Just as each cell within a wall structure can be considered a unit form, each slice in a series of planes or solids can be considered a unit form to be used in a repetitive structure or in gradation of shape, size, color, and texture. As discussed, repetition refers to repeating both shape and size of the unit forms, and gradation refers to the gradual variation of a unit form used in several methods. A unit form can change in gradation of size with repetition of the same shape; it can change in gradation of shape with repetition of the same size; and it can change gradation of both shape and size. All of the above methods can also be affected by gradation in color runs of hue, value, or chroma and in gradation of texture from fine to coarse or in surface treatments from rough to smooth (fig. 8–1A).

VARIATIONS OF POSITION

With a solid such as a cube, prism, or planar form, the positioning depends on the amount of space provided between and around the elements. As with repetitive structures, if no directional variations are introduced, all the cells or unit forms are parallel to one another and each follows the next successively, with an equal amount of space occurring between the forms. For the purpose of initial demonstration, assume that all planes are square and of the same size. If one plane follows another along a straight path, the vertical edges of the planes trace parallel straight lines with the same width as the breadth of the planes. The amount of space between planes can be opened up or reduced to create different effects. If the space is narrowed, a greater feeling of solidity and therefore of volume or implied mass is created while increased space between the forms reduces the impression of mass. One can also change the position of the planes, without altering spacing, by shifting them gradually to

the sides or back and forth, which distorts a volumetric shape or mass. Similarly, each plane can be shifted gradually up and down, as if the forms were supported by wire in open space, or they can be reduced in size on a base plane to imply the effect of their gradual sinking-in by varying their position vertically (fig. 8–1B).

VARIATIONS OF ORIENTATION AND DIRECTION

Solids can also be rotated along each of the three axes—vertical, horizontal, and oblique—to produce variations in orientation. Solids that rotate on a vertical axis are thereby diverted from a parallel to a curvilinear arrangement and create an effect of radiation in one or more directions. The position of such a solid is affected because directional changes simultaneously require positional changes. The horizontal axis provides other variations in orientation that may be included with vertical rotation for a combined effect or viewed as a distinct effect in the plan of mass.

A solid can also rotate on its own plane, which means that the corners and edges gradually move from one position to another without alteration to the established direction of the plane or solid. This can create the effect of a spiral or twisted mass. This variation can also be performed in conjunction with the preceding directional variations of vertical and horizontal rotation and imply a complex and intricate composition of mass (fig. 8–2). The solids chosen may also have the additional dimensional characteristics of curvilinear planes, planes that bend in one or more directions, and gradations of color and texture.

METHODS OF CONSTRUCTION

There are many kinds of materials that can be used in the design and construction of planes, prisms, and solids in mass studies. These include acrylic sheets for transparent effects;

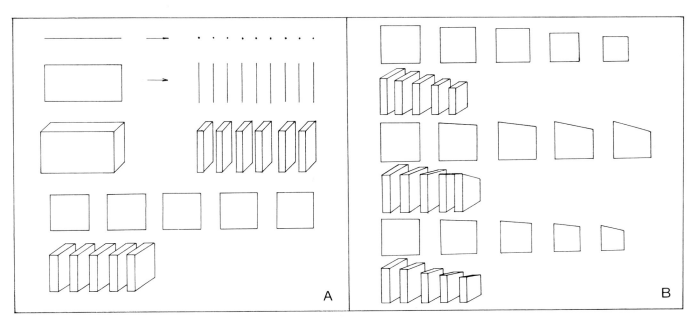

8-1A. Variations in shape and size.

8-1B. Variations of position.

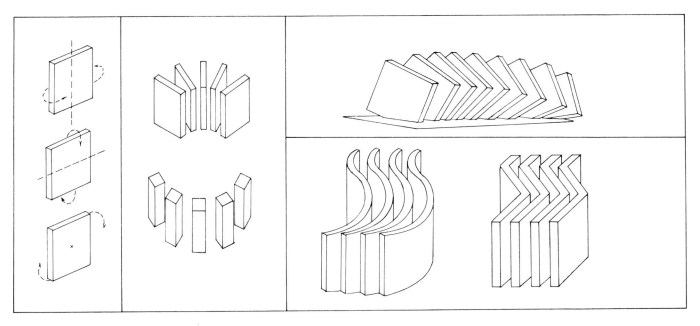

8-2. Variations of orientation and direction.

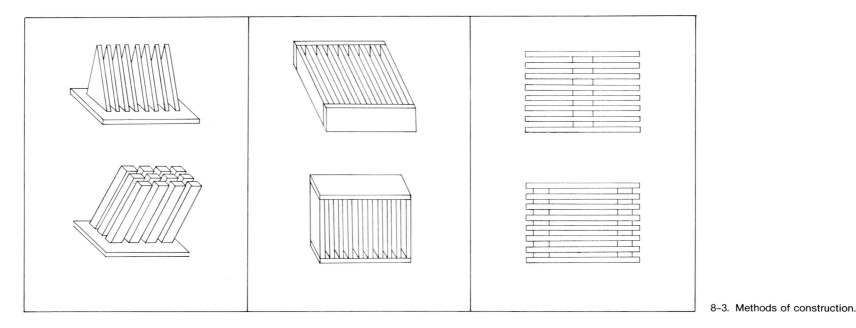

8-3. Methods of construction.

various woods for construction in both large- and small-scale projects; and thick cardboard, which can be treated with paint and paper overlays. The thickness of the material and an appropriate joining technique and adhesive ensure firm attachment to a vertical or horizontal base plane. Solids can also be suspended in the air by wire, thread, string, and acrylic rods instead of relating them to a base. Vertical or tilted elements resting on a base require the precise bevel or fit of joining elements and an adhesive that offers a quick, strong bond. Depending on the arrangement or requirements for an unobstructed view of the visual elements, reinforcements can be used between, at the sides of, or above and below the solid elements. Normally, two or more vertical boards should be used for the support of elements in horizontal arrangements. A freestanding shape can be created with internal supports used between the serial elements (fig. 8-3).

The edges of the elements may not be significant if the planes are very thin, but if they are thick, they may influence a

design. Analogous to the treatment of the ends of linear elements, solids can also be shaped through rounding off, beveling, and/or cutting their edges and faces. A basic example of dissecting a solid is shown in figure 8-4 and provides an idea of the many ways in which a number of planes and solid forms are obtained. Additional treatments through carving, cutting, beveling,

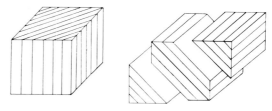

8-4. Dissection of a solid.

and so forth will produce variations to the ends, edges, and faces of each segment of the solid.

BASIC STUDIES

One of the most obvious ways in which a mass can be created is through an arrangement of unit forms in contact with one another. Face-to-face contact provides the densest form of grouping and the strongest impression of mass. As the space between unit forms is opened slightly, the impression of mass is reduced. In this type of arrangement, many opportunities for rhythmic spacing and variations in position, orientation, and direction are possible without diminishing the overall impression of a volumetric form. The organization of unit forms in the first group of studies introduces the arrangement of unit forms with precise location on a symmetrical plan.

The first study, shown in figure 8-5, is made from six acrylic sheets joined with acrylic rods in a horizontal stack and illustrates the principle of gradation of shape. Each of the geometric planes are symmetrical and arranged in a plan for gradation of shape with repetition in size. When viewed from above, the top plane conceals the plan of gradation of shape below. Space provided between the layers suggests the possibility for additional horizontal sheets used in series to further define or vary the existing plan of volumetric form.

Figure 8-6 illustrates a group of solids in wood that have been arranged in edge-to-edge contact. This example demonstrates both gradation of shape and size. A pattern of intersecting circumferential lines form a plan for the symmetrical arrangement of unit forms across the design. Viewed at an angle, however, the height of each of the solids gradually increases and defines the mass in terms of progressive elevation.

In figure 8-7, five studies in the evolution of a volume have been created in paper and enclosed in a transparent acrylic case. The base circumference of each volume is the same, while changes in the shape and size of the internal unit forms produce a different result in mass for each of the studies. Half of each volume is actually constructed in paper. A mirror on the back vertical wall inside the case completes the illusion of the total form of each volume.

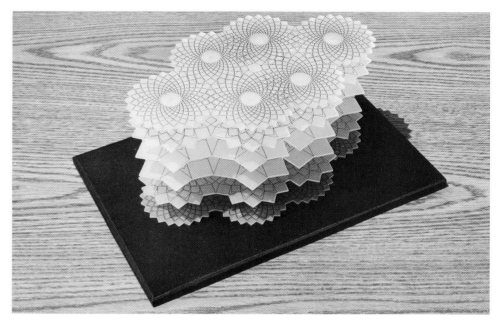

8-5. Acrylic planar study in gradation of shape.

8-6. Wooden solids in gradation of shape and size.

8-7. Paper volumes in gradation of shape and size.

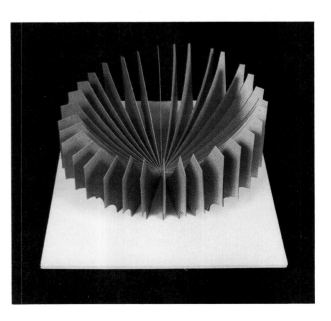

8-8. Chipboard study in radial structure.

PLANAR STUDIES

Planes, by themselves, offer many possibilities for the exploration of mass. The study models in figures 8–9 to 8–11, executed in single-thick chipboard, illustrate a number of ways in which volumetric form can be evolved through variations in size, shape, position, orientation, and direction.

In figure 8–8, the serial planes increase gradually in height from the foreground to the background. The volumetric feeling of the form is not particularly strong because the spacing between planes is relatively wide around the circumferential path of the design.

In figure 8–9, a semispherical shape has been described in the foreground by modified planes that appear to rotate on their own plane and sink into the base plane. A prominent negative shape becomes a focal point in the design and leads the eye to the top of the form at the center where triangular planes, rhythmically spaced, lead farther into the enclosed space within the mass.

In figure 8–10, gradation of shape is used along with a cut dividing the form into two parts. The form rises from the base plane in high relief to accentuate the prominent negative shape.

Figure 8–11 is also split in the middle. In this study, however, the planes change in shape, size, and orientation as they lean against one another from the foreground and background toward the center. Viewed from above, graduated intervals of space between the individual planes progress toward a feeling of spaciousness at the center.

MASS STUDIES IN COLOR AND LIGHT

The following studies of a grouping of planar forms in open composition may be considered polychromatic sculpture. The forms are derived from an exploration of the principles of mass and from experimentation with patterns of shade and shadow.

Figure 8–12 illustrates a group of basic planar forms viewed from above. The strong play of shade and shadow on the forms and ground plane is created by sunlight. Cast shadows can become a very important element in composition. Chapter 1

8-9. Chipboard study in semispherical shape.

8-10. Chipboard study with prominent negative shape.

8-11. Chipboard study with intervals of progressive spacing.

8-12. Shadow and mass.

showed how they were used to define form. They can also add new formal and tonal elements, such as those created by the building up of tones in the shadows through simultaneous contrast by using one hue and an achromatic light source, resulting in a surprising range of subtle color effects.

When working with more than one light source, cast shadows can have two or more values. First, there are shadows that do not receive light from one source but do from the other. In addition, there are absolute shadows that receive light from neither source. Those objects lighted from one side are much more positive in giving induced colors than are absolute shadows. Obviously, when two or more colored sources are used, both half and full shadows result in a rich array of tonal mixtures. Figure 8-13 illustrates the basic principle, using the three light primaries. Three lights are focused on a plane with a free-form

shape suspended in front of them. Where the shape interrupts the light from one source, the result is an additive secondary mixture from the remaining two lights. Where two sources are interrupted by the shape, the result is the primary color of the third light source. Where the shadow is absolute, the result is black, a complete absence of light. Figure 8-14 and plate 56 illustrate a study in mass with shadow patterns on a dull reflective surface (silver mat board) as a means of softening and creating a visual transition between the color composition and the ground plane. The use of rectangular planes and monochromatic color runs in this project are all reflected in the base, extending the color space toward a volumetric color experience.

Plate 57 illustrates a cylindrical form of sculptural or environmental proportions articulated by a strong pattern of vertical planes. This scheme of relatively high key hues has been inten-

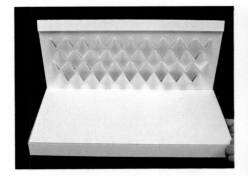

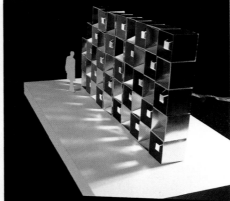

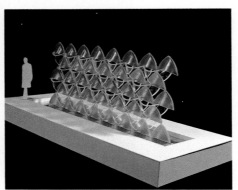

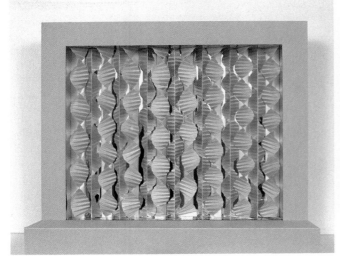

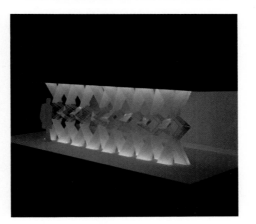

Chapter 7

Plate 44. <u>Upper left</u>: Reflected light from the interior faces of a tetrahedron softly colors the background wall.

Plate 45. <u>Center left</u>: A color run across the rows of prism forms is reflected on the faces of a mirrored necklace within a recessed wall structure.

Plate 46. <u>Lower left</u>: Pleated spiral forms are reflected in the mirrored faces of alternating columns.

Plate 47. <u>Upper right</u>: Freestanding wall structure is designed with reflective hollow cells.

Plate 48. <u>Center right</u>: Each unit of the structure is preformed from acrylic sheet and covered in transparent color films.

Plate 49. <u>Lower right</u>: Compound prism forms are illuminated from above and below with fluorescent light.

Plate 50. <u>Upper near right:</u> Cubes made from acrylic sheet are illuminated from the interior of the base with fluorescent light and from outside the wall structure with diffuse light.

Plate 51. <u>Center near right:</u> Hollow prism forms are illuminated with fluorescent light from inside the base.

Plates 52 and 53. <u>Lower near right and upper far right:</u> "Chromatokinetic" elements in the Union des Banque Suisses by Carlos Cruz-Diez. (Courtesy of the artist)

Plates 54 and 55. <u>Center far right and lower far right:</u> Views of corridor with colored light by Dan Flavin for the Hauserman Showroom in the Pacific Design Center, Los Angeles. (Courtesy of Sunar Hauserman)

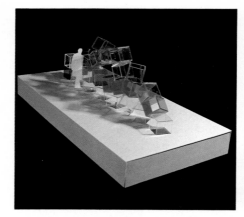

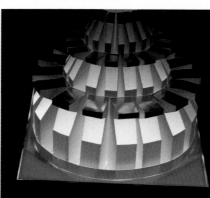

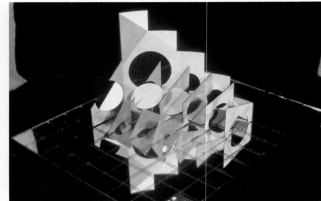

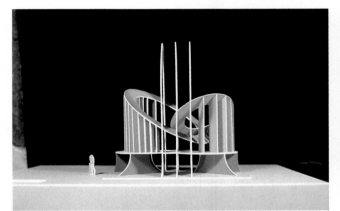

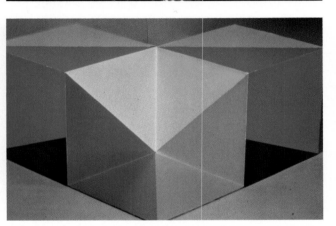

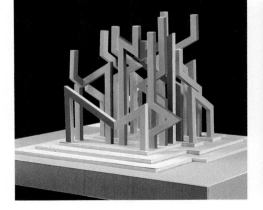

Chapter 8

Plate 56. <u>Upper left</u>: Colored shadow and reflection.

Plate 57. <u>Center left</u>: Bounced light from one vertical to the next in an analogous color run serves to heighten the intensity of hues.

Plate 58. <u>Lower left</u>: Faces are treated with strong hue and value contrasts that are further heightened by diffuse lighting.

Plate 59. <u>Upper right</u>: Mirrored base continues the concept of transparency in color and form.

Plate 60. <u>Center right</u>: Student experiment with color and form under the direction of Lois Swirnoff produces "plastic" illusions of transparency, altering the perception of volumetric forms. (Courtesy of Lois Swirnoff and Pergamon Press, Ltd.)

Plate 61. <u>Lower right</u>: Hue and value contrasts in this student experiment maintain a strong illusion of transparency and alter the perception of form. (Courtesy of Lois Swirnoff and Pergamon Press, Ltd.)

Plate 62. <u>Upper near right</u>: Student project under the direction of Jean-Philippe Lenclos utilizes fragmentation of a volumetric form with patterning based on a color landscape photograph. (Courtesy of Jean-Philippe Lenclos)

Plate 63. <u>Center near right</u>: The consulting work of Jean-Philippe Lenclos is based on color research taken from natural materials in a project-locale and utilizes patterning to fragment and reorganize into a "plastic" whole.

Plate 64. <u>Lower near right</u>: *Sunset Cube,* Oakland University, Rochester, Michigan, by David Barr. (Courtesy of the artist and the Donald Morris Gallery)

Plate 65. <u>Upper far right</u>: Fairlane Town Center sculpture, Dearborn, Michigan, by David Barr. (Courtesy of the artist and the Donald Morris Gallery)

Plate 66. <u>Center far right</u>: Sculpture for the First National Bank, St. Paul, Minnesota, by George Sugarman. (Courtesy of the artist)

Plate 67. <u>Lower far right</u>: Sculpture incorporated in model study for subway station by George Sugarman. (Courtesy of the artist)

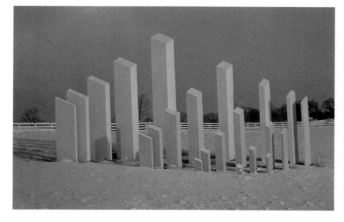

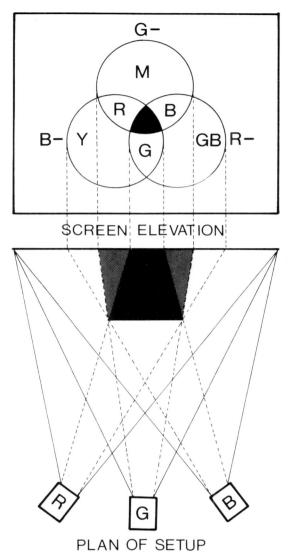

SCREEN ELEVATION

PLAN OF SETUP

8-13. Diagram of basic principle of color shadows (yellow, magenta, green-blue) from light primaries (red, green, blue).

8-14. Planar study in mass with shade, shadow, and reflection.

sified by the result of light reflected from the faces of the colored vertical planes across to adjacent colored faces of similar hues. The orientation of the colored vertical planes in relation to the direction of the main light source acts to intensify the local hue on many of the faces by reflecting colored light, while those faces receiving the full impact of direct light tend to lighten and fade in intensity. Shadow play is also noticeable as it traces a linear path on the verticals and the underside of the large circular shapes.

The piece in plate 58 is formed from balsa wood sticks in geometric columns derived from 60-degree and 120-degree angles. The intention of light and dark value contrast (and

8-15. Planar study in mass with curvilinear direction and colored shade and shadow.

temperature contrast) is to induce a visual connection from column to column that circumscribes a shape or remains a discontinuous and broken part of the shape. This is achieved through a plan for similarity or contrast in color on all faces of the column forms that dominate the various views of the design. The light source causes even greater distinction between light and dark hues, resulting in the light blues fading in value toward white and the dark blues shading in value toward black. The overall effect is a heightened perception of contrast, with little remaining sense of space or volume, and a playful dialogue between geometric shape and line.

In the study shown in figures 8-15 and 8-16 and in plate 59 the relationship of positive and negative form gives the effect of transparency, further extended by the use of high-key color runs across the planar forms. The mirrored base plane heightens the illusion of transparency by extending the relationships of overlapping and penetrating forms into greater volumetric complexity. This study incorporates the play of shadow predominantly from one of its views, in which circular and triangular intersecting planes receive shade and are distinguished from the mirrored base.

PROFESSIONAL PROJECTS

The following professional projects extend the exploration of color, light, and mass into the areas of sculptural and architectural forms. They represent various attitudes and directions that derive significance from each artist's and designer's search, experimentation, and evolution of plastic expression in mass and volume.

8-16. Study drawing in figure 8-15 proposed in the context of an environmental sculpture for the Allen Botanical Park in Southfield, Michigan. (Rendering by Richard Rochon)

TRANSFORMATIONS OF COLOR AND FORM:
THE WORK OF LOIS SWIRNOFF AND STUDENT PROJECTS

An example of the potential power of the illusions of color can be found in the work of Lois Swirnoff and her students. With students of architecture at the University of Southern California in Los Angeles and students of design at the University of California at Los Angeles, Swirnoff has experimented with optical illusions involving the interaction of color and form that show how color can be combined with form in design to serve as an attribute of an object's three-dimensionality.

These experiments involve a three-dimensional object constructed of seven square panels, which are joined to resemble three cubes touching at two of their faces (fig. 8–17). The cube studies are made from seven squares of 6″ × 6″ white mat board. Three of the squares are joined to form a half cube. Two such half cubes are joined along one edge so that the external three sides

of each half cube face frontally, the direction from which the model is to be viewed. The seventh square joins the two half cubes along their bottom inner edges.

The two white half cubes appear convincingly as two cubes and the seventh square appears as the ground plane between them. When the model is viewed monocularly from a distance of about 15 feet, the illusion of the inside of a half cube (concave) is obtained at the center of the model. It is formed by the seventh square and the two adjacent squares, which are also the external faces of the two cubes, leaving a pair of perpendicular squares on the left and right. With continued observation of the model, illusions of the concave half cube and the pair of cubes appear alternately.

The model is then illuminated from one side and placed below eye level to appear monocularly as an isometric projection—that is, so that the three edges forming the far corner at the bottom of the central half cube appears to intersect at 120-degree

8–17. Seven square panels of cardboard are grouped together to create the illusion of three cubes. (Courtesy of Lois Swirnoff and Pergamon Press, Ltd.)

8-18. The appropriate illumination and contrast from a single light source heightens the arrangement of faces that reflect light, middle, and dark tones. (Courtesy of Lois Swirnoff and Pergamon Press, Ltd.)

angles (fig. 8-18). The three faces of the two cubes now appear in light, medium, and dark values, respectively, and the alternating illusions of the pair and half cube seem to increase. Once the alternating illusions are perceived monocularly, they continue to be seen, despite distortions of perspective, when viewers walk from one side of the model to the other along an arc of 180 degrees in front of it.

In plates 60 and 61, the panels are colored in different ways to demonstrate how color can enhance the perception of convex cubes; cause cubes to produce alternating illusions of concavity and convexity; and cause one of the cubes to appear convex, and another to appear flattened. Visual phenomena, such as the effect of transparency, can be produced when colored areas are juxtaposed on a flat surface. With the intention of studying the occurrence of such phenomena on three-dimensional objects and their possible influence on the form perceived, Lois

Swirnoff systematically developed studies in her course Dimensional Color at Harvard University's Carpenter Center.

A visual principle inherent in these studies is that ambiguity in the monocular perception of three-dimensionality may occur when a boundary between two adjacent colors appears more pronounced than a physical boundary, possibly a significant aspect of camouflage. When a color boundary replaces other visual cues for form, such as a physical boundary, an illusion occurs. While viewing the model binocularly restores three-dimensional forms, this can be influenced by viewing distance. At a vantage point greater than 60 feet from a small tabletop, one is more inclined to see a monocular illusion. Swirnoff believes that these experiments ". . . suggest that color can be a significant attribute of form. Clearly, advantage can be taken of this attribute in environmental design. In architecture, for example, the texture of colored surfaces of buildings can be designed to change progressively in appearance during the normal daily variations in daylight illumination. Thus, illusions or transformations which are a visual device in nature, could be introduced to enhance aesthetically the human-made environment."

THE WORK OF JEAN-PHILIPPE LENCLOS AND STUDENT PROJECTS

The following studies were carried out by design students under the direction of Jean-Philippe Lenclos at the Ecole Nationale Supérieure des Arts Décoratifs in Paris. The act of color selection as practiced in the consulting work of Mr. Lenclos is one of developing a tonal base pattern that relates directly to the fenestration of the architecture under consideration. It is significant to restate that the experience of color is a product perceived in association with other colors, forms, and surface textures. The experience is constantly and simultaneously affected by all of the visual elements in a field of view. The student work in figure 8–19 represents an analysis of color in nature and exemplifies the third of the three methodologies Lenclos prescribes in his own practice and which can be described as follows.

1. The expression of pattern inherent in the physical form of an established design.
2. The further development of an inherent pattern through the addition of contrasts in value not present in the existing structure.

8–19. Analysis of color in nature from a photograph applied in value and color patterning. (Courtesy of Jean-Philippe Lenclos)

3. The creation and application of a completely applied pattern, which may dramatically transform the visual impression given by the building.

The student projects parallel the third methodology with an analysis of the color of nature from photographs and an application of pattern to geometric forms, which in turn represent scaled abstractions of buildings (plate 62). The organization of pattern in monochrome is a fundamental step before the translation to color. In many of Lenclos's own projects, monolithic scale buildings are transformed through a basic design attitude in response to "humanizing" the monotonous grid structures of large buildings by attaching a seemingly inexhaustible series of tapestry patterns to their facades. He begins by selecting colors based on the collection of samples of earth taken from the immediate location of a building. These colors together with studio paint samples are compared and color-matched to represent one architectural palette for application to a building. Lenclos's achromatic pattern studies in figure 8–20 illustrate endless variations that can be woven around facades and transform mass and scale through the fragmentation of a building's scale. Ex-

tremes in value contrast are also often reduced in favor of a subtle gradation of value steps in patterning before Lenclos makes a translation into an architectural palette (plate 63). In his students' work, alternate light and dark progressions receive either a value-matched range of saturated spectral hues or a range of hues based on a pattern of graduated steps of value.

An awareness of value as the key color dimension prior to a translation into color plays a significant role in the design process of many of the architects and designers discussed. Following the establishment of tonal patterns in design, variations in hue and chroma can be considered in relation to an existing plan. The predominant forms, patterns, and qualities of light, shade, and shadow can either directly or indirectly influence the degree of contrast between the intervals of color.

THE WORK OF A. C. HARDY

The color projects and student works under the direction of Jean-Philippe Lenclos include the use of models in the development and testing of a proposed design against its setting

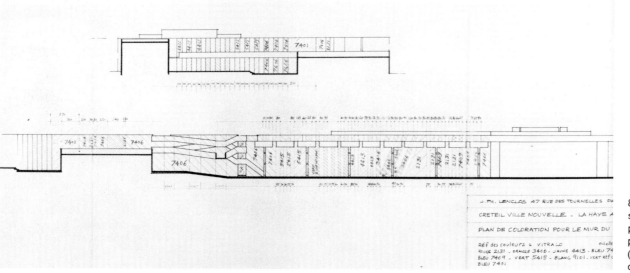

8–20. Achromatic patterning studies are created by Lenclos prior to color translations and application to architectural projects. (Courtesy of Jean-Philippe Lenclos)

8–21. A. C. Hardy's technique for producing composite photographs requires a model setting compatible in scale with the intended setting of the camera viewfinder. (Courtesy of A. C. Hardy)

8–22. Composite photograph. (Courtesy of A. C. Hardy)

8–21

and the communication of the color form through the representational means of drawing, photography and three-dimensional models. A direct method of proposing color concepts of form in their environmental settings is found in the research work of A. C. Hardy at the University of Newcastle upon Tyne in England.

Hardy's studies involve predicting how a proposed building will look in the landscape by creating lightweight models and photographing them outside against a test site. The model is supported on a thin steel strip, the edge of the strip facing the camera so that the support is not visible. The steel strip is fixed to a rigid post with a spike to set into the ground and photographed after its relative scale and size have been determined through the camera's viewfinder (fig. 8–21). The distance of the camera to the model and the distance of the model to a proposed background are aligned to provide a compatible scale with that of the intended setting (fig. 8–22). The results of his work convey a convincing simulation of the color of large architectural form when integrated with its site.

8–22

STRUCTURIST FORMS: THE WORK OF DAVID BARR

The works of David Barr extend across the disciplines of painting, sculpture, and architecture. They are described as structurist, seeking a dialogue between the essential qualities of the structure and harmony of form in nature and the expression of those relationships in plastic form. *Sunset Cube* (fig. 8-23 and plate 64), at the Oakland University campus in Rochester, Michigan, creates an illusion of a volumetric form tipped and sinking into the ground plane. The idea for the form is derived from the basic notion of warping a square into a diamond as a truncated volume with the top plane appearing as though it had been sliced at an oblique angle, reminiscent of the form of an axonometric drawing. The columns stand upright perpendicular to the ground plane and are graduated in height and color from pale yellow on the tallest forms to intense yellow on the shortest forms. The close grouping of the solids and the distinctive color contrasts between the top and side faces heighten the dimensional feeling of the columns and define an overall cubic volume that is tipped and partially submerged in the ground.

Barr's sculpture for Fairlane Town Center in Dearborn, Michigan (plate 65) is constructed from a plan for cubes that have been sliced into halves, quarters, eighths, and so forth and stacked above each other into a column study. The rotation of each cube section against the face of the one stacked above it is based on measurements derived from the Fibonacci Series (1, 2, 3, 5, 8, 13, and so on). Through the stacking of incremental portions of cubic forms from the base plane, a color run from a warm tertiary hue to bright red and back to a warm neutral hue heightens the rhythmic twisting of forms.

A large portion of Barr's work consists of structurist relief sculpture. These projects relate a systematic organization of form to logarithmic spirals and equivalent mathematical structures from nature to form a basis for the orientation of planes and solids in relief. *Structurist Relief # 155* (fig. 8-24) was constructed in mathematical relation to the constellation of Orion and the colors determined from the magnitude of the stars that compose the constellation. In many of Barr's reliefs, a subtle and closely organized color key articulates background planes in space and the juxtaposition of rhythmic intervals of form and color con-

8-23. *Sunset Cube* by David Barr. (Courtesy of the artist and the Donald Morris Gallery)

8-24. *Structurist Relief #155* by David Barr. (Courtesy of the artist and the Donald Morris Gallery)

8-25. Sculpture for the First National Bank, St. Paul, Minnesota by George Sugarman. (Courtesy of the artist)

8-26. View of interior space and sculpture at Greenfield School, Philadelphia, Pennsylvania by George Sugarman. (Courtesy of the artist)

8-27. Sculptural forms installed on exterior walls of the Wills Eye Hospital, Philadelphia, Pennsylvania by George Sugarman. (Courtesy of the artist)

trasts. The work of this artist will be explored further in chapter ten.

ORGANIC SCULPTURAL FORMS:
THE WORK OF GEORGE SUGARMAN

The work of George Sugarman exemplifies an investigation of the role of sculpture and mass as a means to create and activate space. The evolution of Sugarman's language of form can be traced back to abstract expressionism, from which he first absorbed notions of gesture and composition. His use of abundant organic forms and their application to floors, walls, and ceilings are a pioneering effort in the investigation of "sites" for sculptural form. Many of his works begin with studies of three-dimensional cardboard sketches and broadly gestural paintings on paper, which are later translated into aluminum and steel at an increased size. In their lightness and openness, these works read as a direct translation from his maquettes and preliminary studies.

The entryway piece designed for the First National Bank in St. Paul, Minnesota is suspended above the viewer in a dense grouping of brightly colored forms (fig. 8–25 and plate 66). The use of clusters and layers of intense color evoke a tactile quality, drawing attention to the space in front and through to the interior of the bank. Sugarman's work for the Greenfield School and Wills Eye Hospital in Philadelphia, are examples of form applied in patterning to activate architectural spaces as relief wall sculpture. In these works, the use of strong color filling a portion of an architectural space creates an excitement that can be enjoyed by all people (figs. 8–26 and 8–27).

A recent proposal for a sculpture for a subway station in Buffalo, New York shows a trial form of the application of Sugarman's ideas. (figs. 8–28 and 8–29). His planning of large sculptures often includes building architectural models from drawings supplied to him by the architect in order to visualize and sense the full experience of his forms—their effect and interaction with the space and observers (plate 67). His imaginative and energetic exploration of new ways of relating sculptural form to architecture provides visual excitement and awareness of space and has contributed to a unique and compelling form of expression for the public enjoyment.

8–28. Study model for sculptural installation in a subway station by George Sugarman. (Courtesy of the artist)

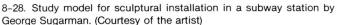

8–29. View from above of proposal for sculpture for a subway station by George Sugarman. (Courtesy of the artist)

9 Enclosure and Volume

Most constructions have meaning to us only as we experience them. They are revealed by the lines and patterns that lead us to, into, through, over, under, or around them. The development of a pattern of "circulation" is a major function in any project because it establishes the rate, sequence, and nature of its sensory reality and visual unfolding.

Objects themselves are perceptible entities that exist in time as well as in space. As discussed at the beginning of chapter 1, an object cannot be comprehended in its entirety at any one instant or from any one point of observation. It is perceived and understood, rather, through a flow of visual impressions. When we are in motion, we see a series of images expand into the visual realization of an object and space. Perception, however, is not a matter of visual mechanism alone. All of our senses of sight, touch, hearing, taste, and smell may be involved. The rate, order, type, and degree of perception are all factors included in the control of a design, which are in turn affected by the plan of patterns of circulation.

Our experience of the visual elements of a design is rarely static. A structure is seen more naturally by people who are moving than by people viewing it from a fixed point in space. The three-dimensional form and modeling of a structure are therefore equal in importance, since both act to define or confuse our perception of volume and space. The plan and arrangement of form outside and around a structure is also experienced from an infinite number of viewing points by those who move through it. If it can be assumed that a fluid plan exists around an open form, the more points of view and, consequently, the more interest and enjoyment can be experienced.

As discussed in chapter 4, movement, in a subjective sense, is an intrinsic part of all visual design. Time and change, the two essential elements of movement, are dimensions of living. They are also objective dimensions of a group of the visual arts—film, theater, and dance. Time and change are also very much a part of painting, sculpture, and architecture, as seen in chapters 6, 7, and 8 in projects involving different sides and angles of view. An investigation of the specific problems of movement as they apply to the "plastic" action of color, light, and form in the fine arts and architecture is pertinent to the present study of three-dimensional design.

THE DIMENSIONS OF MOVEMENT

Direction. The first distinctive characteristic of movement is its direction. Direction can be either along a continuous path or it can change. The change may be one of a regular progression or of opposition. Each of these possibilities has its own expressive nature.

Rate. A second aspect of movement is rate, which may be considered fast, slow, or any intermediate speed and has a pronounced expressive value. The rate can be a constant, or it can be altered in a regular progression abruptly. Changes similar to these can also become part of the pattern of larger rhythms.

Type. Movement circuits can also be characterized as to the kind or type of pattern they create through their direction. They may be continuous in a given direction, linear or rotary. They can also be periodic, like the swing of a pendulum.

Form. When movements are organized together in time, the resulting patterns have a recognizable character of form. If two pendulums of different lengths are suspended from the same support and start out together, the shorter one swings faster than the longer one does and will quickly go out of step with the longer and slower pendulum. Eventually though, they will come back into phase and then go out of phase again. The formal pattern of this fluctuation illustrates two types of form in movement: the simple pattern of the pendulum, and the buildup and loss of phase between the two pendulums. As different movements are patterned against each other, their forms become increasingly complex (as in dancing, where two or more groups perform against each other in different rhythms).

APPLIED KINEMATICS

In relation to an investigation of movement in the exploration of design, Maurice de Sausmarez, in his well-known and concise primer *Basic Design: The Dynamics of Visual Form,* comments:

> In the sphere of three-dimensional structures the mobiles of Calder and early Chadwick would seem to offer suggestions for development, and yet I am doubtful whether it is this construction of mechanisms for actual movement that is the most valuable and most basic experience sculpturally. It would seem to me that the translation and embodiment of the sense of movement into material that is itself static is the subtler and more considerable achievement. To attempt a sequence of relationships of curved rhythms, alternating concave and convex forms, moving through a series of quickly changing axial directions, or to construct a form which has the sense of spinning on a central axis, these and other similar studies involving the sense of paths of movement and forms in the process of change would seem to be relevant.

The various characteristics of motion include the line or trajectory of induced movement, which may be straight, meandering, looping, ascending, descending, zigzagging, or circuitous. The speed in motion may also range from very slow to extremely fast, with numerous terms describing the event such as flowing, forceful, converging, and so on. The nature of these factors—speed and alignment—produce a predictable emotional and intellectual response and should therefore be considered. As abstract visual qualities, the path or line through which a person, object, or space are approached requires a careful plan. If motion is induced, then the plan of spaces must accommodate the nature of the experience. However obvious these concepts may appear, like so many aspects of interior and exterior space, our perception and the plan of color, light, and form all are often overlooked in the design process.

John Ormsbee Simonds, the distinguished landscape architect, teacher, and author of *Landscape Architecture, A Manual of Site Planning and Design,* emphasizes the application of design principles in planning but, moreover, within the design and planning processes stresses an approach to the design of volumetric forms and spaces that encompasses the breadth of human experience. Simonds notes that, "The design approach then is not essentially a search for form, not primarily an application of principles. The true design approach stems from the realization that a plan has meaning only to people for whom it is planned, and only to the degree to which it brings facility, accommodation, and delight to their senses. It is a creation of optimum relationships resulting in a total experience."

THE MODULATION OF SPACE

It is a well-known and established concept in planning that we seek and are therefore attracted to those places and structures that express the qualities of harmony and unity and that we rebel against the intrusion of disjointed or incongruous elements. We also seek a harmonious sequence of transition from one space and group of forms to another. In going from the entrance lobby of a building to the reception desk, a detour through a long hallway is disturbing. When we take our families on a vacation or on a picnic, we naturally avoid business districts and prefer a route such as a parkway or a scenic road to maintain the mood and also to provide a comfortable transition.

The experience of motion offers us great pleasure through sensations of change. Changes can occur in the fluid visual impressions of objects, spaces, and views and in the qualities of light, temperature, and texture. We enjoy areas arranged by shape, line, color, and texture and take pleasure when they are developed into a volume or series of volumes that, by degree or type of enclosure, further describe the plan for their use. Whether moving to and through a space or around or past an object, we enjoy moving from one space to another and respond favorably to a sequence from one space to another.

Occasionally, transitions are very subtle. A sequence of spaces may provide a complete change in use and mood, however, the expression of transition from one space to another may be almost unnoticed. On the other hand, transitions are sometimes powerful. Through the plan for a low, tight, and dark space, one may be led into a lofty, light-filled free space as a dramatic experience. In all cases, the designer creates a plan that includes these human emotions, reflexes, and responses to manipulate, control and orchestrate them much as an experienced musician does with an oboe, violin, or flute.

CONDITIONED PERCEPTION

The nature of a particular object is usually less significant than how we relate to it. If a designer decides to place an object such as a pole, fence, or wall in a space, he or she must consider not only the relationship of the object to the space but also the relationship of the object to those that use the space. Designers must plan for the user's perception of objects through a sequence of established relationships that express its most attractive qualities. It is important to recognize also that our impressions and perception of objects and spaces are conditioned by previous experience as well as by the anticipation of an experience. The crash and spray of waves at the beach are all the more appreciated when we move toward the water's edge after sitting on the hot, dry sand. For the same reason, a foyer or courtyard are all the more enjoyable after leaving the confines of a dark, cool office or hallway. The designer's plan, therefore, should not be for a single space alone, but rather for a sequence of conditioned experiences that give meaning and pleasure to the interaction or impact of each.

SEQUENCE

The term *sequence* concerns a successive group of perceptions that together have continuity. Sequences have little relevance unless we are present to experience them. On the other hand, it is fair to say that all of our experiences are sequential.

In the natural environment, sequences are casual and free. Occasionally, but not always, they are also progressive events. A progression may infer one direction, upward or downward, inward toward a dark interior, or outward toward the light. It may also suggest a progression of enclosure, intensity, and complexity.

The plan for a sequence may be created in either a casual or disciplined manner. In this sense, both are extremely effective design devices because they contain one or both extremes of sequential experience, intentionally rambling or contrived with a high degree of discipline and order. A plan that includes aspects of one or both of these attributes may induce movement, imply direction, suggest rhythm and cadence, create a mood and atmosphere, expose and define an object, and also help to develop and communicate an aesthetic and philosophical concept. A planned sequence requires the organization of design elements in space. Through implied or induced motion, one is compelled to move from the beginning of a sequence to its completion. Once begun, the implied movement and direction should be concluded in a logical and satisfying manner. A well-conceived plan defines the potential for climaxes and their timing, intensity, and transitions through which they evolve. It may be a quite simple sequence of form and space or one that is considerably complex. It can be a sustained event with no interruption or it may be varied with diverse forms of modulation that are either subtle or powerful in appearance.

Most important, a sequence should reveal, interpret, and feature the elements to be perceived and the spaces to be used or traversed. The rhythmic recurrence of one or more spatial qualities—size, shape, color, lighting, or texture—soon results in a cadence with either a slight or very considerable emotional impact upon the moving observer.

THE POSSIBILITIES OF CONTAINMENT

In the broadest sense, space acquires its definition and character through the elements that act to contain it. Although each element will infuse a space to some degree with its own qualities, it must be thoroughly related not only to all similar elements but also to a primary concept for the desired character of a space. All of the visual elements—line, form, color, light, and texture—have an impact on the human senses. If the expression of a given form violates the central expressive purpose of an object or structure, it should be used only with a defined purpose and intent. Every shape, which is part of a structure, has its own abstract design connotation and context within the overall pattern. This must also be in harmony with the intended nature of the object and space.

VOLUMES

Volumes are formed through three elements: the base plane, the overhead plane, and the vertical plane.

The Base Plane. The direction and patterns of movement are established on the base plane. Each object on the base plane has a significant relationship to all other objects. If the object is to be modified, the degree and type of modification must be analyzed. Because the base plane naturally receives the most use and wear, the selection of materials and textures to be applied to this plane should be considered for their permanence and general appearance during all aspects of their projected use. Whether the base plane is level, sloped, or warped, it is the base for the construction of objects placed on, around, or in it. The initial plan of a design is established on this plane.

The construction and material treatment of the ground plane are important to the successful accomplishment of proper transitions. The shapes and patterns of the base plane (ground plane) may relate either a subtle or dominant structural plan to the site and to each successive component. Through the sensitive handling and design of elements that compose the ground surface, we may coordinate, accentuate, and integrate all of the ensuing elements included in the design plan.

The Overhead Plane. In the outdoors, the overhead plane extends to the variable limits of a canopy of trees or the sky. With the requirement of shelter, however, our spaces and volumes must be controlled in height. The character of an overhead enclosure is affected and defined by the form, height, and extent of the overhead plane. This plane may be as translucent and spacious as nylon fabric or as solid as a wooden beam or reinforced concrete. It may also be perforated, pierced, ribbed, or louvered. The

solid overhead plane shields out sun and rain; however, by its degree of translucence or limit of overhang, it also has an effect upon the amount and quality of light. Our appreciation of the effect of light on a given space is based on an awareness of several properties. Light may appear amber, cobalt, lemon, pearl, silver, and in intensity or brightness it may range from soft to brilliant. Light may also appear to suggest motion such as piercing, dancing, scintillating, flooding, or streaming, and may have a distinctive visual character, such as dappled, subdued, harsh, or glaring. Each of these qualities and effects contribute to the many possible moods—gloomy, inviting, exciting, or cheerful—of light.

The overhead plane has three important purposes in regard to light. It may act to shield and therefore modify natural light; it may serve as a plane for reflected illumination; and it may support, contain, or conceal a source of direct illumination. The overhead plane may be pierced and partially open. In this case, it may not be as important as direct light that enters, creating shade and shadow. The overhead plane may be shaped in several ways and made from many materials. It may be a single plane or may be made from multiple planes in various angles; it may be a disk or dome or may appear as a transparent or translucent film, a patterned screen, or an opaque colored surface in varying textures.

The Vertical Plane. Vertical planes divide space and comprise screens, baffles, backdrops, and partitions. The vertical planes are the easiest to control and the most apparent in our visual experience. They also have the most important function in the creation of interior spaces. The verticals contain and articulate areas of usage and may tightly or loosely define and enclose them. Through the design plan, vertical elements may be manipulated to extend and expand areas of use. They also have a role in screening out obtrusive views or revealing expansive features such as a distant view or the spaciousness of the open sky. Vertical enclosure may be as basic as unfinished wood or as sophisticated as a panel of etched glass or ceramic mosaic. The quality and range of materials and forms are almost unlimited. Regardless of the mass or the refinement of the enclosure, its essential purpose is to suit the use of the space.

Whether a space is fully or partially enclosed has little value in and of itself. The degree and quality of enclosure has meaning only in relation to the purpose and function of a given space. Everything that is visible within a space is a function of the space. The extent and nature of enclosure and the quality of revealment should be considered in the plan and proposed use of the space. An object far away may be visually introduced into a space by opening, framing, and focusing on it. In this sense, the object is "brought into" the space. The vertical elements also help to direct the eye into or out of the space. In the most general sense, when interest is to be directed toward objects within a given area, the forms that serve to enclose a space as the backdrop should not compete (in shape, color, and texture) with the interest of the object or objects. When interest is to be directed outward, to an object or view, the enclosing forms are opened to frame and therefore accentuate the subject beyond. Enclosures used as backdrops should be designed to bring out the unique qualities of the object seen against it. Objects that have complex form, intricate lines, dramatic surface texture, and color are usually best displayed in a simple volume in which the spatial relationships enhance the object rather than confuse or detract from it. If more than one object is placed inside enclosing planes, the interacting spaces between objects as well as objects and planes are significant to the design. When the object is planned to dominate, the backdrop becomes secondary in importance. When the backdrop is planned to dominate, however, such as a mural or wall sculpture, the surrounding vertical elements are designed and located so as to heighten the visual impact.

STRUCTURAL AND VERTICAL ELEMENTS

Buildings have a dominant presence whether they are viewed within or surrounding a space. When buildings are to be seen within the context of a larger space, they may be designed as sculptural elements to be fully experienced in the round. In either case, the space is developed in order to focus attention on the most important functions or components and to impel movement toward an entrance or along a directed route. Spaces that are external to a structure are also designed in such a manner as to provide a setting and foreground for the site of a composition. Within this larger setting, the exterior space surrounding a structure is often used as a setting for reference points of natural or man-made origin that provide a relationship to the scale of larger elements. Within a large space, it is useful to furnish many such reference points so as to make human scale evident. Doorways, windows, steps, and adjacent structures also serve to establish a sense of scale.

EYE HEIGHT IN RELATION TO VERTICAL ELEMENTS

Vertical elements generally receive the greatest amount of visual interest and treatment. We are usually far more conscious of them than of either the base or the overhead plane. Our face-to-face relationship with such standing surfaces or objects also presents the greatest number of design possibilities. Those features of greatest interest are often placed or located on the verticals at an average eye height. For one who is seated and for one who is standing, it is obvious that these heights are different. It is worth noting that all too often, however, a vertical plane will terminate at eye height, causing ambivalent reactions from those who see it.

VERTICAL ARTICULATION

The chief relationship of the vertical elements to the base plane is to help explain the use and patterns of the plan. It is the purpose of these elements to suggest direction through sequence, to act as a backdrop against which to view objects, to imply entrance through an open view of space beyond, to direct traffic patterns through shape and form, and to be adapted to the planned use of an area. A plan drawn on the base plane suggests a theme for the entire composition of space and structure, and in this respect the verticals act to articulate the theme and create variation within the plan of harmonious relationships. They also have the important purpose, depending on the degree and kind of spatial enclosure, of control. Wind, rain, sunlight, shadow, temperature, and sound may be diverted or eliminated. Breezes can be directed into or away from interior spaces. Sunlight can be filtered, diffused, blocked, or freely admitted. Similar in purpose to overhead planes, the verticals cast shadows and thereby lend character and pattern to a structure.

Vertical enclosures are seen both from the interior and exterior of a structure. In this sense, their sequence and placement are experienced in the round. Together with the spaces they enclose, verticals can be related to all other elements in a structure in a unified, coherent, and harmonious plan.

THE IMPACT OF SPATIAL ENCLOSURE

Many volumetric structures have been designed in such a way as to inflict disturbing effects on their occupants. John Ormsbee Simonds, writing in *Landscape Architecture,* describes an example of an enclosure having a significant physical and psychological effect on an individual. During the Spanish Civil War, an architect was ordered to design and construct a chamber—a translucent, multicolored polyhedron of crisply defined edges and planes. The size of the chamber was to barely accommodate a locked-in victim so that he would be unable to sit, kneel, or lie down without tilting and therefore tumbling over with the cubicle. In the daytime the surfaces were burning hot and at night they were ice-cold. Whether viewed alone or together, the colored planes were distressing and clashing. Through the discomfort and restrictions this volume imposed, it clearly served its intended purpose of driving its victim mad.

Because human beings are capable of designing these types of structures, they are also aware of their inadequacies and therefore capable of creating enclosures that provide pleasurable experiences. By analyzing a design's purposes and the functions those purposes are to serve, one can design a structure in size, shape, and character that is wholly suitable to a pleasurable experience and to the intended purpose of the design. Many abstract qualities or spatial characteristics of enclosure will induce predetermined responses in a viewer. The following list of characteristics is included as an exercise for the consideration of these purposes.

1. Restful. Basic forms in simple arrangements with subtle variation in size ranging from large to human scale. A sense of stability in the grouping and joining of objects. The use of familiar objects, materials, curvilinear elements, and spaces. Dominant horizontal arrangement of form and space. Subdued lighting and sound.

Relaxing color scheme with subdued, as opposed to intense, hues.
2. Cheerful. Open composition with flowing forms and patterns. Many kinds of movement and rhythm expressed in the structure. Few restraints in the use of forms, colors, and textures that appeal to the emotions rather than to the intellect. Produces a feeling of brightness and spontaneity rather than a subdued and contemplative mood. A warm, bright, and sparkling color scheme with an abundant amount of light.
3. Thoughtful. Few distractions of sharp contrast between relationships of form, color, and texture. Design of spatial relationships provides a sense of privacy, tranquility, and peace. Scale of spaces may either be intimate or large, but forms are not assertive. Diffuse light in combination with low-key color scheme produce a soft and muted atmosphere.
4. Dynamic and Forceful. Strong directional focus established in the composition. Angular and diagonal forms throughout. Evident use of solid materials such as stone, concrete, wood, and steel with rough or natural textures exposed. Internal interest focused on points of activity such as sports field, exit gates, speaker's platform. Implied movement in sequences of form, pattern, and sound. Strong brilliant presence of color in signage, flags, and graphics.
5. Fearful. Twisting, sloping, and broken planes arranged in an unsuitable manner with a sense of compression and confinement. Lack of reference points for the judgment of scale and orientation. Secluded areas that offer the element of surprise. Protruding, dangerous forms with unprotected voids. Symbolism that suggests pain, torture, and the application of force. Intensely bright light in contrast to dimly illuminated spaces. The use of cool temperature hues.
6. Stressful. Forms that appear to be unstable. Compositions that are split, illogical, and complex. Colors of strong intensity that clash and offer few, if any, areas of visual relief. Imbalance in the arrangement of form, color, and texture around a line, axis, or point. Harsh,

bright, or flickering light. Uncomfortable temperatures in the extreme ranges of hot or cold.

7. Spiritual. Large-scale space and form that dominate normal human scale and experience. Obvious contrast of large-scale forms with that of small-scale forms. Visual orientation directed upward toward the sky. Strong sense of compositional order or symmetry. Dramatic use of diffuse and/or focused lighting. Symbolic applications of color.

From the characteristics mentioned, it can be seen that one could experience many emotions simultaneously, such as joy and fright in a carnival haunted house, or joy and spiritual awe in a cathedral, and so on. The variety of suggested spatial characteristics and the measure of precision in which they can be defined are nevertheless surprising. A children's play space, as opposed to a restaurant or residential dining room, should be designed with a variety of textures, bright colors, and intriguing forms such as tunnels, movable objects, and things to climb up and over. Children not only have a fine tactile sense but they also love shapes and bright hues. Their environment should be designed with contrasts—open and closed, high and low, bright and dull, sun and shadow—encouraging excitement and merriment. More relaxing and subdued hues and shapes should be found in dining rooms, where a serene and pleasant atmosphere conducive to conversation is appropriate.

QUALITIES OF SPATIAL ENCLOSURE

A primary quality of a volume is its quality of implied containment. A limited space may be fully enclosed. It may contain, direct, and concentrate interest in the interior. The entire spatial enclosure may be constructed in such a manner as to appear constricted and compressed. Conversely, it may also appear to open out and direct attention to its structural elements and beyond. It may induce directional movement with flowing, undulating, and rhythmic elements. It may appear as a complete or incomplete space within itself and as a setting for objects or people. It may stimulate a prescribed emotional reaction or produce a predetermined sequence of human responses. A space may dominate an object or be dominated by an object. It may have an inward, outward, upward, downward, radial, or tangential orientation. It may

relate to a force, object, or another space and gain its meaning from the relationship between the two. A more complex space can assume the qualities of its component volumes and relate them into a unified entity. In designing a space for any given function, the designer should determine the essential qualities desired and organize his or her approach in order to provide them.

SIZE OF SPATIAL ENCLOSURE

Spaces are most often planned in terms of their relationship to humans. The size of an interior space has a pronounced effect on the feelings and behavior of those who use it. A compressed space, for example, with a low overhead plane conducive to sitting but not for standing does not promote a comfortable and relaxed environment nor a range of human activities that might include sitting, eating, dancing, and conversing. The design plan of exterior spaces requires similar considerations. A timid person in an open expanse feels lonesome and unprotected from nature and the elements, while a bolder person feels challenged with plenty of room for movement and action. The level ground plane, therefore, not only implies but also accommodates action.

An upright object on the bare ground plane is an element of inherent interest as well as a point of orientation. A vertical plane or wall has meaning both as a form of human defense and as a shelter from the elements. Two intersecting upright planes increase our sense of protection by providing a corner from which to survey the outlying plane. Continued attachment of vertical planes increases the definition of spaces and, with the introduction of overhead planes, furthers the control of space.

SPATIAL COLOR

There are many theories and systems of color application for volumetric color design. Early Chinese civilizations cultivated a theory based on colors found in nature, which has become accepted as a rule by many designers today. For the base plane hues and values in earthy colors of clay, stone, sand, and moss are generally used, while blues and greens, reminiscent of the unstable surface of water, are used only in areas where walking is discouraged. Structural elements such as beams and posts are given hues similar to the trunks and limbs of trees, such as deep grays, browns, and ochers. Wall surfaces in atmospheric hues reminiscent of light streaming through the interlacing branches of the forest are colored in warm and light neutrals, while the ceilings reflect the airiness of the sky and range from cerulean blue to aqueous hues and soft white or gray.

Another versatile theory in popular use today supports the concept of maintaining a completely neutral scheme for volumetric enclosures in shades of gray, white, or black. Simply phrased, black, white and gray, are all neutral colors along with gold and silver, and go well together with any other three colors in the same environment. This system proposes that the entire volume is simply a backdrop that allows the objects or persons within to "glow" in their own subtle or vivid hues. It also proposes that exterior views of a neutral color structure will harmonize with other dominant hues in the man-made or natural environment.

An additional theory of psychological origin proposes that spaces and forms be colored with those hues and values that alone or in combination produce a predetermined intellectual and emotional response. In other words, a basic color theme of harmonious hues will have a soothing affect on the observer, while the use of contrasts in hue and value create interest and emphasis.

Some theories of perception propose the manipulation of spaces and objects through a careful and studied application of recessive and dominant values and hues. In these theories, hues and values gain their maximum impact in combination and through carefully devised relationships.

Finally, a more general theory proposes that for a given structure or area of form, one appropriate color can be used as a dominant and unifying point of origin, with all other colors being subtle variations of the hue, value, and chroma of the color of origin. In this type of scheme, color ranges may be used to produce a cohesive system similar to the subtle variations of color found in a tree, plant, or other living form in nature.

All these approaches underscore the idea that spaces or objects within spaces are perceived with meaning only as they are experienced and that, in the creation of spatial experiences, the knowledgeable selection and handling of color is essential. Even though the areas from which a particular type of color scheme are taken are readily observed within the organization of a color solid, a multitude of chromatic possibilities for expression awaits the adventurous designer. In designating colors for use on volumes and in architectural spaces, the designer restructures form and space with light or arranges the reflective characteristics of colors and intervals along their dimensions to emphasize or transform impressions of an environment. On volumetric forms, color can be used to intensify the boundary between planes, to accentuate individual planes in contrast to adjacent planes of a different color, to lighten undulating or indented planes with pastel hues and reveal shadows where dark hues would tend to conceal them, to contrast intense against subdued hues to distinguish details, to adjust the visual position of a plane, and to change the apparent shape of a line, plane, or volume.

Before using colors in combination, one must determine the intervals between the intensity and value levels of selected colors. The previous experiments in this book on training the eye to see how color behaves relatively, demonstrate that an understanding of color interval is of prime importance to color selection and application. An increase in color intensity is perceived when complementary colors are placed together. The effects of afterimage and successive and simultaneous contrast are apparent when bright colors are viewed in isolated areas or in the superimposition of one color over another. Within the design process of the built environment it is important that the designer be fully aware of these phenomena because they can have an adverse effect on individual or groups of colors. For the most part, the environmental design process occurs in the scale of the drawing board, which is similar to the scale in which these phenomena occur. The additional problem of designing for the built environment in a reduced scale is that a successful scheme created with swatches of colors may change in effect when increased to full scale. To some extent, as colors are increased in size, larger areas of color may appear more saturated than smaller swatches. In order to make accurate decisions, samples large enough to offer an impression of the colors as they would appear in the built environment are needed. When considering the differences between increased saturation of color applied on a wall and color applied in a drafting-board scale, one should also take into account the effect of simultaneous contrast. When colors are com-

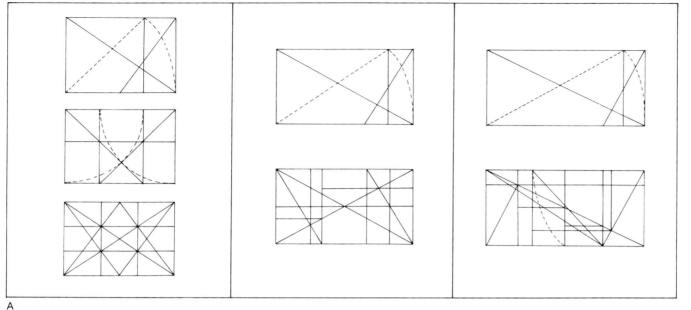

A

9–1A–D. Mathematically derived
linear divisions.

pared in superimposed or side-by-side relationships, the differences between them tend to be exaggerated.

Having experienced the problem of change in color occurring with change in size, many designers first narrow the selection of color to a group of the most appropriate hues and apply a
sample range onto a representative section of an interior wall or
exterior facade as a preliminary study in lighting and spatial conditions. These and other approaches to the use of color in professional practice will be discussed in chapter 10. What appears to
be of broad significance, however, is that the definition of form
and space through combinations of color is based on the use of
contrast in color with particular regard to contrast in value (light
versus dark).

BASIC STUDIES

One of the most basic exercises in the organization of
enclosure and volumetric form is the creation of a space frame.

Similar to the way in which areas are subdivided within a picture,
area divisions within three-dimensional forms are an important
issue because it is the fundamental proportions of containment
that make the first impact on the eye. Any rectangle can be developed in terms of its area division, either systematically on the
basis of mathematical proportion or based on an intuitive bal-
ancing of the parts. A group of mathematically established
squares and rectangles and their subdivisions are illustrated in
figures 9–1A to 9–1D.

SPACE FRAMES

Area divisions with linear and planar elements can be
studied by constructing space frames. With balsa wood, paper,
cardboard, or any lightweight and fairly rigid material, and glue a
rectangular space can be constructed and internally divided into
further spaces by vertical and horizontal rods and planes parallel

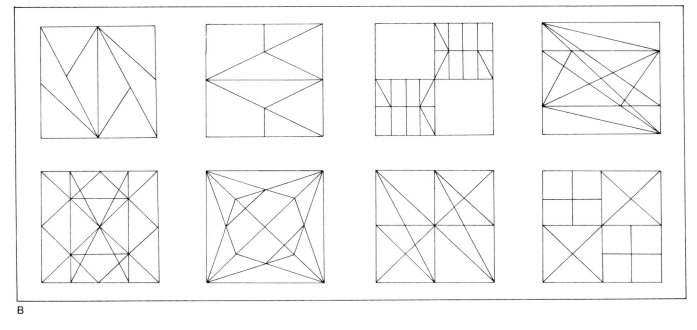

B

to the sides, top, and bottom. The additional use of plywood, acrylic, or metal offers an increased range of materials for experimentation (figs. 9–2A to 9–2C).

A structural exercise with vertical and horizontal planar relationships can also be designed within an imaginary rectangular space, without the enclosing rectangular frame. In this case, the "free" construction of thin solid planes and rods implies containment without an overall enclosing frame (fig. 9–3). Following this exercise, further studies with various rectangular solids and emphasis on size variation and grouping can be created to explore the vertical-horizontal principle, and planes or solids in diagonal orientation can be introduced and studied (fig. 9–4). More ambitious structures might attempt to enclose a spherical frame within a rectangular one or vice versa. In these explorations, as with the previous examples, the criterion is not the ingenuity of invention or construction, but the satisfying quality of visually and sensuously balanced relationships.

Space Frames within Light Chambers. Further effort in the design of space frames can be directed toward the use of colored solids and planes made from paper, cardboard, plastic, and wood combined within the interior of a frame in optically balanced subdivisions viewed from around the full design. An example of a space frame with cubic areas of division and colored forms in the interior is illustrated in figures 9–5A and 9–5B.

The relationships of color and form can be further examined when viewed under the effects of single or multiple directions of light and under white and/or colored sources of illumination. For this purpose, a chamber with a front plane open for viewing the interior, light fixtures with dimmer switches, and a turntable on the base plane acts as a basic means of exploring the effects of illumination on the frame and interior forms. In figures 9–5A and 9–5B colored gelatin filters have been mounted to incandescent fixtures, which are controlled by rheostats (dimmers) that allow the designer to alter the saturation and brightness of colored light. The base plane has been fitted with a revolving turntable and is controlled with a rheostat to allow for slow

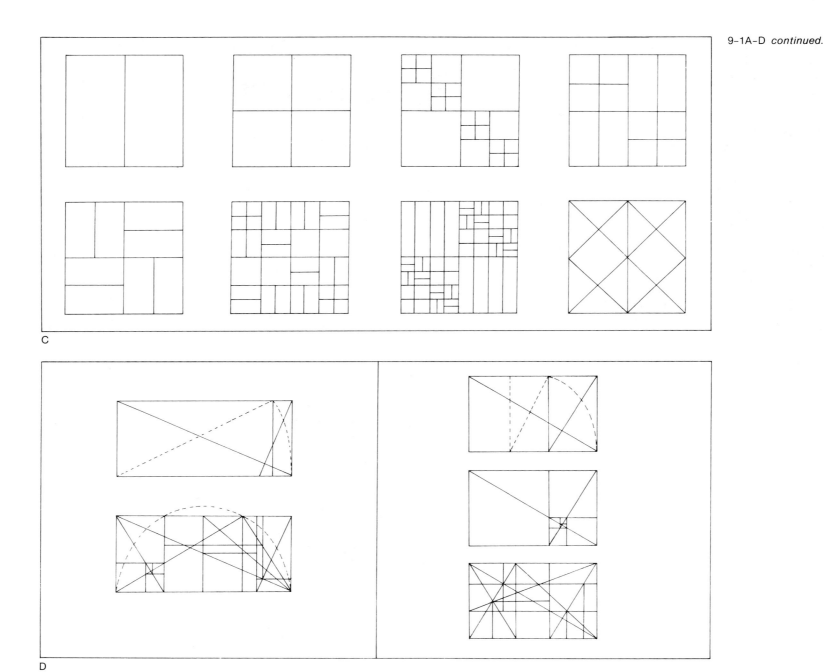

C

D

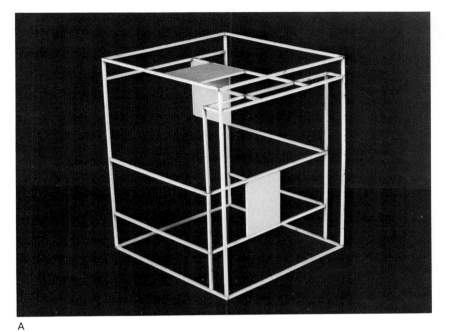

A

9–2A–C. Space frames.

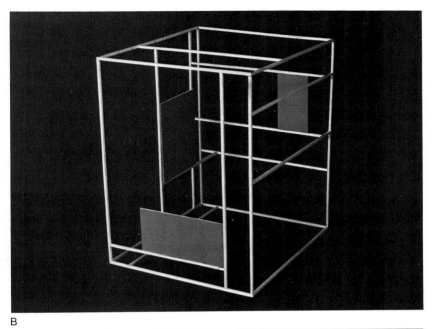

B

C

9-3. These planar forms arranged within a cubic volume of space reflect closed (left) and open (right) possibilities for containment and modulation of space.

and fast revolutions as well as for stopping the rotation of the frame at intervals for viewing.

OUTDOOR VOLUMES

Outdoor volumes that provide shelter and privacy need not be fully enclosed spaces. A pleasant outdoor structure that provides partial shelter from the elements and denotes privacy may be achieved by the careful arrangement of screens or by the grouping of freestanding elements. The following student projects on enclosure in figures 9-6 to 9-9 relate the vocabulary of the elements and principles of three-dimensional design to an ar-

ticulation of form for the enclosure of an outdoor volume that provides partial shelter and privacy—the degree and function of which have been determined by the student.

The qualities of light and spatial color together with a plan for an open or closed form play an important role in the development of each concept and have impact on the experience of each solution. In this sense, the goals inherent in the project are directed toward the plastic experience of form and space and the focus of attention includes a wide assortment of design materials along with the potential of their application to induce a predictable response. Establishing those qualities of form, light, color, and space also requires thinking of and visualizing dominant

9-4. Space frame with diagonal elements.

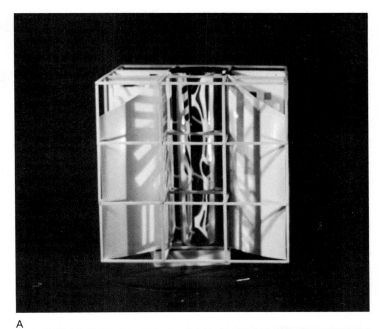

A

B

9-5A-B. Studies in the effect of additive mixing on pigments within cubic subdivisions of a space frame.

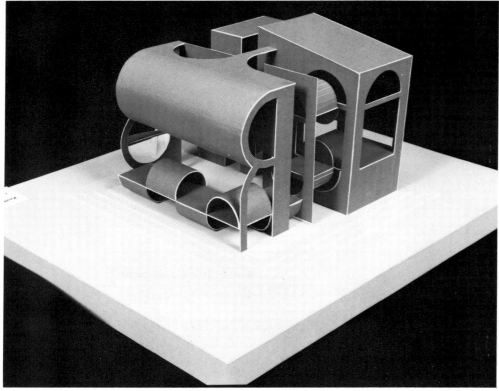

A

B

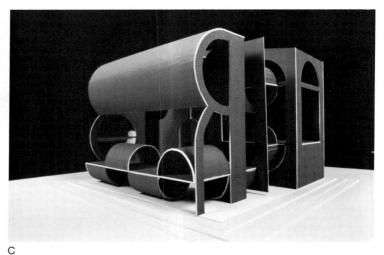

C

9–6A. Overview of a planar structure proposed as a park shelter, integrating the vocabulary of volumes and voids. (Materials are mat board with foam core base.)

9–6B. View of the front elevation.

9–6C. View of the rear elevation.

movement with respect to both the physical and visual approach to the enclosure.

INTERIOR SPACE AND COLOR

The physical size and shape of an enclosed space is a constant; however the appearance of length, width, and height can be altered by the manner in which color is used. Although a closet cannot be transformed into a spacious living room, there are many alternatives for the application of color to interior walls that can make a small space go farther. More specifically and most common are the problems of a long, narrow hallway, a low ceiling, or a boxlike interior shape.

An evaluation of the surfaces that give or define the

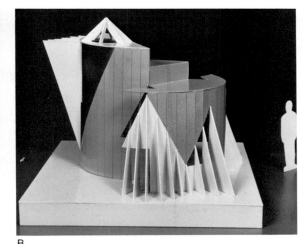

B

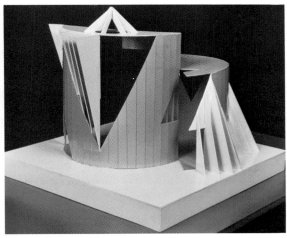

C

A

9–7A. Overview of a planar structure proposed as a park shelter with implied penetration of planar and volumetric forms. (Materials are mat board with lacquer on wooden base.)

9–7B. View of the side elevation.

9–7C. View from the rear elevation.

overall shape of an interior space results in a basic set of six planes—four walls, floor, and ceiling—each contributing to the whole. The visual relationship of the walls to the floor and ceiling planes can be ordered with color to make each appear to advance or recede, to look larger or smaller in comparison to each other, and to connect with adjoining spaces or to distinguish one space from another. Figures 9–10A to 9–10D illustrate the concept of

value planning in relationship to two boxlike, adjoining spaces and the potential impact of value contrast in color as a space-defining element.

The use of any dark hue to define a wall plane in these examples will have a diminishing effect on the perceived space. Therefore, the strength of tone is as important as the intensity of hue to the impact of the space. Lighter tones in this case make

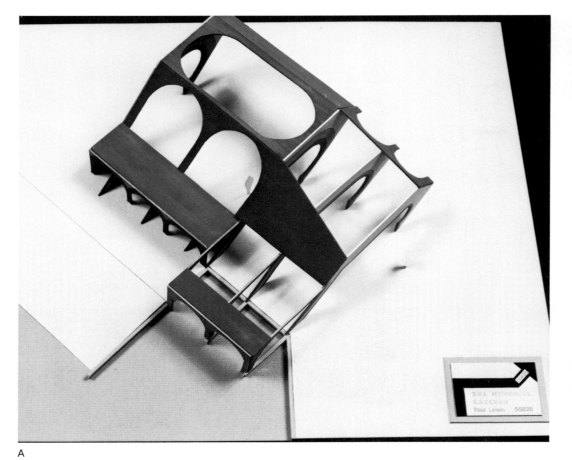

A

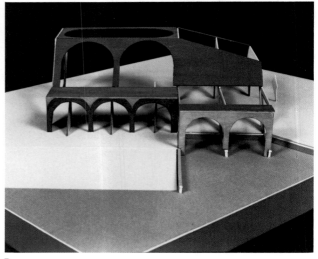

B

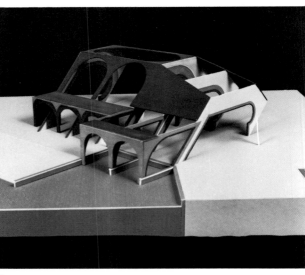

C

9-8A. Overview of an open structure proposed as a waterfront shelter with boat dock and picnic areas. (Materials are balsa wood, designer's gouache, and mat board.)

9-8B. View from the front elevation.

9-8C. View from the side.

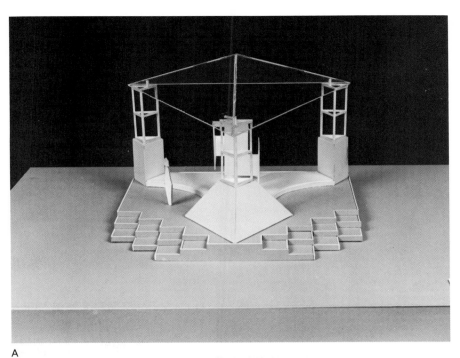

A

B

9-9A. A transparent, highly open structure proposed as a park shelter with interior observation platform. (Materials are acrylic sheet, balsa wood, mat board, and color papers.)

9-9B. View from the side.

9-9C. The model illustrated in the context of a park environment proposed as prototype shelter study for North Campus of the University of Michigan, Ann Arbor, Michigan. (Rendering by Richard Rochon)

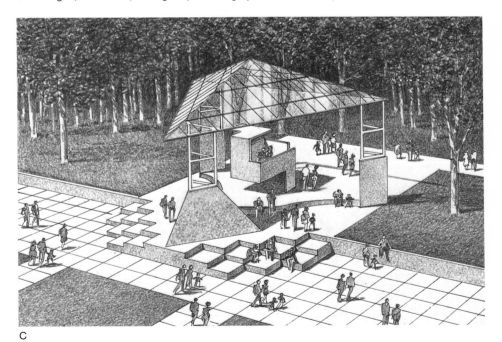

C

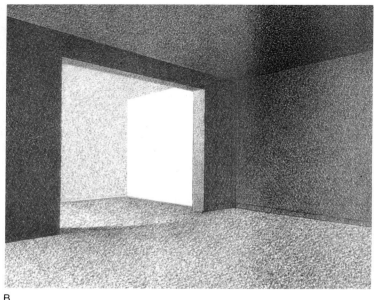

A

B

9–10A–D. Tonal contrasts between the extremes of black and white create special emphasis and awareness of separate or continuous planes.

the walls appear wider or more expansive, and a light-colored ceiling also appears atmospheric and recessive.

In order to lower the spatial effect of the ceiling plane, a dark hue will create a more compressed and perhaps top-heavy feeling in a confined area. A dark value hue for the floor plane grounds the composition and draws the eye downward. In general, the stronger and darker the overall color of a room, the more confined and closed in it may feel, while allover white has the opposite effect, expanding the apparent volume of the adjoining spaces.

Tonal contrasts between the extremes of all black or all white draw special emphasis and simultaneously create awareness of separate or continuous planes. The impression of spaciousness is created in two functionally separate areas and can be unified into a single space.

SPATIAL ACTIVITY MODULE

The student projects in figures 9–11 to 9–15 are based on a plan for an open scheme, with the objective of designing an environment for potential use as a work and study space for an architecture student. Students are encouraged to look at a model as a concept for form rather than to approach form through the traditional use of bubble diagrams, plan and elevation drawings, and then perhaps a model as incidental to the process. The scale of 1½″ = 1′ − 0″ affords an opportunity to explore details of joinery, structure, color, and texture as an extension of conceptual thought. Integrating functional elements, such as structures and areas for drawing, typing, filing, storage, and so on, with the human dimension (ergonomics) is also an important part of the project. The additional consideration of lighting within the open

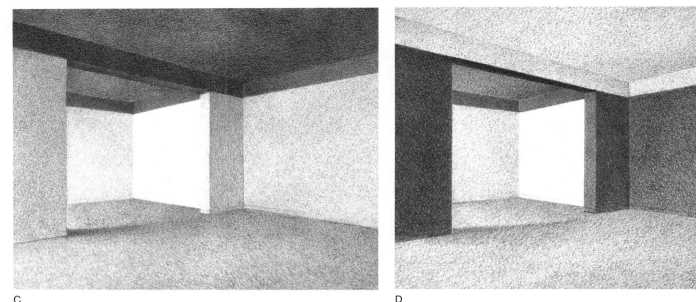

C

D

9-10A-D *continued.*

structure is planned on three levels. Diffuse lighting from outside the module provides overall illumination but perhaps not in sufficient brightness or direction to serve as a useful source for illuminating the interior space. Therefore, the need for central or ambient fixtures within the module to provide general illumination, as well as task-oriented lighting for specific internal functions (typing, drawing, reading), are both necessary considerations. The materials for interior and exterior surfaces, furnishings, and hardware detailing include woven fabric samples that replicate the scaled appearance of furniture coverings, metal hardware adapted from jewelry and silversmith supply houses for structural applications and detailing, and colored papers, cardboards, films, woods, and plastics. The finishing treatments and the level of realism are left up to the students' resources and imagination.

THE SIMULATION OF REAL SPACE

During the exploratory stages of the design process, varieties of expression of an idea, as well as modifications of size and scale, permit the designer to understand the full potential of the idea. Through the visualization of multiple views in two, three, and four dimensions, the designer begins to see the articulation of color, form, and space and to extend his or her comprehension of the dynamic relationships and the "life" of a design concept. Although the method demonstrated in figure 9–16 of using a video camera does not yield a complete likeness of our visual or sensory perception of the world, it does amplify one aspect in common with our experience—that of movement. The designer's ability to simulate motion adds the dynamic relationship of time to our understanding of space and our movement within it.

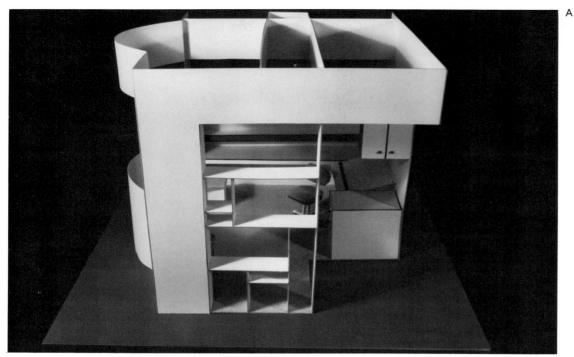

A

9-11A. Spatial modulation of a cubic volume through proportional divisions with planar elements.

9-11B. View of interior from the entrance.

9-11C. View of interior from the side.

B

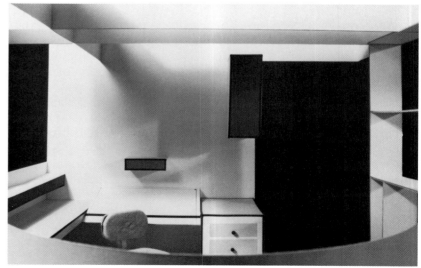

C

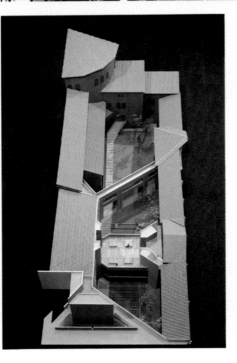

Chapter 9

Plate 68. <u>Upper left:</u> Color saturation chambers by Carlos Cruz-Diez. (Courtesy of the artist)

Plate 69. <u>Lower left:</u> Canopy for summer events at Kennedy Square, Detroit, Michigan. (Courtesy of Kent Hubbell, Chrysalis, Ann Arbor, Michigan)

Plate 70. <u>Upper right:</u> Evening view of Spaceship Earth at Epcot Center illuminated by lights mounted on surrounding buildings. (Courtesy of Walt Disney Productions, photograph by Stan Tracy)

Chapter 10

Plate 71. <u>Lower right:</u> Model of the University Museum Academic Wing, University of Pennsylvania. (Courtesy of Mitchell/Giurgola Architects, photograph by Rollin R. LaFrance)

Plate 72. Upper near right: Interior view of the lobby/garden for the School-House Project. (Courtesy of Graham Gund Associates, Inc., Cambridge, Massachusetts, photograph © Steve Rosenthal)

Plate 73. Lower near right: Interior model for the School-House Project. (Courtesy of Graham Gund Associates, Inc., Cambridge, Massachusetts, photograph © Steve Rosenthal)

Plate 74. Upper far right: Interior of escalator in the Detroit Science Center, Detroit, Michigan. (Courtesy of William Kessler Associates, Inc., photograph by Balthazar Korab)

Plate 75. Lower far right: Interior view of connecting tunnel at the Wayne State University Health Care Institute and Detroit Receiving Hospital, Detroit, Michigan. (Courtesy of William Kessler and Associates, Inc., photograph by Balthazar Korab)

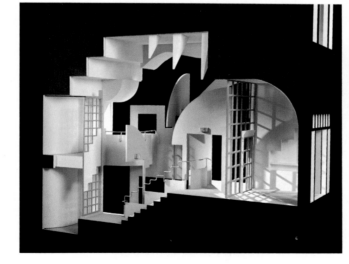

Plate 76. <u>Upper left</u>: Interior view of tunnel intersection at the Wayne State University Health Care Institute and Detroit Receiving Hospital, Detroit, Michigan. (Courtesy of William Kessler and Associates, Inc., photograph by Balthazar Korab)

Plate 77. <u>Lower left</u>: The effect of prismatic light is tested on a full-scale model by Charles Ross for Yeshiva Porat Joseph in Jerusalem. (Photograph courtesy of Joyce P. Schwartz, Ltd.)

Plate 78. <u>Upper right</u>: Skylight prisms by Charles Ross in the atrium of the Spectrum Building, Denver, Colorado. (Photograph courtesy of Joyce P. Schwartz, Ltd.)

Plate 79. <u>Lower right</u>: The light from overhead prisms by Charles Ross creates evolving patterns of color, giving the viewer a personal connection to the substance of light. (Photograph courtesy of Joyce P. Schwartz, Ltd.)

Plate 80. Upper near right: View of the Barr residence, the Villa, related to one of David Barr's outdoor sculptures. (Courtesy of *House & Garden* © 1982 by The Condé Nast Publications, Inc.)

Plate 81. Lower near right: Neutral colors and natural textures are integrated within the plan of interior spaces in the Barr residence. (Courtesy of *House & Garden* © 1982 by The Condé Nast Publications, Inc.)

Plate 82. Upper far right: Presentation model of Wonder Wall. (Courtesy of Charles Moore and William Turnbull with Perez Associates, Architects; photograph © Alan Karchmer)

Plate 83. Lower far right: Detail of Wonder Wall model. (Courtesy of Charles Moore and William Turnbull with Perez Associates, Architects; photograph © Alan Karchmer)

A

9–12A. Slat details of studlike construction used as linear elements to imply enclosure.

9–12B. View of interior.

9–12C. View of interior.

B

C

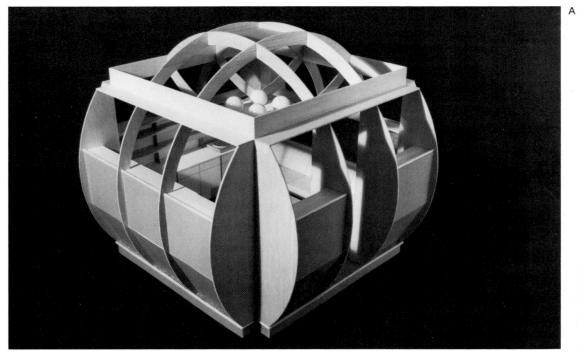

A

9-13A. Nine bay subdivisions of a cubic volume using curvilinear planar elements.

9-13B. View from above.

9-13C. View of interior.

B

C

A

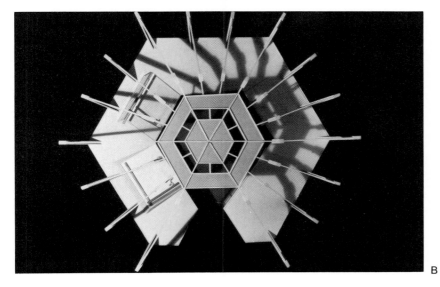

B

C

9–14A. Radial modulation from a hexagonal plan raised into a prism through implied planes of linear elements.

9–14B. View from above.

9–14C. View of interior.

A

9–15A. Spatial concept of tetra-hedrons melded to a linear struc-ture for a dodecahedron. The tetrahedrons are raised from the vertices to interconnect and sta-bilize the structure.

9–15B. View from above.

9–15C. View of interior.

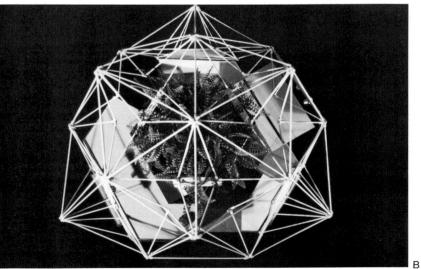

B

C

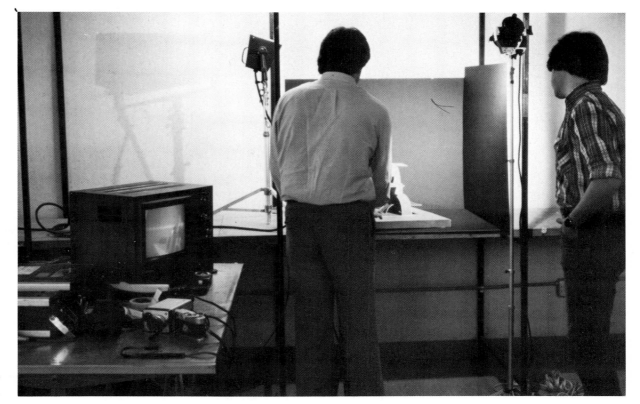

9-16. Model being positioned for videotaping in classroom project.

The eye and the camera may have basic functions in common with one another; however, there are enormous differences between them. For example, the eye has the ability to perceive movement in clearly defined images without the need of a shutter. The idea of placing a camera on a dolly in order to animate the exploration of the spaces inside and outside scale models increases the possibilities of being able to virtually walk through and around the projects. The scale of perception is reduced through the camera lens to the scale of the object being viewed so that the connotation of small-scale objects can be transformed to resemble the open spaces and planar and volumetric forms of the model in a human scale.

The project in figure 9-17 examines the dimension of movement through a model space with a video camera, projected through a television monitor, and a student project chosen from the outdoor shelters discussed in chapter 8. Initial experiments had the camera mounted on a movable dolly (similar to being mounted overhead on a movable gantry or counterweighted boom so that the sensation of walking or driving can be simulated). The camera lens defines the field of vision in a monocular or one-eye theory of examination. All planar relationships in the model are defined at a level of view in context with human scale and in con-

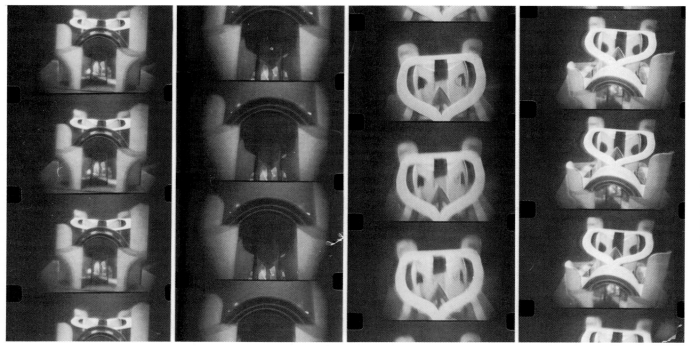

9–17. Outtakes of color footage of a project for an outdoor shelter were transposed from videotape into black-and-white still photographs to represent a motion sequence of four consecutive camera angles. In sequence from left to right: the camera approaches the entry, moves into a close-up, begins again from above the structure, and is lowered toward the entrance. (Courtesy of Ken Paul)

junction with the following attributes of spatial color, which absorb and reflect light applications.

1. Shadows create depth.
2. Highlights control composition.
3. The quality of light presents a mood.
4. The quality of light directly affects color contrast.

Model forms in their fixed positions provide information about the size and distance of planar relationships and how they are perceived from entry into and through interior spaces. Spaces open and close; planar relationships change in size and in their qualities of light and color. The degree to which an overall composition is open or closed becomes apparent and is altered by the movement of the camera through the space. The experience of movement and the related visual qualities become a cinematic experience of time, space, color, and light.

Variations in the direction of the camera through the model can alter the cinematic composition and resulting sense of space. The study of monochromatic schemes, the effects of light and shadow, open and closed relationships of form, and textural finishes without strong chroma are all possible. Studies in color with a video camera can be directed toward spatial compositions with gradual or abrupt changes in hue, and cool/warm color and light treatments along plotted movements that can be replayed and reviewed.

PROFESSIONAL PROJECTS

The final section of this chapter includes professional examples of volume and enclosure that relate a diversity of forms to the creation and control of the qualities of color, light, and movement. In this sense, they serve to increase awareness of traditional forms of enclosure and to expand on these concepts.

VIDEO AS A PROFESSIONAL PRESENTATION TOOL

Ken Paul Associates, specialists in visual communications, have been involved in the use of video as a medium for recording the design process of architectural spaces for study and client presentations. Prior to establishing his own firm, Paul served as director of visual communications at the architectural firm of Smith, Hinchman and Grylls Associates Inc., in Detroit, Michigan, and collaborated at the University of Michigan with Lester Fader, who pioneered in the use of video techniques in architectural education.

The preparation and use of video equipment for model studies requires an understanding of video hardware and its relationship to the physical project under consideration. Goodyear Tire and Rubber Company Technical Center is an example of a project that required an accurate simulation of how a large and antiquated production facility could be reshaped to serve as a research and development center. In figure 9–18, the proposed research and development offices are being videotaped as if one were looking through exterior windows to the proposed underground parking facility. For a major government defense office building, it was necessary to construct a model of the interior

9–18. Videotape of the model for the Goodyear Tire and Rubber Company Technical Center by Ken Paul, and Smith, Hinchman and Grylls Associates Inc.

spaces in order to introduce the client to the design plans for a prototypical information-gathering agency. In figure 9-19 designer James Wright views an auditorium space on a video screen through a camera lens located within the model, showing an accurate representation of scale within the space. In figure 9-20, the camera is moved to locations along a main corridor to test the perception of spatial relationships of movement along its path while the designer observes the taping on the monitor. In both figures 9-19 and 9-20, an analysis of the videotapes made resulted in changes in the design and execution of interior spaces in the final project.

Chesapeake Commons in Baltimore, Maryland is an architectural attempt to restore a girls' preparatory school into a viable complex of apartment dwellings. The use of the video camera was important in both phases of the design process as a study and presentation vehicle and opened an awareness of its eventual use as a tool for presenting the dwelling as it would look to future tenants. In order for video techniques to accurately project interior spaces in scale, the models had to be constructed at a size able to accommodate a camera, simulated lighting, and detailed furnishings. The sequence in figures 9-21A to 9-21D demonstrates four consecutive views of the project, beginning

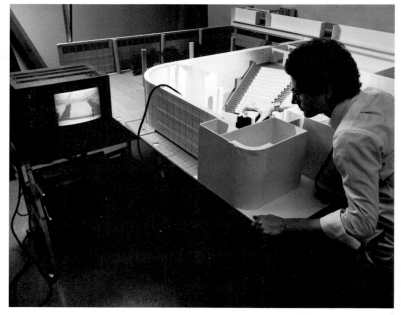

9-19. Videotape of the model of a government office building by Ken Paul and Smith, Hinchman and Grylls Associates Inc.

9-20. Study of the main corridor of the model of a government office building by Ken Paul and Smith, Hinchman and Grylls Associates Inc.

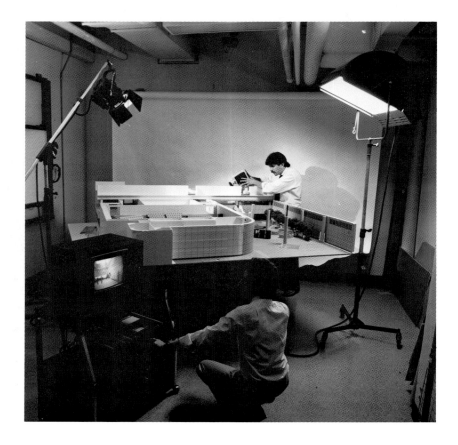

A

B

C

D

9–21A–D. A sequence of views of the model for Chesapeake Commons, Baltimore, Maryland by Ken Paul Associates, The Schneider Group: Developers, Syndicators, Architects, Designers. (Courtesy of Ken Paul Associates)

from a canopied entrance, proceeding into the lobby, entering an apartment, and ending in the living room of one apartment at Chesapeake Commons.

MASSACHUSETTS INSTITUTE OF TECHNOLOGY CORRIDOR PROJECT

Sports stadiums, transit systems, and many large public and private institutions are now planned with color-connected links within interior spaces, which provide a form of visual orientation for leading people to their destinations. For these large-scale applications, color graphics are often designed in chromatic contrast with the surrounding neutral climate of color to function either as signage or as a coding device for orientation within the plan of such spaces.

At the Massachusetts Institute of Technology, the renovation of the main corridor began several years ago as part of a major environmental program to ameliorate the notoriously drab and confusing corridor spaces. Working with the M.I.T. Planning Office, architect Paul Stevenson Oles created the prototype, which

9-22A-C. The offices, hallways, and stairwells along the main corridors at M.I.T. required color and signage to help students, faculty, and staff with easier orientation. (Courtesy of Paul Stevenson Oles, *Architectural Illustration*)

included a color-coded orientation system, a slide projection information system, community opinion feedback devices, and mobile notice kiosks. The project was oriented toward the primary users of the largest networks of interior corridor systems to date—the students, faculty and staff of the M.I.T. community. Preliminary studies showed that users were familiar with only a few frequently used pathways and that minor orientation cues, such as a drinking fountain or bulletin board, were the only visible anomalies in an otherwise repetitive complex of intersecting corridors. Deviation from these familiar paths led to disorientation, even in cases where students and staff were familiar with the general layout of the institute. The steps taken to alleviate these orientation problems included implementing graphic-verbal information (maps, directories, directional signs, building numbers, and floor level identification), as well as a consistent system of nonverbal orientation cues encompassing the main group of corridors and conceptually uniting its disparate paths.

The new orientation system related all parts of the main group of corridors to a Cartesian grid that utilized limited areas of color within a predominantly neutral white field. This nonverbal system was also made available to visitors through the general distribution of small maps of the main corridor group along with larger maps printed in colors corresponding to those used as cues in the system.

Many of the changes to the corridors reflected the primary community concerns of general corridor drabness, locational orientation, and social spaces, which together formed the general criteria for all master planning suggestions. The color system has elicited the almost universal approval of the M.I.T. community and is therefore a useful study for those interested in the application of color to signage and for orientation within a large network of interior spaces.

Figures 9–22A to 9–22C depict the hallways and stairwells of the main corridor at M.I.T., typical of many institutions built in the late nineteenth and early twentieth centuries.

COLOR SATURATION CHAMBERS

Carlos Cruz-Diez's experiments with environmental works take the form of labyrinthine enclosures installed in streets, museums, and schools. His works attempt to lead the spectator to perceive color in isolation, as opposed to perceiving it in nature, in which a color is relative to whatever surrounds it (fig. 9–23). These color saturation chambers are small booths composed of transparent colored sheets, which allow the viewer to observe the surrounding reality transformed by color.

The slits or orifices between the sheets permit the viewer a dual vision: one subtractive and the other "natural," causing a reaction of complementary color vision in the eye. When the viewer is showered by yellow color, the interstices appear blue; but if the shower of color is green, the interstices are red (plate 68). This experiment is connected with the idea that the starting point of all culture has been a primary event, a simple situation that immediately unleashes a whole system of thought, mythology, and so on. As very simple situations of elementary elements

9–23. Enclosed transparent color booths by Carlos Cruz-Diez are situated in city spaces for awareness and use by the public. (Drawing by Richard Rochon, based on photo courtesy of Carlos Cruz-Diez)

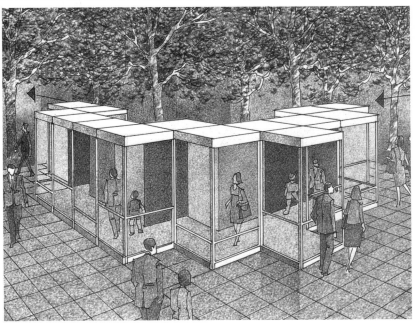

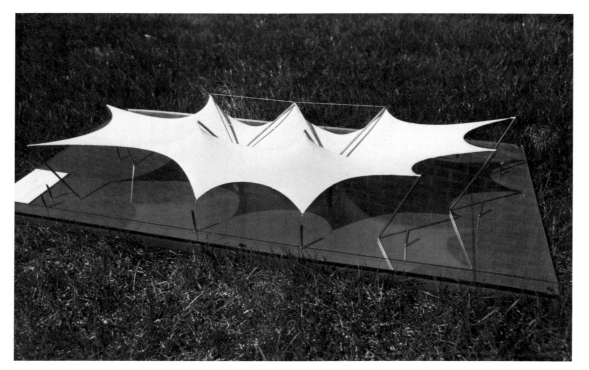

9-24. Canopy model made from swimwear fabric and aluminum for Herman Miller Inc., by Kent Hubbell, Chrysalis Corp. (Courtesy of Chrysalis Corp.)

9-25. Installation view of acrylic canvas canopy for Herman Miller Inc., by Kent Hubbell, Chrysalis Corp. (Courtesy of Chrysalis Corp.)

unsupported by an aesthetic idea or traditional artistic form, they can lead to new ideas and interpretations of chromatic perception.

TENSILE STRUCTURES

A knowledge of shaping fabric, combined with an understanding of basic structural principles, work together in the plan and design of stressed fabric structures. Kent Hubbell, president of Chrysalis in Ann Arbor, Michigan and professor of architecture at the University of Michigan, has been involved in the design and construction of tensile structures throughout his professional career. With a background in architectural principles and an awareness of what is possible, the applications of this form of design are almost unlimited.

9-26. A bright splash of color in a vinyl-coated nylon canopy for Kennedy Square, Detroit, Michigan by Kent Hubbell, Chrysalis Corp. (Courtesy of Chrysalis Corp.)

9-27. Overview of canopy design for Kennedy Square. (Courtesy of Chrysalis Corp.)

Tensile structures enable the designer to create spaces for both short-duration events and for permanent installations. The broad appeal of enclosing structures for short-term public events has resulted in many successful projects in major cities across the country for Chrysalis.

In Zeeland, Michigan, Herman Miller Inc. required an outdoor canopy as a staff lounge during the summer months. A temporary structure in aluminum and fabric was designed so that each tubular support could be anchored to permanent "collars" in the ground and the entire structure erected in half a working day (figs. 9–24 and 9–25). In the fall, the aluminum tubing supports and fabric are dismantled and packed away for storage until the following season.

A larger design for Kennedy Square in Detroit, Michigan, shown in plate 69, also serves as an announcement of spring and as an overhead shelter for public events during the summer months (figs. 9–26 and 9–27). For the Three Rivers Arts Festival in

9-28. Inflated shelter made from vinyl-coated nylon for the Three Rivers Arts Festival, Pittsburgh, Pennsylvania, viewed from offices above. (Courtesy of Kent Hubbell, Chrysalis Corp.)

9-29. View of the shelter for Three Rivers Arts Festival at night. (Courtesy of Chrysalis Corp.)

Pittsburgh, Pennsylvania a bright yellow inflated shelter announces the beginning of the festival and serves as an enclosure for concerts and recitals during the period of the summer fair. The structure is also supported by an interior steel safety frame that together with the inflated shell can be erected within a working day (figs. 9-28 and 9-29).

Chrysalis has also designed permanent forms of stressed fabric structures for use as outdoor shelters and as fabric roof enclosures for buildings. The group's project for the revitalization of the Baltimore Inner Harbor involved the design of three canopies to cover a series of bridges linking the activities of the inner harbor and identifying circulation throughout the extreme ends of the harbor. Shown in figures 9-30, 9-31, and 9-32 are the plan,

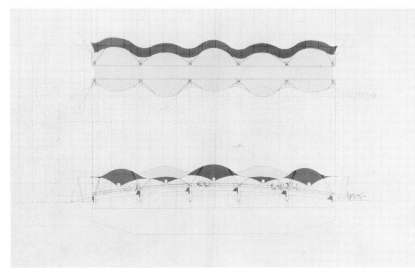

9–30. Plan drawing of bridge canopies for the Baltimore Inner Harbor revitalization project for Charles Center Inner Harbor Management Inc. (Courtesy of Chrysalis Corp.)

9–31. Study model for bridge canopy made of polyester fabric, metal, and wood. (Courtesy of Chrysalis Corp.)

9–32. Installation of bridge canopy for Baltimore Inner Harbor revitalization project. (Courtesy of Chrysalis Corp.)

model study, and the completed design for one of three similar canopies. A vinyl-coated polyester fabric is used along with marine hardware to create an open form in the completed design that provides shelter and also allows views out into the harbor areas.

One of the largest projects attempted to date is the enclosure of the roof of the Comprehensive Health Services of Detroit, Inc. Building within a fabric structure. In this project the owner wanted a thematic building for health services that also would contrast with neighboring building forms and utilize a sophisticated and highly technological building design. The planning model developed for the roof enclosure utilizes acrylic sheet and fabric to suggest a light-filled interior space and did not need

9–33. Project model for Comprehensive Health Services of Detroit, Inc. made of acrylic sheet and polyester fabric. Project Architects: Smith, Hinchman and Grylls Associates Inc. Structural Consultant: Robert Darvas Associates. Fabric Structure Technical Consultants: Chrysalis Corp., Ann Arbor. (Courtesy of Chrysalis Corp.)

to be modified in the final project (fig. 9–33). Several skylights are located at the top of the model and one is above the entrance drive extending to the right (fig. 9–34). In the completed building, a teflon-coated fiberglass fabric with interior insulation and liner were used for the roof, with steel columns supporting the glass skylights. Over the entrance drive, the same fabric, without its insulating liner, is used for a translucent effect, admitting 8 to 15 percent daylight (figs. 9–35 and 9–36).

In all Hubbell's projects, an analysis of structural systems and the qualities of interior light play a major role in the design process. The broad application of fabric structures in architecture is yet to be fully realized. Much of the work presently being done by architects like Kent Hubbell, however, is an effort to create a formal vocabulary, adding to the array of means at the architect's disposal.

DOME STRUCTURES

The multifaceted "dome structures" in figures 9–37 to 9–40 were created by Ernest R. Schaefer of Wayland, Massachusetts. He has been an inventor, engineer, and sculptor, among other occupations in an energetic career. All the models were in-

9-34. Plan view of project model for the Comprehensive Health Services of Detroit, Inc. (Courtesy of Chrysalis Corp.)

9-36. View of steel supporting columns for the entrance canopy of the Comprehensive Health Services of Detroit, Inc. (Courtesy of Chrysalis Corp.)

9-35. View of canopy installed over the entrance drive to the Comprehensive Health Services of Detroit, Inc. (Courtesy of Chrysalis, Corp.)

itially created with Strathmore 2-ply paper (figs. 9–37, 9–38, and 9–39). Beyond their beauty as intricate paper forms and studies in mass, they have a further use as building structures. Writing about *Dome #2* (fig. 9–40), Mr. Schaefer explains that, "every unit is made of wax-coated fiberboard cut to the same pattern. This dome supports steel rods which fit through slits in the fiberboard while concrete is sprayed over the dome in a method called gunite. The outside is then smoothed and when the wax-coated forms are removed from the inside of the structure, an acoustical surface remains in reverse-molded concrete. The steel rods are for reinforcement with the concrete." *Dome #2* spans up to 250 feet and can withstand a 150-mile-per-hour wind and snow load. The process of erection is relatively easy and does not require scaffolding. Each of the units overlap, which prevents water from getting into the structure. Commenting on the simplicity of their construction, Schaefer states, "There is no hardware or gluing or stapling of any kind in my structures; they are completely self-supporting." In all Schaefer's structures, the exploration of both aesthetic and practical issues are evident. His work has been included in major exhibitions, and he is often invited to speak about dome structures at schools of design.

SPACESHIP EARTH AT EPCOT CENTER

The Walt Disney Organization has long been famous for its highly original and innovative work in design. In Florida's Epcot Center, the Experimental Prototype Community of Tomorrow reaches a new plateau for Disney in utilizing the most advanced concepts and technologies available. Built in cooperation with private industry and the advice of experts from around the world, it is a permanent world's fair with two major elements: Future World, a prophetic "community of tomorrow" and World Showcase, an enduring "community of nations." Each of the pavilions in Future World presents its own highly original topic, exploring an issue of vital interest to the future of humanity. In Spaceship Earth the story of communications is told in a ride that spirals through the interior of the globe and encompasses thousands of years, ending in a glimpse of the future. Similarly, insights into the past, present, and future of energy, agriculture, life-styles, the seas, transportation, and technology are all given form in separate pavilions using the imaginative Disney blend of special ef-

9–37. Dome structure made from Strathmore two-ply paper by Ernest R. Schaefer. (Courtesy of the artist)

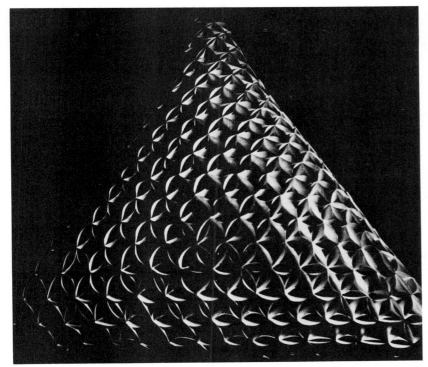

9–38. Triangular structure by Ernest R. Schaefer. (Courtesy of the artist)

9–39. Unit forms in the structures by Ernest R. Schaefer are ordered in a repetitive sequence with gradation in size and shape. (Courtesy of the artist)

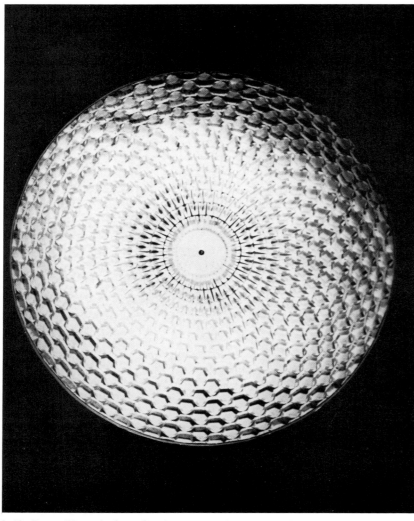

9-40. Dome #2 made from Strathmore two-ply paper by Ernest R. Schaefer. (Courtesy of the artist)

9-41. Spaceship Earth looms 18 stories above ground at Epcot Center reflecting views from the shining facets of its exterior "skin." (Photo © 1982 Walt Disney Productions)

9-42. Solutions to the engineering problems of Spaceship Earth were solved on a carefully designed model of a geodesic sphere. (Photo © 1982 Walt Disney Productions)

fects, film, animation, performers, inventive displays, and the Disney Audio-Animatronics—three-dimensional characters with programmed voices and movements.

Spaceship Earth (fig. 9–41) is the world's largest geodesic sphere. Early in the planning phases for Epcot Center, the original concept of a domed pavilion was replaced by a bolder vision, 180 feet in diameter, rising 18 stories high. As can be seen by visitors approaching the park, it dominates the landscape for miles around with an outside skin of aluminum that reflects diffuse images in its surroundings during the day and the sparkle and illumination of colored light at night from lamps mounted on the rooftops of surrounding pavilions.

Many of the problems in the construction phase arose from the choice of a sphere instead of a dome, an idea which had never been tried (fig. 9–42). The original concept began with plans for creating a highly dramatic entrance from the bottom of the sphere (rather than from the side), which would give visitors the sensation of moving upward into Spaceship Earth. Through a swirl of fog, light, and projected images, visitors begin a trip in a "time machine"—an open train of two vehicles, four persons to a vehicle. Throughout all the pavilions at Epcot Center almost every type of lighting, light source, and method of lighting control is displayed. Inside the pavilions an enormous amount of theatrical or special lighting is used for live shows, animated Audio-Animatronics scenes, and rides. There is also general illumination, maintenance lighting, and display, restaurant, merchandising, exit, and emergency lighting. Exterior lighting includes roadway, walkway, foliage, and tree lighting, pool and underwater fountain lighting, special parade lighting, and dramatic illumination for building exteriors.

The purpose of exterior lighting at Epcot Center is not only to provide necessary levels of illumination for the movement of people but to enhance the aesthetic values of the buildings and to create an overall mood. Spaceship Earth—an enormous freestanding sphere encircled by a monorail—was a difficult task in this respect. Lighting was made even more complicated by the fact that visitors walk or ride completely around the buildings on many different levels, thus producing multiple sight lines and making it somewhat difficult for designers to conceal fixtures and prevent direct viewing of bright, glaring light. A large part of the solution to the problem of lighting the building dramatically with unseen light sources was found in a completely new light source never before used in the United States (although it had previously been introduced in Europe). Known as compact-source iodide (CSI), this 1000-watt HID (High Intensity Discharge) floodlight uses a new metal-halide lamp about the size of a walnut. Seventy 1000-watt compact-source iodide lamps from as far away as 320 feet behave almost like point light sources, making the beam easy to control. The result is approximately 15 to 20 footcandles of light on the sphere's eye-catching surface and the imaginative use of colored light to form a color run across the exterior of the world's largest sphere (plate 70).

10 Expressive Dimensions

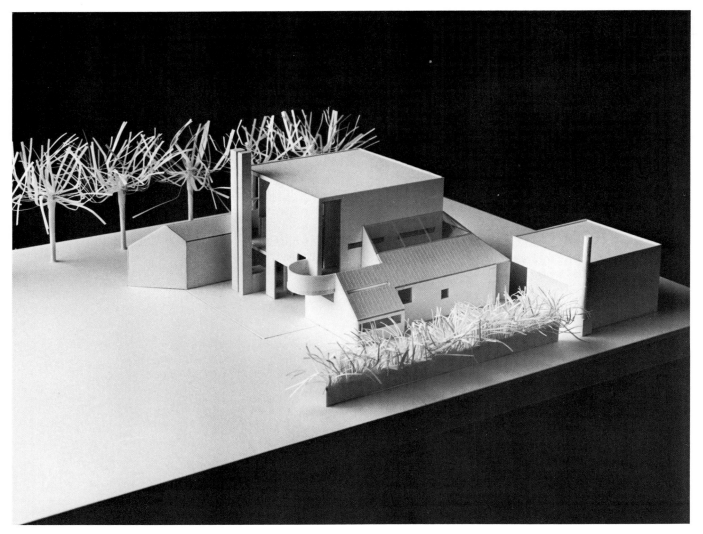

10-1. Retreat House. (Courtesy of Mitchell/Giurgola Architects, photo by Rollin R. LaFrance)

A current concern of designers is finding new ways of shaping, coming to terms with, and understanding the environment. Although the artists and designers included in this book represent a diversity of practices, all of them feel that a color design of good quality not only sets off shapes to their best advantage but also provides a better understanding and access to form as well as arouses enthusiasm.

Chapter 10 includes a summary of broad directions taken by various professionals. Through divergent approaches to fulfilling a client's goal, pursuing artistic purposes, and expressing unique sensitivities to surface, form, and space these designers all seek expression through the careful organization of the elements and principles of design.

SIMPLICITY IN VOLUME

The simplicity and understated elegance of a well-fashioned design can be communicated in the basic materials of paper, wood, and cardboard. The models on pages 217 to 237 were designed by Mitchell/Giurgola Architects of Philadelphia and New York. In addition to their superb execution, the models all express basic patterns that suggest the materials to be used in construction.

The model for Retreat House is constructed from Strathmore paper, scored for the roof details and rolled, cut, and curled for the trees (fig. 10-1). The models for White Marsh Library and the Acadia National Park Headquarters Building are both made with chipboard. The processes for their construction include detailing with scored lines and basswood and creating roof details from laminations of chipboard slices (figs. 10-2, 10-3, and 10-4). In the project model for the National Headquarters Building of the American Institute of Architects, Washington, D.C., a highly refined appearance is achieved by using chipboard laminated with a teak veneer for the building and lead for the trees (fig. 10-5). The presentation model for the Boston 5 Cent Savings Bank takes on a warm appearance from the use of a fine-grain cork veneer applied to chipboard wrapped around basswood (also used for the church steeple adjacent to the bank building). The trees in this model were formed from braided wire, unraveled and shaped to suggest the trunk and limbs (fig. 10-6).

The model project for The University Museum Academic

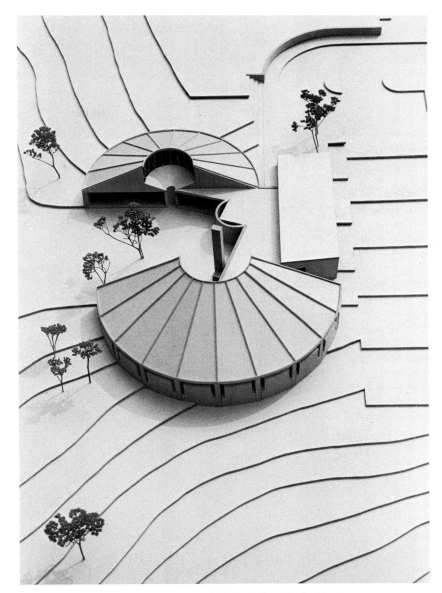

10-2. White Marsh Library. (Courtesy of Mitchell/Giurgola Architects, photo by Rollin R. LaFrance)

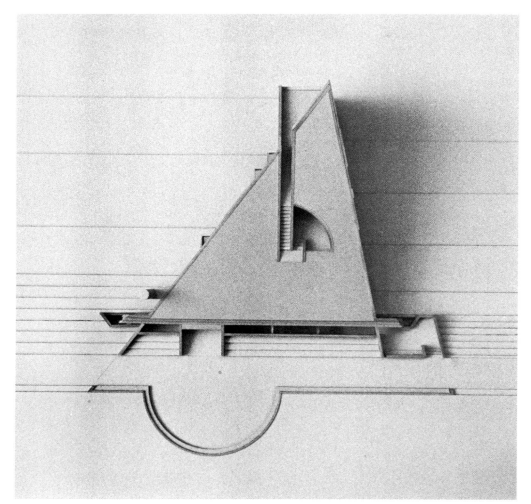

10-3. Acadia National Park Headquarters Building. Plan view. (Courtesy of Mitchell/Giurgola Architects, photo by Rollin R. La-France)

Wing of the University of Pennsylvania, in Philadelphia (plate 71), is also designed largely from paper and cardboard products representing the basic surfaces of building materials and natural textures. The models of the interior courtyards use chipboard with laminated paper, trimmed by scalpel, with the tiled roof simulated in corrugated paper. All of these models use additional details in acrylic sheeting for window treatments, and scaled trees and figures are used sparingly to reflect concern for an overall subtle yet direct statement of form.

SCULPTURAL SPACE

Minuro Yamasaki and Associates, Inc. of Troy, Michigan have long practiced the use of model design as integral to the

10-4. Acadia National Park Headquarters Building. Elevation. (Courtesy of Mitchell/Giurgola Architects, photo by Rollin R. La-France)

overall planning processes of architectural design. In testing and developing concepts of form in three-dimensional space, a well-equipped studio for making models and an experienced staff function together with Yamasaki and specialists from all areas of design development.

The staff's skill and expertise with methods of handling

materials and incorporating them into three-dimensional forms have played a significant role in the reputation of the office as a leader in the design professions. An example of their work is shown in the model and completed project for the North Shore Congregation Israel, Glencoe, Illinois, in figures 10-7 and 10-8. A comparison of the model and finished project is interesting, not

10–5. National Headquarters Building of the American Institute of Architects. (Courtesy of Mitchell/Giurgola Architects, photo by Rollin R. LaFrance)

10–6. Boston 5 Cent Savings Bank. (Courtesy of Mitchell/Giurgola Architects, photo by Rollin R. LaFrance)

10-7. Interior view of the model for the North Shore Congregation Israel. (Courtesy of Minoru Yamasaki and Associates, Inc., photo by Balthazar Korab)

only because the two are so similar but especially because the scaled sculptural elements in the model are closely replicated in the completed project.

One such designer responsible for many sculptural elements in the North Shore Congregation Israel project is Lee Dusell, professor of art at Syracuse University. In developing models of the bimah (platform); lecterns to the left and right on the bimah for reading the Torah; the candelabrum; and the arc, he used a multitude of materials and methods. The lecterns are carved from wood and attached to sculptural pediments made from reinforced plastics (polyester resin molded in plaster casts).

The Hebrew inscription on the back wall was photoengraved and separately adhered. The arc encasement for the Torah was formed in brass along with the candelabrum to its left. The floor and seating in the model were made with colored flocking to represent carpeting and cardboard for the rows of seating.

Several of these elements were also created as full-scale sculptural refinements for the final installation in the completed project. In the model and the completed project the eternal light was completely handcrafted. Through his skills with wood and metal and through his constant search for a final form that expresses the essence of a space simply and elegantly, Dusell ex-

10–8. Interior view of completed synagogue of the North Shore Congregation Israel, Glencoe, Illinois. (Courtesy of Minoru Yamasaki and Associates, Inc., photo by Balthazar Korab)

emplifies the best traditions of the contemporary designer's role in the evolution of an architectural space. His sculptural/design collaborations with Yamasaki and Associates, Inc. can be seen in many other projects throughout the world in which careful planning in model forms has resulted in the successful culmination of the architect's and the client's vision.

DESIGN FOR A "METAPHORICAL GARDEN"

The School-House Project, the conversion of a school building into condominiums by Graham Gund Associates, Inc. of Cambridge, Massachusetts, provides an example of the color transformation of an interior lobby space into what Gund calls a "metaphorical garden."

The rich assemblage of color and form intended to allude to nature is intuitively structured through the juxtaposition of pastel hues and linear and planar elements such as handrails, trellises, posts, beams, and sculpted wall segments in a light-filled space (fig. 10–9).

The lobby/garden is entered through a glass-enclosed trellis that serves as the vestibule wall. Plate 72 illustrates the view of the lobby "garden," which confronts visitors directly

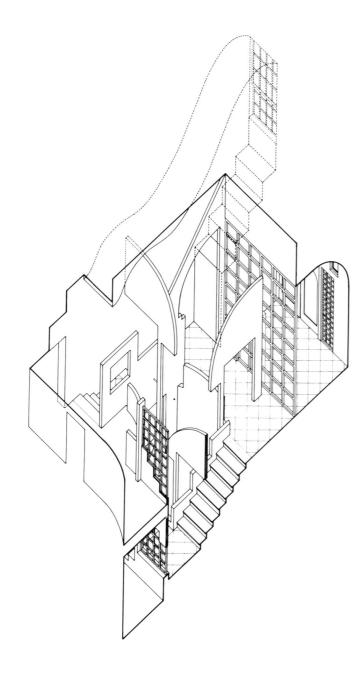

10-9. Axonometric drawing of interior lobby for the School-House Project. (Courtesy of Graham Gund Associates, Inc.)

entering the space. However beautiful, the photograph can only suggest what appears as the full airiness of the three-dimensional space.

Several color schemes in various color keys were tested on the model for their form-defining characteristics and association with a "garden" theme (plate 73). A light-value scheme with warm and cool tertiary hues was eventually chosen to define various linear and planar elements in the composition. The model, based on a scale of 1″ = 1′-0″, measures 15″ × 3′-0″ in the plan drawing. The model itself is made from foam board and balsa wood, which was primed and painted with acrylic paint. Detailing in the model consists of metal trim for the light fixtures, metal solder for the handrails, and a painted floor to replicate the actual granite surface in the lobby.

TRANSITIONAL SPACES IN COLOR AND LIGHT

Our enjoyment of carefully planned transitional links between interior spaces is heightened by the stimulation of self-awareness and the arousal of interest in the environment. In the Detroit Science Center, William Kessler and Associates of Detroit, Michigan, have designed escalator wells that draw the visitor through a shaftlike space emitting a sequence of pulsating colored light. The concept for lighting, initially tested in models (fig. 10-10), incorporates cycling devices that illuminate consecutive segments of the space consistent with the pace and direction of movement of the escalator. One's perception is influenced by the enveloping qualities and intervals of consecutive

10-10. Interior study model of escalators for the Detroit Science Center, Detroit, Michigan. (Courtesy of William Kessler and Associates, Inc.)

colored illumination, which for a few minutes appear to suspend time in an expansive atmosphere of color, light, and space (plate 74 and figs. 10–11A to 10–11C).

In the Wayne State University Health Care Institute and Detroit Receiving Hospital, created by William Kessler's office, the feeling of moving through a closed space is anticipated with an innovative design for indirect lighting and transitional views to the exterior environment. A T-shaped configuration of tunnels, together approximately 400 feet long, connect the major wings of the complex. The tunnels were designed with recessed floor lighting at the base of the interior walls to naturally illuminate their interior surfaces (figs. 10–12A–B). In practice, the plan of indirect lighting serves those nonambulatory patients who are often confronted with direct light from overhead fixtures. At an intersection formed by two of the tunnels, a periscope with mirrored glass was installed above a ceiling skylight to reflect exterior views of the surrounding landscape at grade level for patients and visitors. This project has not only been given a National Honor Award by

A   B   C

10–11A–C. Three consecutive views of the escalators in the Detroit Science Center, Detroit Michigan. (Courtesy of William Kessler and Associates, Inc., photos by Balthazar Korab)

the American Institute of Architects but has also received international attention by winning the first International Color Design Prize 1980/81, sponsored by the Stuttgart Design Center, Baden-Württemberg Land Office of Commerce in Stuttgart, Germany (plates 75 and 76).

PRISM SKYLIGHT SCULPTURE

Light is one of the most intangible subjects for art. Its impact, however, can be as profound as it has been at Chartres Cathedral or in the color-saturated work of the late nineteenth-century French impressionist painters. In the pure color of contemporary designer Charles Ross's prisms, the element of colored light on a human scale leads to the richest of fantasies, overwhelming and intense.

Skylight prisms for the Yeshiva Porat Joseph (a residential college for rabbinical studies), in Jerusalem, Israel, illustrates a fascinating application of the concept. The interior walls of the yeshiva's synagogue are cylindrical shapes capped with skylights, designed by the project architect Moshe Safdie and Asso-

10-12A-B. Wayne State University Health Care Institute and Detroit Receiving Hospital, Detroit, Michigan. (Courtesy of William Kessler and Associates, Inc.)

10–13. View of full-scale model being tested outdoors. (Courtesy of
Charles Ross)

ciates Inc., of Boston, Massachusetts, who in turn commissioned Charles Ross, originator of large-scale prism sculpture, to design prisms to be installed under each skylight. In each of Ross's prism sculptures, tests are carried out on models by means of a machine that simulates the motion of any latitude through any day and season. Each prism is individually placed in the model to carry color through the space in a particular way for a particular season. Experiments for the yeshiva prisms were carried out on both a one-quarter-inch scale model and a full-size mock-up to test whether colored light could overpower sunlight in the interior spaces (figs. 10-13, 10-14, and 10-15). Although the yeshiva is still under construction, the sensitive qualities of artist and architect in collaboration hold promise for a deeply moving experience—one that considers the spiritual expectations of students, faculty, and visitors in a most natural form (plate 77).

10-15. Interior view of ¼" scale study model being tested with prisms. (Courtesy of Charles Ross with Moshe Safdie and Associates, Inc., photo by Joyce P. Schwartz Ltd.)

10-14. Interior view of full-scale test model with canvas liner. (Courtesy of Charles Ross, photo by Joyce P. Schwartz Ltd.)

The Spectrum Building in Denver, Colorado borrows its name from the prism sculpture by Charles Ross at the top of its atrium. In this piece Ross also used a model to aid him in the process of designing a pattern for the angular positioning of the prisms (figs. 10-16 and 10-17). The sides of the prisms are 14 inches wide by 8 feet long, and are mounted 135 feet above the floor. Groups of prisms are focused for different seasons and times of day to create evolving patterns of color that are propelled through space by the rotation of the earth. The fusions of light and color with various surfaces within the atrium space generates ex-citement that comes from confronting a natural event. The art gives the viewer a sense of personal connection to the substance of light, which is the work's real contribution to the architectural environment (plates 78 and 79). The evolving pattern and shape of the spectra through time becomes the work of art.

METAPHORS FOR VOLUME AND ENCLOSURE

Several projects from recent graduate students of the Cranbrook Academy of Art in Bloomfield Hills, Michigan, under

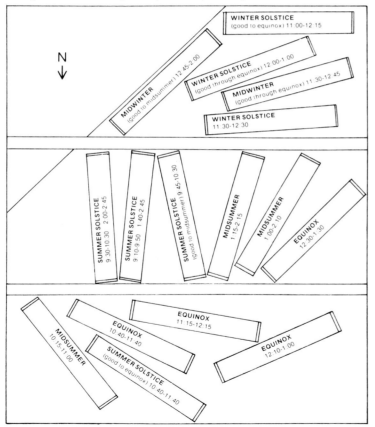

10-16. Groups of prisms are focused for different seasons and times of day to create evolving color patterns. (Courtesy of Charles Ross)

10-17. Ceiling view of prisms suspended beneath the skylights in the atrium of the Spectrum Building, Denver, Colorado. (Courtesy of Charles Ross, photo by Joyce P. Schwartz Ltd.)

the direction of Daniel Libeskind, chairman of the department of architecture, are included as a survey of the evolution of concepts of volume and enclosure. The point of departure for each of these student works is the varied undergraduate and professional architecture training Cranbrook students bring with them. Since classical times, the study of architecture has embodied the roots and concepts of the fine arts, the humanities, and the sciences, with a view toward enriching human life. If each of the following examples of student work share a common belief about architecture, it is that architecture deals with the poetry of place and the myth of dwelling. To emancipate the qualities of architectural design is to capture the spontaneity and poetry of both public and private life. In this sense, the students' aims are to discover the rich history of design, aesthetics, and philosophy and to develop original insights into forms of expression that move beyond mere utilitarian purposes or the traditional values of technology. The following statements are from recent graduate thesis projects, illustrated in figures 10–18 to 10–26, of three architecture students from the Cranbrook Academy of Art.

"Nightmare" by Atsuko Hayashi

Everything here is struggling to find the key to surpass the confusions.
The elements are hung in the air, with the grids as a last sanity.
The forms are growing into their own deformations.
The lines are the last ones to linger with their own clarity in space.

"The Transformation of the Straight Line" by Corvova Choy Lee

An analysis of the paintings of Giorgio de Chirico and readings in *Invisible Cities* by Italo Calvino were the beginnings of my first project. In de Chirico's painting, the cut; the metal connections; the crosses; the vanishing perspective lines; and the tilted plane are situated in a particular space—the super-real of the imagination. This is the site for this project. I then built a model of this "City of Dorthea." Entirely made of aluminum, it is the Urban House, the Garden, and ideas of closure having to do with shallow space (the Cinema, and the Frame).

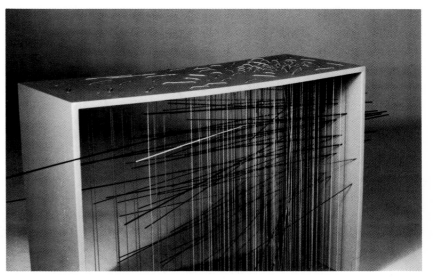

10–18. Model in acrylic sheet, wood, and wire (2″ × 6″ × 6″) by Atsuko Hayashi. (Courtesy of Daniel Libeskind)

10–19. Model in acrylic sheet (6″ × 12″ × 15″) by Atsuko Hayashi. (Courtesy of Daniel Libeskind)

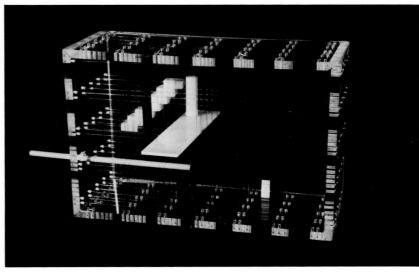

10-20. Model in aluminum (2′ × 2′ × 2′) by Corvova Choy Lee. (Courtesy of Daniel Libeskind)

10-21. Detail of model in figure 10-20 by Corvova Choy Lee.

"The House" by Ben Nicholson

The House reflects that which Man wishes to concern himself with. At best it is also a microcosm of his belief and his relationship to what occurs outside himself.

The Proposed Houses are anthropomorphic, tuned and structured so that they fit upon themselves as a series of wedges; no longer being Stone standing on Stone, but Part wedged between Part, stretching or compressing laterally—without the obvious analogy to gravity. The rooms are both incidental and incorporate.

The Doors are between being a crack for a fly to walk through, and a gaping opening of a deep box.

The Roof is as valid as a lid to a Jam Jar.

The Whole is a composition of resources, and flits in and out of scales, to reveal to the same intensity and purpose of each Act in the House.

The Final House, I propose, having meandered through the tips and vaults of imagination, returns to its original intention of being a place in which to Dwell. By necessity it retains its fireplace, a room to sit in, and a roof.

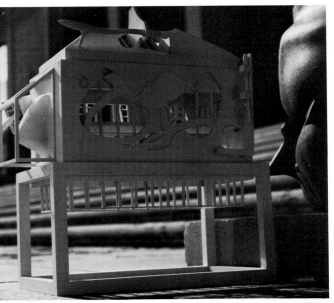

10-23. Grunewald House (side view) by Ben Nicholson. (Courtesy of Daniel Libeskind)

10-24. Grunewald House (rear view) by Ben Nicholson. (Courtesy of Daniel Libeskind)

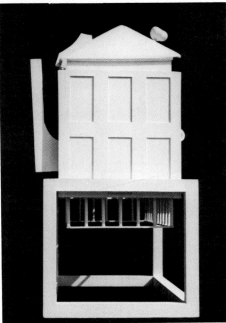

10-22. Model of Grunewald House in painted wood and plaster (9″ × 12″ × 16″) by Ben Nicholson. (Courtesy of Daniel Libeskind)

10-26. Magritte House by Ben Nicholson. Front view from right. (Courtesy of Daniel Libeskind)

10-25. Model of Magritte House in painted wood and plaster (6″ × 8″ × 8″) by Ben Nicholson. Front view from the left. (Courtesy of Daniel Libeskind)

ARTIST'S RESIDENCE/STUDIO

An example of a simplified expression of form and color is found in the collaborative effort between artist David Barr and architect, Laurence Booth of Booth/Hansen and Associates in Chicago, Illinois, in the design and construction of a combined residence/studio for the artist. In this project, the artist wished to unite working and living space, which for him—working in a detached studio space away from his home—had been physically and psychologically separated for many years. Additionally, the villa was to be built by the owner and had to be simple to construct within strict financial limits.

The plan drawing in figure 10-27 shows how the building is divided into two equal parts: a living space and a studio space. The model in figures 10-28A–C shows how the expression of this house is achieved by a half pediment combined with an entry porch and rear deck to unify the composition and recall the traditional American house. Color was chosen to create a gentle and pleasant addition to the flat landscape. As well as recognizing Barr's structurist work, the expression of the house is based in the more general tradition of the American gentleman farmer who lived on the land in buildings that alluded to an earlier civilization (for example, Jefferson at Monticello) (plates 80 and 81).

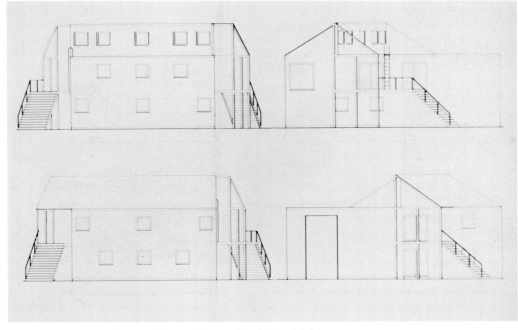

10-27. Plan drawing for the Barr residence Northville, Michigan. (Courtesy of Laurence Booth, Booth/Hansen and Associates)

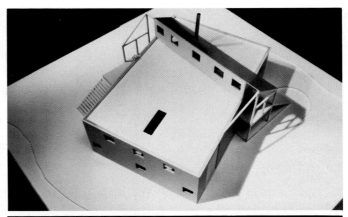

10-28A-C. Project model for the Barr residence. (Courtesy of Laurence Booth, Booth/Hansen and Associates)

WONDER WALL

Wonder Wall, a fanciful center colonnade, 2,300 feet long, stretching across the grounds of the 1984 Louisiana World Exposition, is a beautiful illustration of color planning and metaphor. The many media references to its appearance—"river of imagination," "a parade frozen in time," "the Great Wall of China designed by the Marx Brothers," or even "a 2,300-foot temper tantrum"—have arisen from the excitement being generated for the project, which sprang from the original theme for the exposition, "Rivers of the World: Fresh Water as a Source of Life."

The theme of the exposition generated ideas for the wall

as an "urban river," a fluid, magical procession of color, light, and form. Because water was prominent in the theme, fountains were planned to occur every 24 feet along the path of the wall and serve as public spaces for relaxation. A reference to the *spina,* the barrier wall dividing an ancient Roman circus lengthwise about which the chariot racers turned, is found in the placement of the wall in the center of a wide pedestrian street that extends half a mile from the main entrance of the exposition, passing the New Convention Center to a secondary entrance at the opposite end of the exposition site (figs. 10–29 and 10–30).

The project architects for Wonder Wall, William Turnbull and Charles Moore, enlisted the support of several talented designers and artists for the various phases of preliminary design, model construction, color planning, sculptural details, and lighting. The completed wall is about half a mile long, 15 feet wide, and between 15 and 40 feet high, altering in elevation along its path. The design and construction of the model—at 12 feet long and 2½ feet wide in a scale of ½″ = 1′-0″—by Leonard Salvato, Arthur Anderson, and Rae Kinoshito of Perez Associates in New Orleans is something of a feat in itself (figs. 10–31 and 10–32).

A

B

C

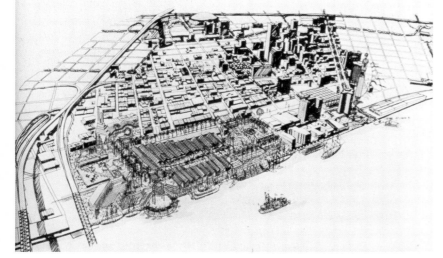

10-30. Early model schemes of Wonder Wall in paper and cardboard. (Courtesy of Charles Moore and William Turnbull with Perez Associates, Architects)

10-29. View of the site for the 1984 Louisiana World Exposition in New Orleans, Louisiana. (Courtesy of Charles Moore and William Turnbull with Perez Associates, Architects)

10–31. Presentation model of Wonder Wall represents a 280-foot section (approximately one tenth) of the 2,300-foot structure on a scale of ½″ = 1′–0″. (Courtesy of Charles Moore and William Turnbull with Perez Associates, Architects, photo © Alan Karchmer)

10–32. Detail of presentation model of Wonder Wall. (Courtesy of Charles Moore and William Turnbull with Perez Associates, Architects, photo © Alan Karchmer)

The materials used for the model include Masonite supported by a wooden frame for the base, perforated steel sheet metal for the main sections of the wall, and plastic scaffolding to represent the final steel scaffolding support system. Model details such as palm trees, people, and lighting were purchased from hobby shops. Miniature light bulbs, called grain-of-wheat bulbs, simulate the incandescent fixtures used in the final project and silhouette the arches, windows, and doorways during the evening hours. Four-ply Strathmore paper is used as a support for color applications and was primed, painted, and adhered to the forms and surfaces at the base of the model. The perforated steel sections of the wall, too difficult to paint with a brush, were painted with sponges that dabbed the color around the perforated openings to prevent dripping and running.

Kent Bloomer, professor of architecture at Yale University, was enlisted as a consultant for the project and commissioned to make sculptural busts of historic figures to be located along various portions of the wall. These were made in a model scale from baby dolls with the hair removed, which were cast in plaster and then painted. An alligator, an animal indigenous to the region, was fashioned by sculptor Joy Wulke from bean bags and covered in nylon, eventually to be made to full size with sandbags sprayed with plastic resin and painted. Many other symbolic references to the region, its lore, history, and the theme of the exposition were incorporated into the wall to create a rich and festive mosaic of images and spaces that could be explored along the ground level (figs. 10-33 to 10-35).

Bloomer's idea of "zones" to represent the heavens, the earth, and the underworld formed the basis for a color palette that would orchestrate the wall's form with pronounced changes in color temperature in a horizontal direction and in changes in color

10-33A-B. Views of Wonder Wall under construction at the Louisiana World Exposition, New Orleans, Louisiana. (Courtesy of The Louisiana World Exposition, Inc.)

10-34A-C. Color "zones" for Wonder Wall were created in drawings done with marker, which corresponded to colored papers and later matched manufacturer's paints. Approximately 45 colors were chosen for the overall scheme. (Courtesy of Charles Moore and William Turnbull with Perez Associates, Architects)

238

key in a vertical direction. Tina Beebe, color consultant for Moore, Ruble, Yudell, Architects, was enlisted to plan color for the zones in several directions (plates 82 and 83). Horizontally, the first story is of the underworld, a murky region where the alligators congregate. The second story is of the temporal world—recognizable, but still partly given to the surreal. Fantasy takes flight on the top story—light and airy, ephemeral and pastel.

"Neighborhoods" were also planned along the wall, reinforced by color. A particular combination of color was used in one area to establish a color key and temperature range and was then changed to a different climate of color—in the words of Josef Albers, "to a cold or warm world." At the main entrance, the wall begins in a sedate color scheme. As one moves further along toward the amusement park, however (where the alligators climb out of the swamp and onto the wall), the wall is transformed into a fantasy larger than life, and the alligators take on appropriately fantastic pink, green, and purple coloring.

10-35. Color designs were fine-tuned at the site to confirm the planning of the color key and color temperature on the wall. (Courtesy of Charles Moore and William Turnbull with Perez Associates, Architects)

10-34A-C *continued.*

Appendix 1:

Munsell Notation for Bainbridge Alphamat and Crescent Museum Rag Mat Boards

BAINBRIDGE ALPHAMAT

Gray Values (warm and cool)
8517   N1
8518   N2.5
8515   N4.5
8548   N7.5   7.5YR 3/2
8558   N5.25   N5
8543   N6   N5.75   10YR 6/1
8544   N6
8522   N7.5   7.5YR 7/2
8523   N8
8555   N7
8505   N7.5
8511   N8.75   N8.5
8519   N9.25
8559   N8.75
8520   N9.25   N9

Warm Tertiaries
8521   5Y 9/2
8547   7.5YR 9/2
8536   10YR 9/2
8509   5Y 9/2   5Y 8.5/2
8535   2.5Y 8.5/4
8525   10YR 8/4   10YR 8/2
8503   2.5Y 8/2
8546   5Y 8/2
8560   10YR 7/4
8514   2.5YR 6/2

8537   10YR 6/2
8508   10YR 6/4
8501   2.5YR 8/6
8553   10YR 6/8
8557   7.5YR 5/8
8532   7.5YR 5/6
8550   5YR 6/4
8556   5YR 6/2   5YR 6/1
8530   2.5YR 5/6
8531   5YR 5/6   5YR 4/6
8538   7.5YR 5/4
8512   5YR 4/4   5YR 3/4
8507   10YR 4/2
8539   5YR 3/4   5YR 2/4
8506   2.5YR 2/2
8546   2.5YR 5/4
8527   10R 4/6

Reds and Oranges
8554   7.5R 5/10
8529   7.5R 5/4
8528   5R 4/8
8552   5R 4/10

Greens and Blues
8502   10Y 8/1   10Y 7/1
8526   5PB 3/2
8551   2.5BG 5/2

8540   10GY 3/2
8524   5GY 4/4
8549   2.5GY 5/6
8516   5GY 6/4   5GY 6/2
8513   10Y 8/2
8534   7.5B 5/4

8541   10B 4/8
8533   2.5PB 6/4
8542   10B 7/4
8510   10B 6/1
8504   5PB 9/1

CRESCENT MUSEUM RAG MAT

Warm and Cool Grays
1577   N2.5
1576   N3.5
1575   10RP 6/1   10RP 5/1
1574   5PB 8/1   5PB 7/1
1573   N8   N7.75
1572   N8.75   N8.5
1571   N9.25

Warm Tertiaries
1570   5Y 9/2   2.5Y 9/2
1569   10YR 9/4
1568   2.5Y 7/2   2.5Y 6/2
1567   10YR 7/4
1566   10YR 8/4   10YR 8/2
1565   10YR 6/4
1564   7.5YR 5/4
1563   5YR 4/4   5YR 3/4
1562   2.5YR 2/2

1561   2.5Y 3/4
1560   2.5YR 6/6   2.5YR 5/6
1559   2.5YR 4/8

Red
1558   5R 5/8   5R 4/8

Yellow
1557   2.5Y 8.5/6   2.5Y 8/6

Greens and Blues
1556   10Y 6/4   10Y 5/4
1555   2.5GY 5/2   2.5GY 4/2
1554   2.5G 3/2
1553   5B 6/1   5B 5/1
1552   5PB 6/6   2.5PB 6/6
1551   2.5 PB 5/6
1550   7.5PB 3/4   7.5PB 2/4

Appendix 2:

List of Manufacturers

Grateful acknowledgment is made to the following manufacturers who have generously given support and product information regarding those materials mentioned in this book.

Ain Plastics Company, 21270 West 8 Mile Road, Southfield, MI 48075

Alvin & Company, Box 188, Winsor, CT 06095

Bee Paper Company, 100 Eighth Street, Box 1016, Passaic, NJ 07055

Beinfang Paper Products (A division of Hunt Manufacturing Company), 1405 Locust Street, Philadelphia, PA 19102

Berol USA, Danbury, CT 06810

Binney & Smith Company, 1100 Church Lane, Box 431, Easton, PA 18042

Bordon, Inc., 180 East Broad Street, Columbus, OH 43215

Bourges Color Corporation, 20 Waterside Plaza, New York, NY 10010

Cello-Tak Manufacturing, Inc., 35 Alabama Avenue, Island Park, NY 11448

Charles T. Bainbridge's and Sons, Inc., 50 Northfield Avenue, Edison, NJ 08817

Chartpak, 1 River Road, Leeds, MA 01053

Chroma Acrylics Pty., Ltd., 615 Deer Road, Cherry Hill, NJ 08034

Color-Aid Corporation, 116 East 27th Street, New York, NY 10016

Color-View Company, 6 North Pearl, Port Chester, NY 10573

Crescent Cardboard Company, 100 W. Willow Road, Box X-D, Wheeling, IL 60090

C-Thru Ruler Company, 6 Britton Drive, Bloomfield, CT 06002

DMI Industries, 1201 East Whitcomb Avenue, Madison Heights, MI 48071

Eastman Kodak Company, Graphics Markets Division, 343 State Street, Rochester, NY 14650

Eberhard Faber Inc., Crestwood, Wilkes-Barre, PA 18773

E.I. Dupont De Nemours & Company, Box 89, Circleville, OH 43113

Faber-Castell Corporation, 41 Dickerson Street, Newark, NJ 07107

General Electric Company and General Electric Lighting Business Group, Nela Park, Cleveland, OH 44112

Georgia-Pacific Corporation, 290 Ferry Street, Newark, NJ 07105

Grossman Knowling Company, 26614 Southfield Road, Lathrup Village, MI 48076

Hunt Manufacturing Company, 1405 Locust Street, Philadelphia, PA 19102, importers of Conté Crayons and Pastels

Iddings Paint Division of Rosco Laboratories, Inc., 69 Beacon Street, Boston, MA 02134

J.S. Staedtler Company, Box 65, Elk Grove Village, IL 60007

Kent Adhesive Products Company, 449 Dodge Street, Kent, OH 44240

Koh-I-Noor Rapidograph, Inc., 100 North Street, Bloomsbury, NJ 08804

Letraset Company, 40 Eisenhower Drive, Paramus, NJ 07562

Loctite Corporation, 4450 Cranwood Court, Cleveland, OH 44128

Magic Marker Industries, 467 Calhoun Street, Trenton, NJ 08618

M. Grumbacher, Inc., 460 West 34th Street, New York, NY 10001

Morilla, Inc., 211 Bowers Street, Holyoke, MA 01040

Munsell Color and Educational Materials, Munsell Color, 2441 N. Calvert Street, Baltimore, MD 21218

National Card, Mat and Board Company, 14455 Don Julian Road, P.O. Box 2306, City of Industry, CA 91746

Northwest-Martin Company, 13450 Farminton Road, Livonia, MI 48150

Paasche Airbrush Company, 1909 West Diversey Parkway, Chicago, IL 60614

Pantone, Inc., 55 Knickerbocker Road, Moonachie, NJ 07074

Pentalic Corporation, 132 West 22nd Street, New York, NY 10011

Pentel of America, Ltd., 2715 Columbia Street, Torrance, CA 90503

Presstype, Inc., 194 Veterans Boulevard, Carlstadt, NJ 07072

Primex Plastics Corporation, 1 Raritan Road, Oakland, NJ 07436

Rich Art Color Company, Inc., 109 Graham Lane, Lodi, NJ 08701

Roberts Consolidated Industries, 600 N. Baldwin Park Boulevard, City of Industry, CA 91749

Rohm and Haas Company, Independence Mall West, Philadelphia, PA 19105

Salis International, Inc., 4093 N. 28th Way, Hollywood, FL 33020

Sanford Corporation, 2740 Washington Boulevard, Belwood, IL 60104

Special Papers, Inc., Box 31, West Redding, CT 06896, importers of Canson & Montgolfier of France

Steig Products, Box 19, Lakewood, NJ 08701

Strathmore Paper Company, South Broad Street, Westfield, MA 01085

Tara Materials, Inc., Fredrix Brand, P.O. Box 646m 111 Fredrix Alley, Lawrenceville, GA 30246

3M, 3M Center, Adhesives, Coatings, and Sealer Division, 220–2W, St. Paul, MN 55144

Transilwrap Plastics, 1605 East Avis Drive, Madison Heights, MI 48071

Union Rubber, Inc., 232 Allen Street, Box 1040, Trenton, NJ 08606

Winsor & Newton, Inc., 555 Winsor Drive, Secaucus, NJ 07094

X-Acto, a subsidiary of Hunt Manufacturing Company, Philadelphia, PA 19102

Zipatone, Inc., 150 Fencl Lane, Hillside, IL 60162

Bibliography

Aach, Herb, and Matthaei, Rupprecht. *Goethe's Color Theory.* New York: Van Nostrand Reinhold Company, 1971.

Albers, Josef. *The Interaction of Color.* New Haven, CT: Yale University Press, 1963.

Arnheim, Rudolf. *Art and Visual Perception.* Berkeley, CA: University of California Press, 1954.

Ballinger, Raymond A. *Design with Paper in Art and Graphic Design.* New York: Van Nostrand Reinhold Company, 1982.

Birren, Faber. *Color, Form and Space.* New York: Reinhold Publishing Company, 1961.

Birren, Faber. *Light, Color and Environment,* Rev. ed. New York: Van Nostrand Reinhold Company, 1982.

Birren, Faber. *History of Color in Painting.* New York: Van Nostrand Reinhold Company, 1965.

Birren, Faber. *Principles of Color.* New York: Van Nostrand Reinhold Company, 1965.

Bloomer, Carolyn M. *Principles of Visual Perception.* New York: Van Nostrand Reinhold Company, 1976.

Ching, Francis D. K. *Architecture; Form, Space and Order.* New York: Van Nostrand Reinhold Company, 1979.

Cohen, Arthur A. *The New Art of Color: The Writings of Robert and Sonia Delaunay.* New York: The Viking Press, 1978.

de Sausmarez, Maurice. *Basic Design: The Dynamics of Visual Form.* New York: D. Van Nostrand Company, 1964.

Dondis, Donis A. *A Primer of Visual Literacy.* Cambridge MA: The MIT Press, 1973.

Doyle, Michael E. *Color Drawing.* New York: Van Nostrand Reinhold Company, 1982.

Duttman, M., Schmuck, F., and Uhl, J. *Color in Townscape.* Translated from German by John William Bagriel. San Francisco: W. H. Freeman and Company, 1981.

Ellinger, Richard G. *Color Structure and Design.* New York: Van Nostrand Reinhold Company, 1980.

Escher, M. C. *The World of M. C. Escher.* New York: Harry N. Abrams Publisher, 1971.

Gerritsen, Frans. *Theory and Practice of Color.* New York: Van Nostrand Reinhold Company, 1975.

Gibson, James J. *The Perception of the Visual World.* Cambridge MA: Houghton Mifflin Company, 1950.

Gregory, Richard L. *The Intelligent Eye.* New York: McGraw-Hill Book Company, 1970.

Hohauser, Sanford. *Architectural and Interior Models: Design and Construction.* New York: Van Nostrand Reinhold Company, 1970.

Itten, Johannes. *The Art of Color.* New York: Van Nostrand Reinhold Company, 1973.

Itten, Johannes. *Design and Form: The Basic Course at the Bauhaus and Later.* Rev. ed. New York: Van Nostrand Reinhold Company, 1975.

Itten, Johannes. *The Elements of Color.* New York: Van Nostrand Reinhold Company, 1970.

Janke, Rolf. *Architectural Models.* New York: Architectural Book Publishing Company, 1978.

Jones, Tom Douglas. *The Art of Light and Color.* New York: Van Nostrand Reinhold Company, 1972.

The Josef Albers Foundation and François Bucher. *Despite Straight Lines.* Rev. ed. Cambridge MA: The MIT Press, 1977.

Katz, David. *The World of Colour.* New York: Johnson Reprint Company, 1970.

Koffka, Kurt. *Principles of Gestalt Psychology.* New York: Harbinger Book, Harcourt, Brace and World, 1935.

Kueppers, Harald. *The Basic Law of Color Theory.* New York: Barron's Educational Series, Inc., 1982.

Lam, William M. C. *Perception and Lighting as Formgivers for Architecture.* New York: McGraw-Hill Book Company, 1977.

Libby, William Charles. *Color and the Structural Sense.* Englewood Cliffs, NJ: Prentice-Hall, Inc., 1974.

Libeskind, Daniel. *Between Zero and Infinity.* New York: Rizzoli International Publications, Inc., 1981.

Lighting Business Group, General Electric Company. *Light and Color,* NELA Park, Cleveland, Ohio (TP–119), February 1978.

Minnaert, M. *The Nature of Light and Color in the Open Air.* New York: Dover Publications, Inc., 1954.

Moholy-Nagy, Laszlo. *Vision in Motion.* Chicago: Hillison and Etten Company, 1947.

Munsell, A. H. *A Grammar of Color.* New York: Van Nostrand Reinhold Company, 1969.

Munsell, A. H. *A Color Notation.* 12th ed. Baltimore: Munsell Color Company, 1975.

Neuman, Thelma R. *Plastics as an Art Form.* Rev. ed. Philadelphia: Chilton Book Company, 1972.

Oles, Paul Stevenson. *Architectural Illustration: The Value Delineation*

Process. New York: Van Nostrand Reinhold Company, 1979.

Ostwald, Wilhelm. *The Color Primer.* New York: Van Nostrand Reinhold Company, 1969.

Pearce, Peter, and Pearce, Susan. *Experiments in Form: A Foundation Course in Three-Dimensional Design.* New York: Van Nostrand Reinhold Company, 1980.

Porter, Tom. *Architectural Color: A Design Guide to Using Color on Buildings.* New York: Whitney Library of Design, 1982.

Porter, Tom. *How Architects Visualize.* New York: Van Nostrand Reinhold Company, 1979.

Porter, Tom, and Mikellides, Byron. *Color for Architecture.* New York: Van Nostrand Reinhold Company, 1976.

Pugh, Anthony. *Polyhedra: A Visual Approach.* Berkeley CA: University of California Press, 1976.

Rood, Ogden N. *Modern Chromatics: Student's Textbook of Color with Application to Art and Industry.* New York: Van Nostrand Reinhold Company, 1973.

Rotzler, Willy. *Constructive Concepts: A History of Constructive Art from Cubism to the Present.* New York: Rizzoli International Publications, Inc., 1977.

Simonds, John Ormsbee. *Landscape Architecture, A Manual of Site Planning and Design.* 2nd ed. New York: McGraw-Hill Book Company, 1961, 1983.

Smith, Charles N. *Student Handbook of Color.* New York: Reinhold Publishing Company, 1965.

Smith, J. Ritchie. "Process CAN be Style," *Landscape Architecture* Magazine, May/June 1983.

Smith, Patricia Beach, ed. *Gerhardt Knodel Makes Places to Be.* Bloomfield Hills, Michigan: Cranbrook Academy of Art, 1982.

Swirnoff, Lois. "Experiments on the Interaction of Color and Form," *Leonardo,* Vol. 9, pp. 191–195, Pergamon Press, Ltd., 1976.

Thompson, D'Arcy Wentworth. *On Growth and Form.* London: Cambridge at the University Press, 1961.

Thurstan, J. B., and Carraher, R. G. *Optical Illusions and the Visual Arts.* New York: Van Nostrand Reinhold Company, 1966.

Varley, H. Editor. *Color.* London: Marshall Editions Limited, 1980.

Verity, Enid. *Color Observed.* New York: Van Nostrand Reinhold Company, 1980.

Wong, Wucius. *Principles of Three-Dimensional Design.* New York: Van Nostrand Reinhold Company, 1977.

Zeier, Franz. *Paper Constructions: Two- and Three-Dimensional Forms for Artists, Architects, and Designers.* New York: Charles Scribner and Sons, 1980.